D1206911

The Population Ecology of Interest Representation

# The Population Ecology of Interest Representation

## Lobbying Communities in the American States

Virginia Gray and David Lowery

*Ann Arbor*

THE UNIVERSITY OF MICHIGAN PRESS

Copyright © by the University of Michigan 1996
All rights reserved
Published in the United States of America by
The University of Michigan Press
Manufactured in the United States of America
⊗ Printed on acid-free paper

1999   1998   1997   1996      4   3   2   1

*A CIP catalog record for this book is available from the British Library.*


Library of Congress Cataloging-in-Publication Data

Gray, Virginia.
    The population ecology of interest representation : lobbying
communities in the American states / Virginia Gray and David Lowery.
        p.   cm.
    Includes bibliographical references (p.   ) and index.
    ISBN 0-472-10683-X (acid-free paper)
    1. Pressure groups—United States.   2. Pressure groups—
Environmental aspects—United States.   3. Population biology.
I. Lowery, David.   II. Title.
JK1118.G73   1996
324'.4'0973—dc20                                                    96-4459
                                                                      CIP

For Our Parents

# Contents

## Preface and Acknowledgments

This project has its origins in a paper written in 1986 on interest groups and state economic growth. Frustrated by our null findings, we then turned to tracing the origins of interest communities in the 50 states, especially accounting for the density and diversity of state interest communities. Even with some empirical successes, however, we were frustrated by the lack of a theory to explain these system-level properties. We turned to population biology for solace. (Actually, one of us first turned to gardening, and thence to the scholarship on ecology; the other sought solace in golf, thereby sentencing herself to eternal frustration.) This eventually led us to organizational ecology as developed in our sister discipline of sociology. This book is the result of our search for a theory to explain why interest communities are constructed as they are.

Population ecology theories, whether used in population biology or organizational ecology, are theories of context. Their central premise is that such population-level properties as density and diversity are most fundamentally shaped by environmental constraints. The environmental forces of space, energy, and stability determine both how large and how diverse populations can be, whether they be biological or organizational populations.

Applying population ecology thinking to communities of interest organizations necessarily leads us, then, to an abrupt departure from how we have traditionally analyzed interest representation. Rather than focusing on the individual-level incentives of individual members of interest groups, leaders of interest organizations, and elected officials, the models we develop and test address contextual forces bearing on interest organizations as organizations—the number of potential constituents available to be mobilized by interest organizations, what government is doing or not doing of relevance to those constituents, and how likely it is to continue doing or not doing it. These variables determine the carrying capacity of political systems for interest organizations and, thereby, determine the density and diversity of interest communities.

Organization ecology models cannot be inconsistent with what we know about individual-level behavior, nor can they be encompassed by existing theories designed to address individual-level questions. In short, we address a topic that is new to the literature on interest representation. Along the way, we discover a world that is more complex and much more interesting than we had imagined. Simply put, population thinking often leads to quite surprising inferences about population outcomes, inferences that differ sharply from those derived from models focusing exclusively on individuals. Population diversity, especially—when viewed through the lens of population ecology—becomes a far more complicated phenomenon than ever imagined by Truman (1951) or Olson (1965).

Perhaps our most surprising and hopeful finding given pervasive fears of special interests and hyper interest group politics is that the environment governing interest organizations is highly constraining. Interest communities are unlikely to grow in an unlimited fashion. Moreover, the political influence of even dense interest communities is highly restricted—restricted by their very density. This optimistic assessment of the role of interest organizations is something less than the benign pluralism of Truman (1951) and Dahl (1961), but it also offers more promise for democratic government than the gloomy pessimism of a generation or more of scholarship on interest representation by political scientists and, especially, economists.

Some portions of our analysis have appeared in print in different form and/or with somewhat different data. Portions of chapters 3, 4, and 7 were adapted from David Lowery and Virginia Gray, "The Population Ecology of Gucci Gulch, or the Natural Regulation of Interest Group Numbers in the American States," *American Journal of Political Science* 39, no. 1 (1995): 1–29; © 1995; reprinted by permission of the University of Wisconsin Press. Portions of chapters 4 and 6 were adapted from Virginia Gray and David Lowery, "The Demography of Interest Organization Communities: Institutions, Associations, and Membership Groups," *American Politics Quarterly* 23, no. 1 (1995): 3–32; copyright © 1995 by *American Politics Quarterly*; reprinted by permission of Sage Publications, Inc. Portions of chapter 5 were adapted from Virginia Gray and David Lowery, "Stability and Change in State Interest Group Systems, 1975–1990," *State and Local Government Review* 25, no. 2 (spring 1993): 87–96; reprinted by permission of the authors and the Carl Vinson Institute of Government, University of Georgia. Portions of appendix 1 were adapted from David Lowery and Virginia Gray, "Do Lobbying Regulations Influence Lobbying Registrations?" *Social Science Quarterly* 75, no. 2 (1994): 382–84, by permission of *Social Science Quarterly* and the University of Texas Press. Portions of chapters 4 and 8 were adapted from Virginia Gray and David Lowery, "Environmental Limits on the Diversity of

State Interest Group Systems: A Population Ecology Interpretation," *Political Research Quarterly* 49, no. 1 (March 1996): 103–18; reprinted by permission of the University of Utah, Copyright Holder. Portions of chapter 10 were adapted from Virginia Gray and David Lowery, "Interest Representation and Democratic Gridlock," *Legislative Studies Quarterly,* 20, no. 4 (November 1995): 531–52; reprinted by permission. And portions of chapters 4 and 9 were adapted from Virginia Gray and David Lowery, "A Niche Theory of Interest Representation," *Journal of Politics* 58, no. 1 (February 1996): 91–111; reprinted by permission of *Journal of Politics* and the University of Texas Press. We thank the editors and reviewers of these journals for making our thinking more precise.

Our work was aided by numerous individuals and organizations. At the University of Minnesota, several graduate students served as coders over the years—Robert Paolino, Paul Kramer, Steven Taylor, and Amanda Bryant—while Keith Katko and Jennifer Alstad served as undergraduate coders. Stacey Hecht answered various calls for help. At the University of North Carolina at Chapel Hill, graduate students Ruffin Hall, Jonathan Jordan, Yun-Jie Lee, and Kristin Siebenaler conducted the mail survey, with the able assistance of Julie Daniel. We appreciate the dedication and creativity of all of these people.

The students were supported by financial assistance from many sources. At the University of Minnesota, the sources included the Undergraduate Research Opportunities Project, the Department of Political Science, the College of Liberal Arts, and the President's Office. During academic year 1993–94, Virginia Gray was able to visit Chapel Hill under a grant from the National Science Foundation's Visiting Professorship for Women Program, supplemented by a sabbatical grant from the University of Minnesota. The University of North Carolina at Chapel Hill provided office space and four research assistants. The mail survey and the bulk of the manuscript for this book were completed during this leave, and the golf game was much improved due to the tolerance of the "Friday morning group." The authors appreciate the generosity of these institutions.

A number of colleagues provided encouragement and advice along the way. Among interest group scholars, Sarah Morehouse, Ron Hrebenar, Clive Thomas, Bill Browne, and Bob Salisbury were especially helpful. Among University of North Carolina colleagues, the Comparative Politics Discussion Group as well as Mike Munger provided valuable criticism. Ann and Andy Scott loaned David Lowery their wonderful cabin in Nova Scotia, where a good portion of one of the intermediate drafts of this book was completed. In the "real world," Virginia Gray learned a lot from four years of lobbying the Minnesota legislature with

Donna Peterson and from reflecting on that experience (otherwise known as "talking politics") with veteran lobbyists Joe Bell in Arkansas and Wyman Spano in Minnesota. We also thank Shirley Kessel for compiling the index. Finally, we thank the fellow members of the Elijah Mitchell Society—Pam, Donald, Caryl, and Mel—for good meals and conversation in Chapel Hill.

# Tables

# Figures

# CHAPTER 1

## The Importance of Populations

The essential requirement of democratic politics is that citizens to some degree control their government and influence its decisions. Election of public officials is the primary tool democratic political systems use to ensure that citizens have both voice and authority. But the infrequency of elections and the inability of voters to provide detailed and nuanced signals about citizens' preferences means that more is required for the realization of democratic rule. In modern scholarship on democracy, great emphasis has been accorded the role of interest organizations in providing a second and supporting channel of citizen communication and control. In the 45 years since David Truman's *Governmental Process* brought renewed salience to the topic, social scientists have argued long and sometimes fiercely about the benefits and costs of relying on that channel. We have learned a great deal about interest representation since Truman. Success on two research topics is especially noteworthy. First, based largely on Olson's (1965) influential account of the collective action problem governing the formation of membership groups, a generation of scholars has developed a deep understanding of the origins of interest organizations (Moe 1980; Wilson 1973; McFarland 1984; Berry 1977; Walker 1983; Hansen 1985). Second, while theoretically integrated to a far lesser degree, research on the activities and impact of interest organizations has also taught us much. We know a great deal about leaders of interest organizations, lobbying, and the influence of campaign contributions on elections and public policy (Malbin 1984; Austen-Smith 1987; Munger and Denzau 1986; Bauer, Pool, and Dexter 1968; Milbrath 1963; Hall and Wayman 1990; Wright 1985; Wright 1990). Though theoretical and empirical controversies abound within each of these domains of research (Cigler 1994; Salisbury 1994; Tierney 1994; Berry 1994), they are of a kind that is indicative of a healthy and prosperous research program. Thus, it requires little in the way of charity to conclude that each program is a social science success story.

What is missing, however, is any connection between them. While this is usually evident only in a negative sense, via our treatment of the two as distinct topics (Cigler 1991), it is especially obvious in the few efforts that have been made to connect the two elements of interest representation. The canonical example here is Mancur Olson's failed effort in *The Rise and Decline of Nations* to bridge the gap between research on the micro-level incentives of mobilization and macro-level research on interest organization impact. Extrapolating from his successful micro-level theory—presented in his *Logic of Collective Action*—to the societal level, Olson argued that interest organizations will accumulate over time, that they will pursue policies that inhibit collective productivity in favor of selective protection, and that they will do so even until economies collapse. Despite the initial flurry of attention accorded Olson's analysis of *institutional sclerosis,* empirical tests failed to find evidence supporting it (Gray and Lowery 1988), and it has since disappeared as an object of serious research. The short life span of the institutional sclerosis model illustrates well our failure to link individual-level analyses of interest organization formation with macro-level theories of interest organization impact.

Is this such a terrible problem? Perhaps not. After all, we have judged the two domains of scholarship on interest organizations to be successes. Even without a linkage, we know already a great deal about mobilization and about interest organization influence, and the research agendas of each of the distinct domains remain full.

Still, we cannot help but feel that we are missing an important opportunity by not bridging this gap. We believe that many interest organization scholars share our suspicion, given that most seem to take as axiomatic that the different levels at which we study interest organizations are related to one another. Moe (1980, 224), for example, argues persuasively that we cannot understand the behavior of membership group leaders without understanding why and how members join interest organizations. Browne (1990, 499–500) similarly explains the balkanized structure of legislative policy systems in terms of powerful incentives bearing on interest organizations to maintain well-defined issue identities. Both hint, then, at the possibility of an integrated theory of interest representation, a theory that will enable us to move freely and with confidence from individual-level decisions about joining interest organizations to the behavior of interest organizations and their impact on policy and governance, drawing inferences along the way about how changes at one level influence patterns of behavior at the next and succeeding levels.

We attempt to close the gap between our two domains of knowledge about interest organizations with the theory and empirical analyses presented in this book. Our central argument is that we cannot proceed *directly* from the individual level of mobilization to the macro level of interest organization behavior and impact. Indeed, Olson's failure to bridge the gap with *The Rise and Decline of Nations* resulted strictly from his effort to make such a direct connection between micro and macro levels of behavior. Rather, a distinct body of theory and research that falls between the two existing domains is required as an indirect or mediating link. This new theory, inspired by research in population biology and organization ecology, is about interest organization *populations*—how they are comprised, how they confront the political system, and how they influence governance and public policy.

**Why a New Theory Is Needed**

A new theory is required because it is unlikely that we will be able to move directly from knowledge about the individual-level incentives of interest organization mobilization to inferences about interest organization impact. Perhaps the best way to illustrate this difficulty is via an analogy with a well-known episode in biology—the disastrous introduction of rabbits from Great Britain into Australia. The facts of this episode are easily summarized. When a number of shy, retiring, and generally well-mannered rabbits emigrated from the home islands to Australia to provide sport for colonial gentlemen, the long-eared rodents ran amok. Tens of thousands, hundreds of thousands, millions of rabbits wreaked ecological devastation on the grasslands of the island continent. Devastation stopped only when the rabbits were inoculated with a highly contagious and lethal disease.[1]

The primary elements of the analogy are easily identified. First, we know a great deal about how rabbits are put together—their genetic makeup, physiology, and breeding patterns. We know a great deal as well about how interest organizations are put together—the incentive structures that govern mobilization. Both theories are micro-level theories in that they tell us how individual units of two entities are constructed. Second, we also know a great deal from ecology about the impact millions of rabbits will have on unprotected grasslands, just as we know much about the behavior and influence of interest organizations within democratic political systems. These are macro- or societal-level theories of impact.

The point of the analogy is just this—we cannot make inferences about what happens at the macro or societal level simply from knowledge about micro-level processes governing how rabbits or interest organizations are constructed. For rabbits, the explanatory problem is accounting for why animals that were rare, shy, and meek in England became a numberless horde in Australia. The answer cannot be found in how rabbits are put together. The genetics, physiology, and breeding behavior of British and Australian rabbits is identical since they are conspecifics, members of the same species. By the same token, we cannot explain why one interest organization system has few organizations and other systems many simply by reference to theories about how interest organizations are put together. The micro-level incentives governing interest organization mobilization are likely to be the same in Arkansas, a state with few lobbying organizations, as in Michigan, a state with many.

Most readers will by now have little trouble accounting for the divergent experiences of England and Australia by filling in the missing link between knowledge about how rabbits are put together and knowledge about how rabbits influence their habitat. The environmental constraints that controlled rabbit populations in Great Britain were absent in Australia. When confronted with few competitors, few predators, and abundant food, rabbit populations exploded. The important point of this explanation, however, is that our theories about how rabbits are constituted—their genetics, physiology, and breeding behavior—say nothing about the variables that prove essential in accounting for the divergence of the British and Australian cases—the role of competitors, predators, and food.

In short, we need another type of theory altogether—one telling us how rabbit *populations* are formed—to understand variance in the density of rabbit populations. Such a population-level theory will identify environmental factors governing properties that emerge at only the population level—population density and diversity, especially. Population biologist Paul Colinvaux (1978, 12) has expressed the relationship between the reproductive behavior of animals and ecology: "the way an animal breeds has very little to do with how many of it there are. This is a very strange idea to someone new to it, and needs to be thought about carefully. *The reproductive effort makes no difference to the eventual size of the population.* . . . The numbers that may live are set by the environment, and these are quite independent of how fast a species makes babies." Colinvaux's point is simple: population-level outcomes are more than simply aggregated consequences of lower-level, individual-level processes.

The same is likely to be true for interest organizations. If we wish to understand how different configurations of interest organization populations influence patterns of governance and policy, we must start by understanding how interest organization *populations* are constructed, especially how environmental forces determine their size and their composition. Population density and diversity are properties that emerge only at the population level. We are unlikely, therefore, to account for population density and diversity if we rely solely on our knowledge about how individual interest organizations are formed, no matter how sound that knowledge is. There is simply little in our theories of individual-level mobilization processes that speaks to environmental context and its influence. This does not mean that these theories are wrong, only that they cannot be used to do more than they were designed to do, as was made painfully evident by Olson's attempt to extend his analysis in *The Logic of Collective Action* to the macro level with *The Rise and Decline of Nations*.

A population ecology theory of interest organizations—a theory attentive to environmental context—*may* provide the missing body of knowledge linking research on interest organization formation with research on interest organization influence and impact. If considered together and fully integrated, we *may* then be able to combine these separate bodies of knowledge into a general theory of interest representation. This expectation is qualified, for our findings suggest that the several domains of research on interest representation can be only incompletely and partially linked through analyses of populations. But even if such a general theory does not emerge, a new and distinct research program on interest organization populations should contribute to both of the existing areas of inquiry. We think it unlikely that we can fully understand interest organization mobilization or interest organization impact without understanding the dynamics of interest organization populations.

If the gap between existing research programs is so obvious, why hasn't a theory of interest organization populations been developed before now? Certainly, the very real difficulties of measuring population-level properties across multiple populations has inhibited such research (Salisbury 1994, 13). While this explains better why population-level theories have not been tested, rather than why they have not been developed in the first place, it remains the most likely cause for what is to us a rather glaring gap in interest organization research. As Cigler (1994, 29) has noted, "In large measure, data availability has been the major determinant of the interest group politics research agenda, framing both the questions we explore, and the topics we avoid."

This does not mean that students of interest representation have been totally silent on population issues. Schlozman and Tierney (1986) and Walker (1991), especially, have addressed these issues in their analyses of the Washington interest community. Unfortunately, their analytic focus was essentially descriptive in offering opposing responses to Schattschneider's assertion (1960) of interest community bias, instead of theoretical in providing an account of how the Washington interest organization population is comprised. Other scholars—most notably Laumann and Knoke (1987), Browne (1988, 1995), and Heinz, Laumann, Nelson, and Salisbury (1993)—have carefully studied several subpopulations of interest organizations. But again, their theoretical questions did not include asking how the interest organization communities they studied were constituted. In large part, the simple and controlling reason for this failure was that all of these studies examined the Washington interest organization system, a single population in which the environmental forces governing population density and diversity are constants.

The studies that are most closely related to our purpose are those on state interest organizations, especially the work of Morehouse (1981) and the several studies by Hrebenar and Thomas (1992, 1993a, 1993b; Thomas and Hrebenar 1990, 1992). Other useful studies compare firm participation in PACs across economic sectors (McKeown, 1994; Malbin 1984; Grier, Munger, and Roberts 1994). And there are a limited number of studies by organizational ecologists on national trade associations (Aldrich and Staber 1988; Aldrich et al. 1990, 1994). Each of these research programs examines multiple populations of organizations, either across space or across time, in a manner at least potentially appropriate for addressing how environmental forces determine population density and diversity. We will have occasion to comment on all three of these literatures as our analysis proceeds. Yet, only the last, because it is couched in a population ecology framework, offers a broad-ranging and rigorous theory of populations. It is to population ecology, then, both in biology and organization theory, that we turn in the chapters that follow, as we develop a theory of lobbying populations.

### Defining Populations of Organized Interests

We are interested in interest organization populations and what accounts for their growth and change, which necessitates that we examine multiple populations of interest organizations.[2] This focus alone need not rule out examination of the Washington, D.C., interest community. Most research in organization ecology (Hannan and Freeman 1989; Hannan and Carroll 1992) examines single populations *over time* to ensure variance in the environmental forces governing population growth and change. But the very practical difficulties of gathering valid and comparable time series data on Washington lobbying organizations effectively precludes its use in testing population ecology models (Schlozman and Tierney 1986).

We turn, then, to the American states and their 50 populations of interest organizations. While we are longtime students of state politics, we did not select the states as our laboratory for this project for that reason. Rather, comparative state analysis offers a nearly ideal vantage point from which to study multiple populations of organized interests. The similarities of American state political institutions, traditions, and practices enhances the degree to which we can compare apples to apples. Yet, at the same time, the apples come in a number of varieties: state interest communities vary considerably in density and diversity. It is this variation that we hope to explain.

To begin, we must identify in much more precise terms the populations we study. First, we do not study lobbyists—although lobbyists and lobbying are important subjects; rather, we study lobbying organizations. Second, it should be obvious that not all organizations are *interest* organizations in the sense of engaging the political system by monitoring and/or influencing the course of government decisions. Moreover, there are surely gradations in the intensity of engagement on the part of interest organizations, with some only passively monitoring public decisions, while others work legislative offices day after day in the pursuit of specific policy actions. And intensity of engagement can change with time as issues of concern to organizations enter and leave the public policy agenda. So, how are our boundaries to be defined? In other words, what signifies inclusion or exclusion in our population?

Measures sometimes used to assess population-level theories of interest representation are not appropriate to the task. For example, despite his explicit theoretical focus on populations of interest *organizations*, Olson's test (1982) of the institutional sclerosis model for the American states uses data on organization *membership*, clearly confounding two distinct levels of analysis (Gray and Lowery 1988). Other scholars employ reports of Political Action Committees (PACs) to define interest organization populations. But while PAC populations also merit study, they are not coterminous with what we mean by populations of interest organizations. In our survey of leaders of interest organizations registered to lobby state legislatures, which is described more fully in chapter 9 (see also the text in app. 2), only a little more than a third of the respondents reported that their organizations sponsored a PAC. Political behavior by organizations includes more than operating a PAC. More importantly, it seems reasonable to expect that the subpopulation of registered interest organizations utilizing PACs may be unrepresentative of the universe of organizations engaged in political activity.[3]

The most valid indicator of broadscale political activity now available is provided by lobby registration rolls, and these define the populations we either study directly or sample from in the analyses that follow.

More specifically, most of our empirical analyses employ the universe of organizations registered to lobby state legislatures in all 50 states in 1990 and in 44 states in 1975 and 1980. Other analyses examine subsets of these data. In chapter 6, we track the life histories of all of the interest organizations registered in 6 states from 1980 to 1990—North Carolina, Arkansas, Michigan, Minnesota, South Dakota, and Pennsylvania. Some of the models tested in chapter 7 and 8 examine data on interest organizations in only six economic sectors in all 50 states in 1990. And in chapter 9, we report the results from a survey of interest organization leaders in 6 states. In the chapters in which the data from these several samples are used, we discuss the rationales supporting the selection of these samples and describe the procedures used to construct them: each is founded ultimately on state lobby registration rolls.

These data have the advantage of measuring the number of interest organizations where they come into contact with state political systems, thereby excluding organizations that are largely local in orientation or nonpolitical. At the same time, lobby registration rolls capture broad engagement with the political system. As Salisbury (1992, 97) has observed, "Although most interest groups will tend to prefer one institutional branch to another, most of them will try to attain and utilize access across the whole system." Thus, we expect registration rolls to capture attention by interest organizations to state government in its entirety. Legislatures are merely the institutions that happen to require the legal recording of that attention.

There are, of course, variations in the restrictiveness of lobby registration laws as well as variations in the rigor of their enforcement. Fortunately, these variations seem to have little impact on numbers of either registered lobbyists (Hunter, Wilson, and Brunk 1991) or registered interest organizations (Paolino 1991). Still, given the importance of this potential source of systematic bias in defining our populations, appendix 1 presents a more complete defense of the validity of lobby registration lists. A fuller discussion of coding procedures is presented there as well.

This does not mean that lobby registration lists faithfully record the names of all politically active interest organizations in the states. We will see in chapter 6, for example, that institutions in particular move on and off the registration rolls as issues of importance to them move on and off the political agenda. When off, they still retain the ability to reenter the political market. Thus, our boundaries are not hard or fixed; there is a gray area, just off the registration rolls, where organizations with latent interests reside. Still, as Hrebenar and Thomas (1992, 322) have argued, "It is . . . state lobby laws that provide the most specific and comprehensive information about interest organizations activity."

A final set of data used in our analysis is only indirectly built on lobby registration lists. These are the insights of 23 contract lobbyists in six states—the same six states noted earlier—interviewed by phone from April through September 1994. From lobby registration lists, we determined which contract lobbyists had the most clients in each state, and we sought to include the top four or five in our sample. This information was supplemented by inquiries to other lobbyists as to who had a reputation for influence and by reputational mentions in the state politics literature.[4] In structured interviews lasting from 12 to 56 minutes, averaging around 25 minutes, the lobbyists were asked open-ended questions about changes they have observed in their lobbying communities, their business practices, and the influence of interest organizations.

Why talk to lobbyists in a study designed to analyze populations of interest organizations? Simply put, analyses of populations of lobbying organizations can be highly abstract at times, far removed from the real world of lobbying and being lobbied. Talking to lobbyists, we hope, will insure that our speculations and conclusions do not stray too far from that reality. Our sample of lobbyists is not representative. Indeed, the respondents are some of the most successful lobbyists in their states. But they are all well-experienced, senior observers of their lobbying communities and their state governments. So, while we do not analyze their responses systematically, we use their insights from time to time to comment on the plausibility of arguments that scholars, including ourselves, have raised about lobbying communities.

## An Outline of Our Analysis

In developing and testing a family of population ecology models of interest organizations, we begin in chapter 2 with what is traditional in scholarly analysis—a literature review. The literatures on interest organizations can be divided and subdivided on many dimensions: economic or political science in origin and/or theoretical orientation; impact or mobilization in explanatory focus; case analytic, empirical, or formally analytic in methodology; and so on. And there are any number of excellent reviews of the literature along these dimensions (Mitchell and Munger 1991; Walker 1991, 41–56; Cigler 1994; Browne 1990, 477–82; Heinz et al. 1993).

So, why do another? Unfortunately, none of these reviews examines existing scholarship from a population perspective, exploring what existing accounts can tell us about the formation of interest organization populations under different environmental conditions, how this formation influences the diversity of represented interests and the structure of interest organization communities, or how these population properties constrain the influence of interest organizations on issues of governance and public policy. It is necessary, then, to examine the literature again, this time from a population perspective.

In chapter 3, we examine the nature of population ecology models by reviewing their development in population biology over the course of this century and in sociology's research program on organization ecology over the last two decades. The two literatures are closely related intellectually, with sociology's founded on insights developed by population biologists. Given the close connection of our topic to those studied in organization ecology, some may wonder why it is necessary to proceed into the unfamiliar intellectual territory of biology. Part of the answer is that we developed our own thinking about ecological models directly from population biology, only much later exploring the growing literature on organization ecology.[5] More telling, however, the organization ecology research program in sociology only partially matches the rich set of topics considered in population biology. By studying population biology, we can gain many theoretical insights relevant to the study of politically interesting populations, some of which would be missed if we only reviewed the derivative literature on organization ecology.[6]

Chapter 4 presents the core of our theoretical analysis, in which we apply population thinking to interest organizations. Hypotheses are developed on five related topics: (1) interest organization population demography, or why some lobbying organizations survive while others do not; (2) interest organization population density, or why interest organization populations expand or contract; (3) interest organization population diversity, or how the mix of interests represented within a population is determined; (4) interest organization community structure, or how and why interest organizations interact with each other and the political system in some ways and not in others; and (5) interest community impact, or how different configurations of interest organizations influence governance and public policy. While developing these hypotheses, we contrast population thinking to standard interpretations within the literatures on lobbying organizations.

Several important properties of populations of organized interests in the American states in 1975, 1980, and 1990—especially their density and diversity—are described in chapter 5. Several measures of each of these properties are developed using state lobby registration data. The measures are assessed in terms of their value in both describing and explaining population-level properties of interest communities and their impacts on politics and governance.

Using these measures, chapters 6 though 11 comprise the empirical portion of our analysis, addressing, in order, the sets of hypotheses developed in chapter 4. Chapter 6 focuses on questions of demography. We track interest organizations' patterns of entry into, survival in, and exiting from lobby registration rolls from 1980 to 1990 in six states. We use these data especially to assess the role of organizational mortality in shaping interest organization populations and to test a population ecology explanation of the source of variations in mortality rates across populations.

Chapters 7 and 8 test population ecology's Energy-Stability-Area (ESA) model of population density and diversity. The density model is tested in chapter 7 with two sets of regression analyses. First, a somewhat simplified version of the ESA model is tested using 1975, 1980, and 1990 data on all registered interest organizations in the states. The second set of analyses test a better-specified model using six subpopulations of interest organizations comprising roughly a third of the entire population of interest organizations in the states. As alternatives to the ESA model, we simultaneously assess the population density hypothesis implicit in Olson's theory of institutional sclerosis (1982) and a Virginia School account (Mueller and Murrell 1986) that indicts the growing size of government as the most proximate cause of expanding interest organization populations.

The results from these tests provide the foundation for a series of simulations presented in chapter 8, simulations that explore the density models' implications for understanding the diversity of interest organization populations. In this exercise, we contrast the population ecology interpretation of diversity with Truman's assertion (1951) that diversity faithfully reflects the complexity of social and economic interests in a polity.

Our attention shifts away from representation and toward issues of policy and governance in chapters 9 through 11. In chapter 9, we explore the nature of interest organization community structure using a population ecology theory of niches, an interpretation that builds on Browne's niche concept (1990). We explore the niche concept and its implications for explaining policy balkanization within legislatures. The data employed in these analyses were developed from surveys of leaders of registered interest organizations in the same six states used in the demographic analysis presented in chapter 6. Chapter 10 examines whether interest community density and diversity are responsible for variations in legislative activity, low levels of which some have labeled gridlock. This hypothesis is tested against an alternative that focuses on divided government as the cause of gridlock. Chapter 11 extends this analysis by examining the consequences of density and diversity for economic

growth, the size of government, the adoption of protectionist regulations and subsidies, and the perceived power of interest communities.

Chapter 12 summarizes our findings and presents a population ecology research agenda for the study of interest representation. These are
traditional tasks of concluding chapters. More importantly, perhaps, we
interpret our findings in terms of their implications for democratic government. Despite Truman's optimistic assessment (1951) of the role of
organized interests in democracies, more than a few political scientists,
most economists, and certainly many of our fellow citizens are increasingly suspicious of what they suspect is government by special interest.
To foreshadow our conclusion, we argue that our findings suggest that
these fears are at least overstated. We find that the environment of
interest communities is a highly confining one that limits the possibilities
of interest community influence.

## A Caveat

Before we begin our analysis, we should acknowledge and justify a
recurring and by now obvious pattern in our terminology—our persistent use of *interest organization* rather than the more familiar label
*interest group*. The term *interest group* has a solid pedigree in political
science and is readily used even in journalistic reports on lobbying,
although *special interest* and *pressure group* seem to enjoy even more
frequent use. All other things being equal, we would be loath to abandon a label that is so widely employed and has such shared common
meaning, especially for such an inelegant semantic construction as *interest organization*.

*Interest group,* however, is fundamentally misleading as a characterization of what we study. As Salisbury (1984) pointed out more than a
decade ago, most interest organizations are not membership *groups,*
representing individuals banded together to influence government policy, but institutions, such as banks, industrial firms, universities, local
governments, or hospitals. Many other interest *groups* are associations.
While they may have individuals as members, the membership of many
associations is comprised entirely of institutions: associations of businesses, university consortia, or federations of local governments. This is
amply demonstrated by our data. In 1990, for example, only 22.78 percent of registered lobbying organizations in the states were membership-
based groups, with associations and institutions comprising, respectively, 28.20 and 49.02 percent of lobbying organizations. Thus, while
*interest organization* may seem somewhat awkward at first, it offers a far
more accurate description of what we study than does *interest group*.

# CHAPTER 2

## Conventional Research and Population Questions

As a first step toward examining interest organization populations, we review how the existing literature addresses population-level issues. We focus on four key population-level questions and their relation to several issues in the literatures on interest representation. How do levels of interest system density vary under different population-level conditions? How do population-level dynamics generate the diversity of interests that we find represented in different political systems at different times? How do the dynamics of population growth and change affect interest organizations in their interaction with the political system? And how do these population-level phenomena structure organized interests' impact on governance and public policies?

In reviewing how scholars have addressed these questions, we draw a divide between two very different literatures. The first relies heavily on deductive analysis and is typically, although not exclusively, the work of economists. The second literature is primarily empirical and inductive in approach and is typically the work of political scientists and a few sociologists. The two literatures also tend to divide in their normative evaluations of the influence of interest organizations. While there are a number of important exceptions, political scientists often view the machinations of interest organizations far more positively than our more pessimistic cousins in the dismal science. For convenience, then, we use disciplinary labels to distinguish the two literatures, although the labels do a minor injustice to some of our colleagues laboring in another discipline's vineyards.

With the major exception of common attention to Mancur Olson's *Logic of Collective Action*, the two literatures rarely speak to each other. Economists tend to studiously ignore the vast political science literature on interest organizations. In contrast, political scientists will more often cite economists—but only grudgingly. For instance, Salisbury (1994, 14) has written, "Messrs. Stigler, Becker, Peltzman, Buchanan, Tullock, Tollison et al. have remarkably little to teach political scientists regarding the fundamental processes of interest representation." It is clear, however, that both sets of scholars have completed important studies on interest representation that bear, if often indirectly, on how we understand interest communities.

## Density of Interest Representation

Why do some political systems have more interest organizations than others? While on first blush this may seem a trivial question, it is not. To see why, consider the cases of Pennsylvania and Arkansas. Pennsylvania had 69 registered interest organizations attentive to banking issues in 1990, while Arkansas's legislature registered only 11. Yet, both states had similar numbers of banks operating within their borders during the same year—298 and 239, respectively. Such unexpected patterns occur frequently when we examine populations of interest organizations across political systems. Thus, while it may be trivial to ask why New York has more manufacturing firms than does Mississippi, it is not trivial to ask why New York has more manufacturing lobbying organizations than does Mississippi.

### Political Science Explanations of Density

Traditional political science analyses of interest organizations did not address population density until recently. To Bentley (1908), Latham (1952), and Truman (1951), the formation of interest organizations was regarded as neither puzzling nor especially interesting. It was assumed that those with common interests joined together to further those interests. As a result, pluralist analyses of membership group mobilization were largely tautologous—there are interest organizations, so there must be interests.

This changed, of course, in response to Olson's startling account of membership group mobilization in *The Logic of Collective Action.* In Olson's model, the individual-level incentives governing mobilization render membership group formation something far less than inevitable and, therefore, of great explanatory interest. Political scientists quickly adopted Olson's model as their own and generously extended it (Salisbury 1969; Wilson 1973; Moe 1980; Walker 1983; Berry 1977). At the same time, political scientists pointed to the importance of studying the mobilization of nonmembership organizations (Salisbury 1984). But even when transformed via Olson's new perspective on the economics of mobilization, political science explanations of interest organization formation retained something of a tautologous flavor, arguing that since there are interest organizations, there must be material, solidary, and/or purposive incentives sufficient to induce members to join them.

Not coincidentally, this theoretical revolution occasioned an explosion of research in political science. Much of this work involved searching for the specific incentive structures assumed to be supporting existing membership groups (Berry 1977; Cook 1984; Moe 1980; King and Walker 1992; Rothenberg 1992). Other analyses reported surveys of the populations of selected interest representation systems—almost always Washington, D.C.—to describe the population-level outcomes of the incentives presumed to be governing mobilization (Walker 1991; Schlozman 1984; Schlozman and Tierney 1983; Browne 1990; Heinz et al. 1993), most often finding the continued dominance of economic interests first noted by Schattschneider (1960). Some scholars also reported that membership groups, the typical focus of theoretical inquiry in mobilization research, constituted only about half of the interest organizations lobbying in the nation's capital (Schlozman and Tierney 1986, 49).

Clearly, political science has much to say about the mobilization of membership groups. But just as clearly, little of this work directly addresses our question, which concerns variation in the densities of populations of interest organizations across time and/or space. First, it is obvious that interest organization population density is more than the sum of the outcomes of membership group mobilization processes. We must also account for the mobilization of institutions and other nonmembership entities. Furthermore, a satisfactory explanation of density must take into account the mortality of interest organizations. We need to know how many interest organizations "demobilize" over time, why they do so, and whether different kinds of organizations are more fragile than others.[1]

Second, and even more importantly, it seems implausible to expect that population-level traits, such as density, can be explained satisfactorily using theories exclusively attentive to individual-level incentives. We take as a given that the incentives individuals confront are highly conditioned by the environments in which interest organizations find themselves. Such environmental conditions can be safely ignored as a constant when the focus of inquiry is a single membership group and the individual's decision about joining it. They can also be ignored when looking at a single population of interest organizations at a single point in time. But it seems implausible to expect that they can be safely ignored when attention shifts to interest organization populations.

To understand this point, it may be useful to consider again the analogous relationship that exists, in the biological study of populations, between genetics and physiology at one level of analysis and ecology at another. Knowledge of genetics and physiology are obviously important in explaining why some animals survive and others do not. But we would be missing something crucial if we tried to account for differences in the size of polar bear populations found in Greenland and North Carolina solely by reference to the genetics and physiology of polar bears. There are clearly unaccounted for and important contextual forces, such as average mean temperature and its interaction with physiology and genetics, that are relevant to the explanatory problem. If the kinds of analyses provided in the mobilization literature comprise the genetics/physiology of interest organizations, then we must realize that we cannot explain variation in interest organization populations via exclusive reference to the incentive structures governing membership mobilization. Reference to environmental context is needed as well.

Although interest organization analyses addressing environmental context are rare, they suggest how important such forces can be in accounting for variations in the density of interest organization populations. Certainly Truman (1951), Walker (1991), and Salisbury (1992) have theorized in general terms about a number of contextual variables. Salisbury (1992, 85–86), for example, asserted that more interests will emerge where the scope of government is wide, because more people will be affected by government. A few others have focused on these speculations in empirical analyses of interest organizations. Conover and Gray (1983, 184), for example, examined the role of "threatened goods" in abortion group mobilization, showing that pro-family mobilization occurred in states where the feminist movement posed a threat to policies they valued. Similarly, King and Walker (1992, 420) demonstrated that purposive incentives operate more effectively in conflictual policy environments.

These disparate findings suggest that many students of interest representation have implicitly recognized that context matters, but they rarely take the next step of explicitly incorporating context into their theoretical and empirical analyses. As Hansen (1985, 82–83) has written, "a theory that looks only at benefits or only at costs misses a great deal of what is important. Benefits and costs do not simply exist; rather they exist in particular milieux."[2] The constraints imposed by the environments within which interest organizations find themselves almost certainly condition mobilization and mortality processes. Thus, attention to the incentive structure of a single membership group at a specific point in time, while useful for other purposes, will not enable us to account for population-level variance in interest organization populations.

## Economic Explanations of Density

The economic literature also has produced few accounts of variations in interest organization populations. Like political scientists, economists typically assume that interest organization populations are comprised of simple aggregations of membership groups arising separately and individually from the play of micro-level incentives of group formation. This ignores the mobilization of nonmembership groups and mortality among all types of interest organizations, and, perhaps more importantly, it says nothing about context. Indeed, only two economic models of interest representation address larger environmental conditions that might influence variations in populations of represented interests over time and space.

The first is developed in Olson's *Rise and Decline of Nations*, which suggests that the key environmental constraint—indeed, the only constraint—on the growth in the number of organized interests is the length of time since formation of the political system or since its disruption via war or some other crisis. Time interacts with the probability that latent groups will solve the incentive problems of organization, so that numbers of organizations increase over time. Or, numbers increase until instability resets the clock on the system, and interest group formation must begin anew. This is a Cretaceous extinction model of interest organization populations. The incentives governing membership group formation outlined in Olson's *Logic of Collective Action* lead to increasing numbers of organizations until the political system collapses, just as biological processes lead to increasing species diversity until, as Walter Alvarez (1992) phrased it, "Every so often there's a really bad day when a big rock falls out of the sky." While the advent of political collapse is obviously important, too sharply confining ourselves to that factor restricts consideration of plausibly important contextual factors.

Alternatively, the Virginia School's model of interest representation (Mueller and Murrell 1986; Coughlin, Mueller, and Murrell 1990; Mitchell and Munger 1991) highlights the size of government as the critical, and perhaps the only, contextual factor of importance. The model has both a strong and a weak form. In the latter, government is a passive attractor of lobbying organizations and a goad to their formation, as a result of its increasing potential to redistribute wealth as it grows larger. One Arkansas lobbyist (phone interview, 4 May 1994), when asked why interest communities have expanded, noted: "Simple, there is a bigger pie for the tax receivers and a bigger bite for the taxpayers." Not a common opinion among the contract lobbyists we interviewed, this is a vision of government as a lottery winner who suddenly finds that he or she has more friends and relatives than previously imagined. Politicians, the Virginians then argue, have sufficient electoral incentives to respond to the demands of these newfound friends and relatives in exchange for resources needed to enhance their chances of reelection.

The strong form of the model allocates an even more active role to elected officials, suggesting that they purposively seek out existing organized interests or even assist the organization of latent interests so that they may extort rents then used to enhance reelection chances (Grier and Munger 1991). As Shugart and Tollison (1986, 113) put it, "each legislator/broker searches over his constituency, identifies those groups that are net demanders of wealth transfers and those that are net suppliers, and develops a legislative agenda—a level and pattern of wealth transfers that maximizes his political majority." The essential motivating force in this model is the vote-maximizing politician. This form of the Virginia School model might best be characterized as the "Hey kid, want to buy some drugs?" account of populations of organized interests, with size of government acting as the only constraint on the politician as pusher.

In either form, the Virginians propose to restrict the influence of narrowly constituted interest organizations by restricting the size of government. As Mitchell and Munger (1991, 531) note, "their single most important proposal for reform is the adoption of constitutional amendments that limit the powers of government to tax and spend. Tollison and the other Virginians maintain that the basic source of rent seeking is found in an ever-growing government with the power to spend on specific groups while taxing everyone through general taxes." Burn the lottery winnings, and unwanted friends and relatives will disappear. Intercept the drugs, and the drug merchant will go out of business.

Like the political science explanations, the accounts offered by economists are unlikely to help us understand variation in the densities of interest organization populations. At the most general level, the Olson and Virginia School models are not primarily about interest organization populations but about the impact of interest organizations on economic growth and/or the dangers of excessive government. This is especially true of Olson's model. Despite the central role he assigns to *numbers* of membership groups, he did not include the number of interest organizations in his empirical tests of his model. As a result, it is not surprising that Olson's model, or at least that part of it linking time to number of groups, has generated little empirical support when tested with appropriate data (Gray and Lowery 1988).

The Virginia School interpretation also has its own unique liabilities. Simply put, the Virginia School model, at least in its strong form, rests on what many political scientists (Lowi 1969) and at least some economists (Stigler 1971; Peltzman 1976) consider rather implausible assumptions about how political systems operate.[3] These assumptions address what ecologists (E. O. Wilson 1992, 170–73, 392) refer to as *community assembly rules,* the sequential order in which new species are added to an ecological community. When a barren piece of land—a new island for instance—becomes available for colonization, different types of species become established in order over time. Predators, for example, do not become established first and survive, because there is nothing yet to prey on. Assembly rules are equally important in the case of political communities.

Are the assembly rules underlying the economic models plausible? Hansen (1985, 94) summarized their implicit assembly rules by asserting that "There is, in sum, a Say's law of interest groups: supply creates its own demand." The Virginia School model assumes that interest organization leaders, with supplies of selective incentives, and/or politicians, with policy favors to exchange for rents, somehow induce interest organizations into existence.[4] This implies that elected officials arrive first and then stimulate interest organization entrepreneurs to find members or sponsors.

These are the opposite of the assembly rules implicit in pluralist models of interest organization formation. In Truman's interpretation (1951, 104–5), real problems give rise to organization formation and the pursuit of collective solutions via government. Thus, government size may be a consequence of government's response to demands for policy solutions (Berry and Lowery 1987). Many other political scientists have noted that preexisting organizations approach government only after *specific* political benefits of interest to them (or the potential for increased *specific* benefits) are provided (Truman 1951; Haider 1974; Copeland and Meier 1984; Walker 1991, 95). Thus, we have little evidence that membership groups are induced into existence by an opportunity to grab whatever might be picked up from a bloated government. And it does not seem likely that they are enticed into lobbying efforts by electorally motivated politicians seeking to extort rents. When taken together, these arguments and empirical findings suggest that the economic accounts of interest organization density rest on a rather odd model of how the political community is constituted.

Most of the contract lobbyists we interviewed agreed, arguing that internal changes in legislatures had little to do with growth of organized interest populations. And, with perhaps a single exception, those who did see some impact of internal changes within legislatures failed to note the kinds of factors—such as alterations in committee jurisdictions—that are central to the Virginia School explanation. Rather, they noted changes in legislative membership—especially the rapid influx of minorities, women, and urban legislators—which have brought new issues to prominence. They also noted that there are more hearings and longer sessions, which have necessitated closer monitoring of legislation. None of these changes speak to increased rent seeking.

In sum, we have few answers to the question of why some states have many more interest organizations than others. Indeed, the lack of serious attention to the role of environmental constraints on population size is evident in the broadly held assumption that the potential size of the interest organization population is essentially infinite, or that there is no meaningful *carrying capacity* of political systems for interest organizations. Truman (1951), for example, assumes that the total number of interest organizations is limited only by the diversity of interests in society. Olson's model, especially, rests on an assumption of unrestricted growth in interest populations, even to the point that economies collapse. And Browne (1990, 503–4) notes that "Private interest niches . . . allow for an *almost unlimited number* of interests to become organized around specific policy rewards within a single policy domain" (emphasis added). Given the many constraints imposed by environmental conditions on other biological and social populations, such faith in the unlimited growth of populations of organized interests seems misplaced.

Finally, perhaps the most insightful research program on interest density falls outside the traditional economics and political science literatures. While most of the organization ecology literature that we examine more fully in chapters 3 and 4 focuses on such private economic institutions as breweries, newspapers, and banks, Aldrich and his colleagues (Aldrich and Staber 1988; Aldrich et al. 1990, 1994) have intensively studied national trade associations, organizations that often engage in lobbying. We will examine this research program in some detail when we present the population ecology approach.

### Diversity and Interest Representation

A second population characteristic that we are interested in is diversity. More so than density, the diversity of interest organizations can be understood in a number of ways depending on the referent used: class interests, the regional base of interests, or some other basis on which we partition society. Still, most analysts of interest organizations assume that the fundamental basis of interest representation is economic (e.g., Schattschneider 1960; Schlozman 1984, 1011–15; Zeigler 1983, 98–104) and interpret diversity in terms of representation of the complexity of economic interests, a tradition that we follow.[5]

Given this orientation, what accounts for the diversity of interest organization populations? Oddly enough, this question is rarely asked. Instead, studies of interest organization populations at the national level typically document and lament a lack of diversity in the seemingly universal dominance of traditional economic groups (Schattschneider 1960; Schlozman 1984; Schlozman and Tierney 1983). Yet, we will see that surveys of state interest organization populations report a great deal of temporal and spatial variation in diversity. While traditional economic organizations typically dominate, the makeup of state interest populations is neither uniform nor static, and it does not vary in obvious ways with population or wealth. Arizona and Colorado, for example, are similar in many ways. Yet, fully 24.5 percent of Colorado's organized interests in 1990 represented governmental entities, while only 2.1 percent represented construction interests. At the same time, only 11.0 percent of Arizona's interest population represented government organizations, and fully 5.7 percent was concerned with construction. There is variation in diversity, and variation calls for explanation.

Once we turn our attention to explanation, however, we run into an even more severe problem: our stock of theory about variation in the diversity of interest communities is surprisingly thin. As with density, there is almost complete inattention to plausible environmental constraints on the carrying capacities of political systems for different types of interest organizations, the aggregated outcomes of which necessarily define system diversity.

## Political Science Explanations of Diversity

Truman offered two explanations of the diversity of interest organization populations. His first hypothesis—one focusing on countermobilization of threatened latent interests—predicts increased diversity over time. Truman (1951, 59, 503–16) argued that as interest organizations increase in number, they tend to disturb the social equilibrium and to stimulate other interests to organize. And because the newer interests are countervailing, an increase in numbers automatically generates greater diversity among the types of interests represented. This explanation is rarely tested (see, however, Aldrich et al. 1994, 234), but it is an essential element of pluralist conceptions in interest representation.

The second explanation is rather mechanistic, suggesting that diversity of interest representation naturally arises from and reflects the diversity of interests in society. Thus, Truman (1951, 53) asserted that "complex civilizations necessarily develop complex political arrangements. Where the patterns of interaction in a society are intricate, the patterns of political behavior must be also."

Truman's hypotheses have been echoed in nearly all subsequent political science assessments of interest organization population diversity *at the state level.* Zeigler (1983, 111), for example, asserted that "the most important aspect of a state's socioeconomic structure concerning interest groups is its level of complexity." In *State Politics, Parties, and Policy,* one of the most influential recent works on state interest organization systems, Morehouse links socioeconomic diversity with interest organization strength. And in their more recent comparative analysis of interest organizations in all fifty states, Thomas and Hrebenar (1990, 138; 1995) conclude that economic and social development will render interest systems more pluralistic or diversified. Thus, we conventionally assert that economic complexity is associated with diversity of representation.

While the linkage between economic complexity and diversity of representation is part of our conventional wisdom, it is not well established either theoretically or empirically. First, economic or socioeconomic complexity is a very broad and imprecisely used concept. Truman (1951, 52) quite intentionally called it "ambiguous." Indeed, he offered only several quite general examples by way of illustrating complexity, and most of these concern a single dimension of complexity: specialization of labor. Later analysts tend to be equally vague. Morehouse (1981, 49) comes closest to offering a more detailed characterization in her assessment of the link between interest system power and industrialization, social integration, and income distribution. Yet, the theoretical linkages between the elements of these compound independent variables and the broader concept of representational complexity are more assumed than demonstrated.

Second, the empirical demonstration of this linkage is at best weak. The central evidence cited for an association between economic complexity and interest organization population diversity is provided by Morehouse's tabular analysis of her presumed indicators of complexity with a reputational measure of interest organization power. The key problem with this evidence is that it entirely skips over the mediating concept of interest organization diversity. And as our example of Arizona and Colorado clearly suggests, the mix of interests represented in states is unlikely to be simply or directly accounted for by the size and complexity of state economies.

More importantly, this account ultimately is not satisfying theoretically. There is a large and underspecified gap between the interest organization population property of diversity and such macro-level traits as economic and societal complexity. Most scholarly analyses implicitly assume that the causal linkage flows through simple mobilization processes whereby interests in society become represented via interest organizations either in an automatic manner, as suggested by Truman (1951), or in a more complex manner through play of the individual-level incentives governing interest organization formation, as discussed by Olson (1965). But given our earlier critique of the limits of individual-level mobilization analyses for understanding interest organization population density, the plausibility of this linkage is questionable. And without a well-established theoretical account of the linkage between interest organization population diversity and the macro-level variables of wealth and complexity, even strong empirical correlations among them are of little interest.

The national-level literature, while also attentive to Truman,[6] seems far more focused on Schattschneider's (1960) assertion about the dominance of economic interests. Indeed, this literature is highly focused on the narrow empirical question of whether the explosion in the *number* of organized interests over recent decades has led to more or less diversity of interest representation. Walker (1983; see also Hansen 1985) suggests that greater access to patronage has enabled nonprofit and citizens' membership groups to more easily overcome the diseconomies of organizing. This in turn, he argues, has facilitated their growth as a proportion of the interest organization population, while business representation has declined, at least relatively. Others (Schlozman 1984; Schlozman and Tierney 1983) conclude the opposite—that the explosion of interest organizations has led to an increased concentration of business interests and hence no greater diversity.

Clearly, the work of Walker and Schlozman and Tierney addresses as directly as anything else in the literature the issue of interest community diversity. Unfortunately, the authors' narrow focus on the simple empirical question of whether the dominance of economic interests has diminished or increased distracts us from the more important theoretical question of explaining diversity. Moreover, we will see in far greater detail in chapter 6 that their empirical analyses—because of partial and noncomparable samples and inadequate measures—provide an inadequate foundation on which to either assess the degree of dominance of economic interests or adequately test theoretical accounts of interest organization diversity.

### Economic Explanations of Diversity

Unfortunately, economists rarely address the issue of diversity directly. As we have seen, the Olson and Virginia School models focus far more on numbers of interest organizations than on their diversity. But their thinking almost certainly parallels that found among political scientists who treat diversity at the population level as an artifact of individual-level mobilization processes. Thus, Olson might argue that any particular balance of interest organizations observed in nature must be a simple cumulative function of their separate processes of mobilizing. More to the point, Olson argues that small groups can mobilize more easily than large groups, which implies that narrow interests will be well represented in the lobbying universe, while broader interests (e.g., consumer, environmental, and other public interests) will be underrepresented. Olson's theory, then, predicts that diversity among represented interests will be limited, and it provides a micro-level theoretical foundation for Schattschneider's (1960) claims about the dominance of traditional economic interests.

Perhaps the sole exception to this negative interpretation within economics is found in Becker's resurrection (1983, 1985) of Truman's hypothesis (1951, 59, 503–16) that interests mobilize in response to perturbations created by other interest organizations. In sharp contrast to Olson's assertions (1982) about the economic consequences of growing interest communities, Becker assumes that the deadweight costs imposed by government's pandering to narrow interests will stimulate countermobilization by encompassing interest organizations. Unfortunately, Becker's work is deficient because it provides no empirical test of this hypothesis.

With respect to diversity, then, the literature leaves us unable to explain why some populations of interest organizations are more diverse than others. Moreover, the literature provides us little in the way of theory to guide empirical analysis. Whether from Truman's perspective or Olson's, diversity is a simple aggregate function of individual-level processes of mobilization. Theories of individual-level mobilization are clearly an important part of our stock of knowledge about interest representation. Nevertheless, they are unlikely to provide us a complete account of properties like interest organization population density and diversity, properties that have meaning only at the population level.

How, then, shall a more satisfying account be developed? Our earlier discussion of interest organization population density points to several opportunities. The primary answer, we believe, lies in greater attention to environmental limitations on the pace of growth of interest organization populations. There is no reason to suppose that these limits constrain different types of interest organizations equally. Indeed, most analyses of membership group mobilization processes assume that the probabilistic rates of mobilization of different types of groups are themselves different (Salisbury 1969; Wilson 1973; Moe 1980; Walker 1983). This makes it a very small step, indeed, to further suppose that the distinctive impacts of environmental constraints operating on the mobilization of different types of interest organizations indirectly determine the mix of interest organization that we observe in our state and national capitals.

A full account of interest organization diversity must also include the mobilization of institutional actors into the lobbying scene. Salisbury (1984) implied that institutions have fewer collective action problems to overcome than do membership groups; thus, they will come to dominate the lobbying universe. He further characterized them as lending a "conservative bias" to politics, which seems to imply a lack of diversity. And to the extent institutions are spurred into action by policy threats (as hypothesized by Salisbury), environmental conditions will influence mobilization rates.

And again, we need to be more attentive to the potential impact of mortality on the diversity of interests represented in the political system. At present, our theoretical knowledge about interest organization mortality is limited to Salisbury's speculation (1984) that institutions are more durable than voluntary associations. If so, institutions will exhibit greater survivorship over time, thereby reducing diversity. His reasoning reflects that of most analysts: organizations with the highest probability of forming will have the easiest time surviving. But no one really knows if this prediction is borne out empirically.[7]

**The Interest/Government Interface**

One of the most contentious issues in the interest representation literature concerns the way in which interest organization communities are structured, with much of the literature focused on the *balkanization* of the policy process—the degree to which legislative consideration of policy issues is structured so that there is little actual conflict between organizations with competing interests. From Truman (1951) through Schattschneider (1960) to Walker (1983), our assessment of the degree of interest organization balkanization has undergone dramatic swings over the course of the postwar period. For the most part, however, this literature has been descriptive, with scholars examining how levels of policy conflict among interests vary across policy domains. Despite the importance of this line of inquiry, it is surprising that much less attention has been devoted to *explaining* why balkanization may or may not occur.

Political Science Explanations
of Interest/Government Interface

Political Science perspectives on policy balkanization have traversed a wild course over the last four decades. It starts, once again, with Truman's model of interest representation. One of its key features was the notion of interest organization competition: "the activities of political interest groups imply controversy and conflict, the essence of politics" (Truman 1951, 502–3). The pluralist school founded on Truman's analysis proved to be short-lived, however. By the next decade, "plural elitists" (McFarland 1992)—Schattschneider (1960), McConnell (1966), Lowi (1969), and Cater (1964)—argued that interest systems are only weakly organized for contention over policy and that politics is fragmented into many isolated decision arenas. Clearly, this balkanization thesis nearly entailed a complete rejection of Truman's analysis.

Scholarly interpretations, however, changed once again through the 1970s and into the 1980s. A new conventional wisdom emerged, a kind of neopluralism, in which students of interest organizations (Walker 1983) noted the dramatic expansion of the interest system and the emergence of sources of countervailing power in the form of new citizens' membership groups. At the same time, at least some scholars who studied the bureaucracy (Heclo 1978) noted the demise of classic subgovernments and their replacement by issue networks or policy subsystems that were more fluid and more open. While something less than Truman's contentious policy arena, the neopluralist model called into question the prevalence of policy balkanization among interests.

Has more recent research on interest organizations supported the neopluralist perspective? The answer is ambiguous. Although there are more organized interests, more engagements in political activity, and more elements of conflict and controversy, many studies in the 1990s suggest that organized interests are not competing directly against one another over a broad spectrum of issues. Scholars find that (1) organized interests specialize in relatively narrow issue domains where some conflict and cooperation among interests occurs, with variations in their levels across domains (Heinz et al. 1993, 249–59; Browne 1990; Browne 1995); (2) within these narrow areas, interest organizations are connected to their allies but do not often relate to their adversaries in a directly competitive manner (Heinz et al. 1993, 308; Browne 1990; Browne 1995, 217–18); (3) there is no central power broker mediating interests (Heinz et al. 1993, 377; Browne 1995); and (4) government is neither the pluralists' neutral umpire nor captured by private interests but rather an independent actor in policy debates (Heinz et al. 1993; Laumann and Knoke 1987; Browne 1995). The image that emerges is still essentially that of balkanization, although a more fluid and less temporally rigid sort.

While neopluralist research describes a very different world than one governed by *iron triangles,* it has not ended debate over policy balkanization. Browne (1995, 215–17), for example, clearly views agricultural policy domains as something far more fluid and unstable than anything that can be described as a subgovernment. Yet, his analysis of agricultural policy still emphasizes only limited conflict among competing interests (Browne 1990; Browne 1995, 217–18). Heinz and his colleagues (Heinz et al. 1993), in contrast, see far more interaction, including conflict, among interests within at least some domains. Both perspectives can be legitimately described as neopluralist, but they disagree, at least to some degree, in their assessments of levels of policy balkanization in the Washington interest community.

These competing perspectives seek to describe levels of policy balkanization in a single interest community. However, the most important question facing us concerns explaining variations in balkanization, whether of the strong sort described by Cater (1964), the modified, neopluralist sort described by Browne (1990, 1995), or the much weaker form described by Heinz and his colleagues (Heinz et al. 1993).

Browne has pursued this question most thoroughly using his theory of policy niches. His study of American agricultural policy (1988, 247) concludes that "organized interests simply find their substantive policy niche and usually fight to stay there as long as staying is feasible. Their greatest competition is heard among the babel of both posturing and active interests, not as a result of their engagement in conflict over policy matters." The seeking of niches, Browne argues, is what accounts for the very high level of balkanization he finds in the agricultural policy domain.

To explain what underlying theoretical mechanisms account for this, Browne points to two survival advantages accrued through a strong identity, suggesting that narrow issue niches benefit an interest organization both with its constituency or patrons (Berry 1977) and with policymakers (Hayes 1981). Browne (1990, 501) pays far less attention to the former, although it is implicit in his conclusion that interest organizations are attentive to issues "that enhance or expand their internal resource base." In this vein, a well-defined issue identity is advantageous because it provides a strong signal to potential members and patrons about what an interest organization does. Still, Browne (1990, 500) places special emphasis on returns on investments in identity during interactions with government officials, suggesting that "organized interests develop issue identities—indeed are compelled to do so—because their representatives must have something recognizable to market within some one or more relevant networks of decision making." In short, the identities of interest organizations are founded on issues.

Those organizations lacking well-established identities, Browne (1990, 501) suggests, face severe difficulties: "New participants to a recurring issue have an entry problem because they have made no gains from production costs sunk as investments in previous deliberations. But long involved participants have maintenance problems because if they redefine or select a new issue during the course of a transaction, or allow either to be done for them, they may well lose their expertise and reputation as part of the settlement. If an interest's representative selects such inappropriate issue choices and loses, neither the investments made nor the benefits of the targeted issue can be recovered. Restricting issue choice is the only rational act." Thus, Browne relates his empirical findings of issue balkanization directly to the transaction between policymakers and interest organization entrepreneurs. Narrow issue identities enhance interests' reputations when engaging in transactions, thereby enhancing their chances of being successful.

While Browne's is surely the most satisfying account of balkanization now available, we have several reasons to question its completeness. The first inheres in the ubiquitous issue of generalizability. Browne studied agricultural policy in Washington. We have good reason to believe that some policy domains are more easily segmented than others (Cigler 1991, 120–25), and that the agricultural sector, in particular, is far more balkanized than many others (Heinz et al. 1993, 247–61). We need to examine populations, then, not narrow subpopulations of a single interest organization population, if we are to adequately test hypotheses about balkanization.

More than any of our other sets of questions, research on the interest organization/government interface is dominated by analyses of the Washington interest system, and the Washington locus may have produced findings that are less than typical of other governments. Specifically, the Washington policy system is highly stable, with issues and actors persisting from year to year (Browne 1990, 501). In contrast, the prevalence in states of high turnover, part-time legislators, and short legislative sessions with necessarily narrower and more restrictive legislative agendas may depreciate the value derived from a reputation for expertise if that reputation is tied to a narrow policy concern.

Second, while development and maintenance of a well-defined issue identity certainly has potential advantages for an interest organization, it also has obvious costs. Internally, a strong policy signal to potential constituents may scare away as many or more potential members or patrons as it attracts. Externally, having a strong reputation with policymakers in one arena may mean that an organization has no reputation in others. Should the arena in which the policy is discussed change—and such changes are not unknown (Mucciaroni 1995; Baumgartner and Jones 1993; Heinz et al. 1993, 396–97)—the organization will be at a serious disadvantage. It may be that the benefits of a narrow issue reputation exceed the costs.

Third, basing interest organization niches on control of a narrow set of issues may undermine organizational identity. On the one hand, for example, Browne (1990, 500) notes that specialization in a narrow issue agenda by interest representatives sends out "messages as to what their organization is all about. Allies and adversaries can be categorized as a consequence." On the other hand, however, Browne (1990, 492) observes that these specialized agendas "may be so narrow that issues seldom overlap from interest to interest. Therefore, the proliferation of issues may not bring with it conditions of routine interorganizational cooperation and conflict." Highly specialized and nonoverlapping issue agendas, therefore, may preclude the very type of interactions that define allies and adversaries (Browne 1995, 217). If there is any truth to the saying that we are best-known through the friends we keep and the enemies we earn, then issue specialization may actually undermine establishment of a strong organizational identity.[8]

Fourth, Browne's central concept of "niche" is defined only intuitively. We will see that there are several plausible interpretations of the niche concept, emphasizing, respectively, an interest organization's place in the policy process, its pattern of maintenance, or some combination of the two. At best, Browne addresses only the first of these. More to the point, we will see that more complex interpretations will allow us to consider multiple dimensions on which interest organizations' identities might be established.

This echoes an older, albeit undeveloped, interpretation of interest organization identity. James Q. Wilson (1973, 263), for example, observed more than twenty years ago that interest organizations are risk averse: "the easiest and most prudent maintenance strategy is to develop *autonomy*—that is, a distinctive area of competence, a clearly demarcated and exclusively served clientele or membership, and undisputed jurisdiction over a function, service, goal, or cause." Wilson (1973, 265) further speculates that in developing autonomy, newer organizations must adopt a strategy of *resource conflict* with older organizations to secure a viable niche. Conflict over one or all of these dimensions could serve as the basis of a well-defined organizational identity. Thus, Wilson uses the concept of niche in a fuller, multidimensional sense and offers a specific hypothesis about the strategies that are used to establish niches. We will see that this broader interpretation of the niche concept provides a far more powerful theoretical handle for understanding how interest organizations deal with their complex internal and external environments.

## Economic Explanations of Interest/Government Interface

Turning to the analyses offered by economists, only the Virginia School offers a well-articulated account of interest organizations' interface with government. In contrast, Olson (1982) and Becker (1983, 1985) have little to say about how interest organizations interact with government in policy making, although presumably Olson's encompassing groups operate in a manner approximating the role that political scientists assign them in neocorporatist systems. Both analysts seem to accept the interface as essentially uninteresting, as a given resulting from the pursuit of efficient strategies of extraction by either interest organizations or elected officials.

The Virginia School explanation, we have seen, comes in two flavors. The weak form of the model—government as a lottery winner with a sudden collection of friends and relatives—also has no real account for the balkanization of interests once they interface with the policy process. At best, such issue segregation might be an efficient outcome of pigs scrambling to feed at a trough. In contrast, the strong form of the model implies a specific account of the observed segregation of interests in the policy process. In this form, as augmented by principal-agent analysis (Moe 1984, 1987; Weingast and Moran 1982; Shugart and Tollison 1986), the balkanization of interests serves the interests of politicians. If politicians induce the formation of interest organizations to begin with (by providing government benefits in order to extract rents to support politicians' reelections), rational legislators would then use their institutional positions and their monopoly power over issues to claim credit in the benefit exchange. Their goals are best achieved, it is argued, if issues and jurisdictional responsibilities are divided narrowly.

This approach has, however, many problems beyond the theoretical conundrums associated with the principal-agent model raised by Moe (1987) and the plausibility of the model's implicit community assembly rules. An even more fundamental problem is that rational behavior on the part of politicians cannot account ultimately for the resulting fragmentation of interests. Empirical analyses of interest communities have observed patterns that are highly stable (Browne 1990; Heinz et al. 1993). But if the goal of politicians is to extract as many resources from organizational interests as possible, the best arrangement would be to routinely auction among several interest organizations the legislator's monopoly rights over issues. But in a balkanized setting, the interest organization can offer a price that the legislator is forced to accept. If he or she does not, there is no alternative interest organization from which to extract rent. Stable patterns of issue segregation imply that legislators face monopoly interests expressing policy demands, thereby canceling the legislator's presumed power to extract rents.[9]

Given these theoretical and empirical problems in both the political science and economic literatures, how are we to account for the often-documented pattern of limited competition among interest organizations? While a more complete answer must await the development of our own model in later chapters, it is worth reemphasizing that Browne's insightful analysis suggests that policy niches must be explained in terms of the survival value they afford organized interests. But even with this insight, many parts of the puzzle are missing. Do some political systems have more issue niches than others? If issues can be cut into infinitely small pieces as suggested by Browne (1990, 503), and if rapacious politicians have an incentive to extract as many rents as possible, why would political systems vary in niche density? Are niche formation and issue segregation related to the processes of interest mobilization and organization maintenance that generate interest organization populations? And most fundamentally, just what is a niche anyway?

### Organized Interest Populations and Their Impact

While impact is not the sole reason for studying interest organizations, it is probably true that most scholars are attracted to the topic because they are interested in the impact of lobbying on public policy. And over the course of decades, the impact literature has been one of the most productive components of the interest representation research program. Much of this literature examines the specific impact of particular interest organizations on narrow policies. While clearly important to a complete understanding of interest organization politics, such studies are of little direct interest when approaching the topic from a population perspective. Many other theories and a few empirical studies, however—studies ranging in emotional tone from giddy optimism to blackest despair—attempt to gauge the policy and governance impacts of entire populations of interest organizations.

### Political Science Explanations
### of Organized Interest Impact

The history of political science thought on interest group pluralism starts with the vision of benign social balance offered by Truman (1951) and Dahl (1961), moves through the diminished possibility of popular sovereignty of plural elitism as interpreted by Lowi (1969) and others, and arrives at the guarded optimism of modern neopluralists like Dahl

(1982) or Salisbury (1990). Throughout this cycle, empirical research has proceeded on three levels: case studies of individual lobbying efforts on specific policy issues, midrange analyses of specific patterns of influence, and system-level analyses of the broader impact of the interest organization populations taken as a whole.[10]

The first lengthy analysis of note was Bauer, Pool, and Dexter's study (1963) of foreign trade policy. They found that the business community was so internally divided and lacking in resources that it was incapable of influencing Congress. Milbrath's portrait (1963) of Washington lobbyists that same year depicted them as benevolent figures with limited impact on public policy. Since then, case studies have reported more mixed evidence of interest organization influence (see, e.g., Rothenberg's study [1992] of Common Cause), leading researchers to focus on the conditions under which organized interests influence policy choice, rather than on blanket statements about impact.[11] This contextual focus rather naturally steers researchers away from case studies and toward midrange studies.

The authors of midrange studies select an array of issues or a set of policy domains and seek to discover when and under what conditions organized interests have influence. For example, at the state level, Wiggins, Hamm, and Bell (1992) analyzed a sample of bills introduced in three state legislatures. They determined the positions (pro or con) of lobbyists and of the governors and legislative party leaders on each bill. They found that broad interests represented within political parties can thwart special interests represented by interest organizations.

At the national level, Heinz and his colleagues (Heinz et al. 1993) looked at interest organization success on a number of issues in four policy domains—health, agriculture, labor, and energy. No single category of interests proved more successful than others in achieving its policy objectives. Using a broad range of explanatory variables, the analysts had great difficulty in accounting statistically for variance in success rates, leading them to conclude that determinants of success are situation-specific (Heinz et al. 1993, 351). Thus, mixed results abound at this level of analysis too, results that suggest to some scholars that we must return to case studies to find evidence of influence.

Of course, studies at these two levels of analysis do not address our question—what is the impact of *populations* of organized interests on political *systems*? Nor do these results address the central normative concern of pluralism's many critics—the overall corrupting impact of organized interests on democratic governance. Fortunately, a few scholars cast their inquiries at the system level. While their empirical analysis places their work among the midrange studies, Heinz and his coauthors (Heinz et al. 1993) generalize from their findings to hypothesize that there may be cycles in interest organization influence on policy. Increased lobbying introduces greater uncertainty into the policy system, thereby spurring the countermobilization of other interests. This then leads to even greater lobbying efforts, which again increases uncertainty and spurs even further countermobilization. In such a cyclical pattern, a pattern that echoes Truman's (1951) ideas, more activity on the part of interest organizations actually acts to "cancel out" interest organization influence. As Salisbury (1990) succinctly wrote, "more groups, less clout."

A few other scholars reinforce this judgment about the policy impact of dense and active populations of interest organizations. At the state level, Thomas and Hrebenar's large-scale studies (1990, 147; 1995) sampled experts' ratings of the overall influence of interest organizations on politics and policy in each state. Fewer systems were rated as dominant by Thomas and Hrebenar than in Morehouse's 1981 study, and more were rated as complementary/subordinate in influence. Overall, states moved toward the weak end of the continuum where the interest organization system as a whole has less impact.

In an explanation that echoes well the conclusions of Heinz and his colleagues (Heinz et al. 1993), Thomas and Hrebenar (1990, 138) argue that economic and social development has made the interest organization system more pluralistic or diverse, which has undermined at least some of the power of traditionally dominant interests, especially business. As a result, the strength of interest organizations as a whole has declined. At the same time, however, Thomas and Hrebenar (1995, 13–14) note that "a good case can be made that individual groups are more powerful than ever. . . . [The] contradiction is that because of this increased pluralism group systems as a whole may be gradually exerting less influence on their state political systems as groups cancel each other's power."

Peterson (1990–91) reached a similar conclusion about the lessened impact of special interests in Washington, D.C. In an innovative study, he estimated special interest influence by the percentage of gross national product (GNP) the federal government spends on discretionary programs. He found that this measure of special interest spending declined during the 1980s, which he interprets as a function of declining political influence on the part of interest organizations. Peterson, like many other scholars, credits policy retrenchment, stronger political parties, and Reagan's centralization of policy decision making for this triumph over special interests.

Although research at these three levels cannot provide a definitive answer to our questions, the overall trend recently is toward less pessimism among scholars of interest representation. This is in marked contrast to views common among the general public, as well as among some politicians who characterize the role of special interests in nearly apocalyptic terms. At least part of political scientists' optimism must arise from their studied inability to find evidence that more interest organizations lead to more interest organization influence. Another part may be due to the widely perceived strengthening of other political institutions representing broader interests. This reminds us that measuring interest organization influence is always tricky given its relative nature and multiple meanings (Thomas and Hrebenar 1994).

### Economic Explanations of Organized Interest Impact

The economic literature on the policy and governance impact of interest organization populations also varies in its optimism, with at least some analysts holding to Truman's vision. Such optimism is not evident, however, in either traditional economic analyses following the ideas of Stigler (1971) and Peltzman (1976) or the Virginia School literature on interest organizations. While they disagree about whether politicians or interest organizations are the first actors in the process, both view the consequences of interest representation in starkly negative terms.

To Stigler (1971) and Peltzman (1976), these consequences entail regulation not in the public interest but in the interest of the regulated. To Virginia School analysts (Mueller and Murrell 1986; Coughlin, Mueller, and Murrell 1990; Shugart and Tollison 1986), the combination of organized interests and vote-maximizing politicians leads to almost inevitable deadweight losses to society such that only drastic restrictions on the power of government are likely to prevent social and economic collapse (Mitchell and Munger 1991, 531). To Virginians, interest fragmentation and issue niches preclude the balance of interests envisioned by pluralists; acceding to one special interest cannot be balanced by acceding to another. In reference to pluralism's claims, Mitchell and Munger (1991, 528) note, "Virginians would gainsay this, claiming that the self-regarding activities of special groups generally cannot be balanced by encouraging more to be organized. One group who seeks a protective tariff, for example, will not be balanced by another that opposes the tariff. Instead, the opposition group will most likely receive some protection or subsidy of its own, worsening rather than improving the situation." Out of such pessimism arises, of course, Virginians' advocacy of constitutional amendments restricting government size.

Nearly as pessimistic as the Virginia School, Olson, in his second book, *The Rise and Decline of Nations,* focuses on the growth-depressing effects of dense interest organization populations, arguing that they reduce efficiency. Over time, the accumulation of special interest organizations increases the complexity of governmental regulation, especially regulations that protect the inefficient, thereby reducing the rate of economic growth. Olson does allow for a potential constraint on the growth-inhibiting effects of rapacious interest organizations—in the moderating actions of encompassing groups that, because they internalize multiple policy interests, are able to limit the pernicious consequences arising from narrowly self-interested behavior. But Olson (1982, 47–53) never explains how these encompassing groups evolve in the face of the disincentives noted in his earlier work, *The Logic of Collective Action.*

Becker (1983, 1985; see also Mitchell and Munger 1991) offers the most optimistic perspective within the economic interest organization literature, via his reconceptualizations of Olson's analysis of encompassing groups and Truman's (1951) hypothesis about countermobilization. Relying on Coase's analysis (1960) of the allocation consequences of the distribution of property rights and on a maximizing objective somewhat different from that of Olson, Becker demonstrates that the deadweight/efficiency losses associated with the pursuit of narrow interests *should* encourage the development of new, more encompassing interest organizations that will counteract the effects of issue fragmentation. In Olson's terms, the efficiency consequences of issue and policy fragmentation will generate the incentives needed to spur the development of encompassing interest organizations. But Becker's analysis rests ultimately on faith that "waste" cannot be tolerated in a market. It is an outcome that is implicit in his very definition of how markets work. Without explaining how such countervailing interests will overcome the many disincentives to organization demonstrated by Olson (1965), Becker's analysis represents more of a hope than a solution.

There is, however, an even more troubling problem applicable to the interest organization impact literature in its entirety: all of these analyses depend on the very fragile theoretical linkages that tie the several impact hypotheses to variations in organized interest system density, system diversity, and the structure of the government interface. *If* there are environmentally determined capacity limits on the density of interest organization populations, then Olson's (1982) expectation that interest organization pluralism will strangle economic growth will need to be rethought. *If* the number of issue niches and their character is ultimately dependent on the processes that govern the growth and the diversity of interest populations, then the prospects for pluralism may be more, or even less, bleak than the models suggest. *If* the diversity of organized interest systems changes in predictable ways as interest systems become more dense, then their impact on government and the economy may be different—for better or for worse—from those outlined by Becker, Olson, or the Virginia School. To the extent that these issues are unresolved, each of these linkages must be viewed as a potential weakness of the impact models.

### Toward Better Theory

In sum, many questions about organized interests remain. Until we can explain how the incentives of interest organization mobilization interact with environmental conditions to generate specific patterns of interest organization population growth and density, specific patterns of population diversity, and specific modes of interaction with government, any answers in the literature are at best partial and incomplete. In large part, this disappointing conclusion arises from our focus at the population level. And unfortunately, the literature has little to tell us about populations of organized interests.

Some may find this rather dismal conclusion surprising, noting that the broad theories of Truman in *The Governmental Process* and Olson in *The Rise and Decline of Nations* are clearly focused at the population level. Becker's work also, as well as that of the Virginia School, addresses the population level of analysis. While such a characterization is accurate, it is also true that most of the empirical work on the politics of interest organizations is founded on individual-level theories about mobilization, examines individual decisions about joining membership groups, or assesses the influence on policy of one, or at most a few, interest organizations. When it comes, then, to empirically well-established answers to population-level questions, the political science and economics cupboards—with, we have seen, some notable exceptions—are all too bare.

This disjunction between our most broad-gauged theories about interest organizations and the more narrowly focused models motivating actual research suggests that we could profit from developing a new midrange theory of interest organization populations to bridge the gap. Such a midrange theory should provide clear guidance about answering population-level questions, while at the same time being consistent with what we know about how micro-level incentives govern interest organization formation. Simply put, we need an ecological theory of interest organization politics. We explore the nature of ecological theories in chapter 3 as a necessary prelude to building an ecological model of the politics of interest representation.

CHAPTER 3

# The Population Ecology Approach

If we are to understand better the population-level dynamics of interest organizations, we need to employ theories and methods designed to answer population-level questions. The population ecology research program provides such theories and methods.[1] We explore, therefore, the nature of population ecology in this chapter as a necessary prelude to developing a model of interest organization populations. In the first two sections, key definitions and assumptions underlying population ecology are discussed. We then consider a range of ecological processes using concepts from traditional evolutionary biology and modern ecological theory. In the fourth section, we examine how species density and diversity are determined using the population ecology's Energy-Stability-Area (ESA) model of biodiversity. And finally, we tackle two broad criticisms of applying population ecology models to the study of human organizations.

Prior to beginning our review, however, two caveats deserve note. First, population ecology models were developed by population biologists over the course of this century and only applied by social scientists to the study of organizations in the last few decades.[2] Because the latter are derived from the former, we give priority to the more original contributions of population biologists. Second, population ecology, especially as developed in population biology, is a large and dynamic field, making it difficult to fully characterize its diversity of thought. We focus, therefore, on very traditional or core elements of population ecology thinking.[3]

**Key Definitions in Ecological Analyses**

The basic conceptual building blocks in population biology are *species.* There are, however, many overlapping and competing definitions, none of which has proven to be entirely satisfactory or without controversy.[4] Still, most population biologists accept the *biological-species concept,* which confers species-status to "a population or series of populations of organisms that freely interbreed with one another in natural conditions but not with members of other species" (E. O. Wilson

1992, 405). Relative consensus, however, has not obviated the problems with this definition, perhaps the most important being its restrictive attention to reproductive issues. Thus, Eldredge and Grene (1992, 26) argue that "it is economic as well as reproductive properties that mark off the organisms of one species from its congeners." To encompass such properties, E. O. Wilson (1992, 405) also offers a much more general definition of species as the "basic unit of classification, consisting of a population or series of populations of closely related and similar organisms."

If species constitute the basic conceptual building blocks of population biology, its explanatory foci are *populations, communities,* and *ecosystems.* Indeed, it is their attention to explanation at these levels that sets population biologists apart from their disciplinary colleagues. Populations are simply "any group of organisms belonging to the same species at the same time and place" (E. O. Wilson 1992, 404). Communities, suggest Begon, Harper, and Townsend (1990, 613), are partial or complete assemblages "of species populations which occur together in space and time," while ecosystems "comprise the biological community together with its physical environment."

To some biologists—especially those who view species only in terms of changing gene frequencies—populations, communities, and ecosystems hold little intrinsic interest. They merely reflect the outcomes of biological processes occurring at lower levels of analysis, especially the genetic level. Other biologists (Eldredge and Grene 1992, 2–5, 18–20; Mayr 1988, 10–11, 453) emphatically reject this reductionist approach. Thus, Begon, Harper, and Townsend (1990, 613) argue that, "The nature of the community is obviously more than the sum of its constituent parts. It is their sum plus the interactions between them. Thus, there are *emergent* properties that appear only when the community is the focus of attention." Most population biologists apply the same logic of emergent properties in justifying special attention to populations and ecosystems as distinctive units of analysis.

In further analyzing populations, communities, and ecosystems, ecologists often use another set of terms to define specific economic relationships, settings, or activities. While typically defined in less precise terms, these include *guilds,* which are sets of species "that make their living in the same way," and *trophic levels,* "which may be thought of as feeding levels" (Ehrlich and Roughgarden 1987, 322). *Species flocks,* according to E. O. Wilson (1992, 110), "comprise relatively numerous species of immediate common ancestry and are limited to a single well-isolated area." We will have occasion to use some of these terms as well as several others from the biological literature when our analysis turns to interest organizations in chapter 4.

The basic conceptual building block in organization ecology is the individual organization, which corresponds poorly to species as defined by the biological-species concept. Indeed, of all of the concepts we will consider, viewing organizations as species is probably the one for which there is the least natural congruence between biotic and organizational phenomena and the one that has, not surprisingly, received the most criticism (Young 1988, 3–4). Obviously, organizations do not have genes to be recombined and passed on in lineages, which precludes use of the biological-species concept.[5] Instead, organization ecologists (Hannan and Freeman 1989, 45–53) typically employ a definition of organizations as species that reflects well E. O. Wilson's (1992, 405) focus on biological species as "populations of closely related and similar organisms," where similarity is defined in terms of both the internal content or function of organizations and the nature of their external relations.[6]

A potential problem with this definition lies in the fact that species might be viewed as collections of individuals or as classes, while organization ecology's definition places the individual organization in the position of species. This, however, is far less of a problem than we might think, once we recognize that biologists often conceptualize species as individuals for purposes of considering properties emergent at only the species level (Hull 1976; 1978; 1980; 1988, 213–23; 1992). Unlike classes, species are individuals in that they have beginnings, endings, and a unique history between those two points. Accordingly, biological theories addressing species must treat them as conceptual individuals. The same is true for organizations, and their common individuality at the conceptual level, not numbers of units, enables us to define organizations as species.

Turning to higher levels of analysis, Hannan and Freeman (1977, 934) note, "Populations of organizations must be alike in some respect, that is, they must have some unit character. Unfortunately, identifying a population of organizations is not a simple matter." Organization ecologists address this problem by defining populations of organizations as those exhibiting a similar form in a common environmental setting. Thus, Hannan and Freeman (1977, 935–36) note that "systems relevant to the study of organization-environment relations are those usually defined by geography, by political boundaries, by market or product considerations, etc. Given a systems definition, a population of organizations consists of all the organizations within a particular boundary that have a common form." With this definition, it then follows that communities of organizations are partial or complete assemblages of populations of organizations in specific temporal and spatial settings. Applying these definitions in specific settings, of course, can be very difficult (Zucker 1989, 543), but this difficulty is hardly a fundamental criticism.

Critically, and like population biologists, organization ecologists argue that population- and community-level phenomena cannot be analyzed solely in terms of concepts and methods appropriate for lower levels of analysis (Carroll 1984, 90). Thus, Hannan and Freeman (1977, 933) argue that "ecological analysis is conducted at three levels: individual, population, and community. Events at one level almost always have consequences at other levels. Despite this interdependence, population events cannot be reduced to individual events . . . and community events cannot be simply reduced to population events." In short, concern for reductionism in explanation is as evident in organization ecology as in population biology.

**Key Assumptions of Ecological Analyses**

In understanding the dynamics of species, populations, communities, and ecosystems, ecologists typically adhere to several important assumptions, the most general of which is the *isomorphism principle* (Hannan and Freeman 1977, 957; Meyer and Rowan 1983, 28). In biology, in fact, this principle is so deeply ingrained that it is rarely expressed explicitly (for an exception, see Eldredge and Grene 1992, 17). Thus, one of the more complete definitions is provided by Hannan and Freeman (1977, 938–39) in their application and extension of Amos Hawley's work (1944, 1950) to the sociology of organizations: "Hawley answers the question of why there are so many kinds of organizations. According to Hawley, the diversity of organization forms is isomorphic to the diversity of the environments. In each distinguishable environmental configuration one finds, in equilibrium, only that organization form optimally adapted to the demands of the environment." On the basis of this assumption, population ecology seeks to discover, analyze, and articulate the ways in which environmental forces influence the properties of species, populations, communities, and ecosystems.

The second critical assumption, and one that biology shares with economics and organization ecology, is *resource scarcity* (Hannan and Freeman 1977, 940–41). The resources that organisms, species, and populations require to survive are assumed to be limited in supply. As Eldredge and Grene (1992, 110) note, "Traditional, too, in the Darwinian heritage is to see energy resources as perhaps the most important limiting factor of local conspecific population size." While this assumption is simply stated, we will see that it does much to guide ecological analyses of population dynamics.

There is, however, one potential problem in the way in which this assumption is applied in organization ecology. As Young (1988, 22) states the issue, "For both human ecology and population ecology the fact that human beings and organizations can alter and create resources means that their models are at the outset very different from the biological version." But Young is wrong; this is not a property unique to human populations. Indeed, conventional views of ecological succession view resources not as strictly exogenous but as something created by the biological community itself through modification of the physical environment (Odum 1969, 262).[7]

A third critical assumption is about *equilibrium*. As E. O. Wilson (1992, 406) defines the term, species equilibrium is "the steady state number of species, or biodiversity, found on an island or isolated patch of habitats due to a balance between the immigration of new species and the extinction of old residents." Equilibrium is an assumption often found in analyses of communities as well (Ehrlich and Roughgarden 1987, 403). Thus, Eldredge and Grene (1992, 110) note, "It is conventionally assumed that local populations are at or near their maximum population size, given the 'carrying capacity' of the local environment, that is, the energy resources available to organisms with a given set of economic adaptations." Such steady states are generally taken as a given and become, for the population ecologist, the object of explanation. Given an observed ecosystem, the population ecologist attempts to explain how it reached its present state of development (Odum 1969, 266).

This does not mean, however, that populations, communities, and ecosystems are static; equilibria are only local and temporary. Ecological succession has been a major focus of study for most of this century (Clements 1936; Odum 1969), and ecologists have long recognized the importance of environmental disturbances. Thus, Begon, Harper, and Townsend (1990, 740) note, "The truth is that investigators who focus attention on equilibrium points have in mind that these are merely states towards which systems tend to be attracted, but about which there may be greater or lesser fluctuation." This approach matches well with contemporary understandings of equilibrium in organization ecology (Carroll 1984, 74, 85). Just as importantly, because any particular equilibrium condition of an ecosystem is observed does not imply that a given set of initial starting conditions determined it (Park 1948). More recently, ecologists have begun to recognize the importance of different initial starting conditions and the possibly chaotic features of population growth and change (May 1974; Real and Levin 1991, 183–84). Still, given the difficulty of experimentally manipulating whole ecosystems, concepts of species population and community equilibria continue to dominate the literature and, on the whole, have provided a useful starting point for ecological analysis.

## The Dynamics of Ecological Processes

### Population Biology

To account for interspecific and intraspecific interactions that produce populations, communities, and ecologies, population biologists use the conceptual tools of traditional Darwinian analysis as elaborated on and extended by such influential twentieth-century ecologists as G. Evelyn Hutchinson (1957, 1959). Thus, the driving force motivating ecological interactions is the *competition* arising directly from the scarcity of resources within an ecosystem (Eldredge and Grene 1992, 110). As Keller (1992a, 69; see also MacIntosh 1992, 67) has written, "So automatic is the association between scarcity and competition that, in modern ecological usage, competition has come to be defined as the simultaneous reliance of two individuals, or two species, on a finite resource that is limited in supply. . . . Because the scarcity of resources can itself hardly be questioned, such a definition lends to competition the same a priori status."[8]

Population biologists note two important but nonobvious characteristics of competition. First, they follow directly in Darwin's footsteps by assuming that the locus of competition is largely within species (MacIntosh 1992, 61) or among those relying on similar resources. Species relying on different resources have no reason to compete, because access by one does not exclude the other from what it needs to survive. This sharp distinction between competition as an intraspecies phenomenon and either *predation* or *mutualism* (Boucher 1992) as forms of interspecific interaction is characteristic of population ecology interpretations of communities.

Second, and in large part as a consequence of viewing competition as restricted to those using similar resources, population ecologists observed that competition rarely involves direct combat but most often involves avoidance via segregation into distinctive niches. Thus, Colinvaux (1978, 144) notes, "A species lives triumphant in its own special niche from which none can displace it. Only the stragglers into the niches of others must be removed by brutal struggle. Natural selection designs different kinds of animals and plants so that they *avoid* competition [as overt conflict]. A fit animal is not one that fights well, but one that avoids fighting all together." This is especially so in intraspecies competition over common resources. Here, physical combat would reduce the energy available to be invested in offspring, to the advantage of those members of the species that avoid overt conflict. Competition still occurs, but it is generally ritualized so that energy for reproduction is conserved.

In this competition, what constitutes *fitness*? As in the case of species, we might think that biologists would have developed an agreed-on definition of fitness long ago. But, as Diane Paul (1992, 112) has observed, "'Fitness' is perhaps the most contentious concept in evolutionary biology." Indeed, multiple and competing definitions have been employed since Darwin's time (Paul 1992; Keller 1992b; Beatty 1992). But given the synthesis of evolutionary biology and genetics in the middle part of this century, most biologists have come to view fitness in terms of the propensity of passing on genes to future generations and, accordingly, to view competition as the process that leads to differential fitness (Beatty 1992). This, of course, is a definition of fitness that is especially well suited for a biological-species definition of species. But consensus on this definition has by no means eliminated all controversy, and there are still frequent calls for alternatives. One of the more recent interpretations (Cooper 1984) entering the fray offers a long-term view of fitness as "expected time to extinction" (ETE), a definition that will prove useful when we consider nonbiological fitness.

What makes population ecology models Darwinian are, of course, the selection and adaptation implications of competition for scarce resources among differentially fit individuals. It is through the mechanisms of selection and adaptation that competition produces isomorphism with the environment. Indeed, the concept of natural selection is so important an animating force behind population ecology's isomorphism principle and its assumption of species equilibrium that most definitions of *selection* are explicitly predicated on prior notions of competition and fitness. Endler (1992, 220; see also Burian 1992, 7), for example, defines natural selection as "a *process* that occurs if and only if these three conditions are present: the population has (a) variability among individuals in some attribute or trait (phenotypic variation); (b) a consistent relationship between the trait and mating ability, fertilizing ability, fertility, fecundity, and/or survivorship (fitness variation); and (c) a consistent relationship, for that trait, between parents and their off-spring." In effect, these concepts are defined in terms of each other to such an extent that they form an interlocking conceptual system of unusual power.

At least three aspects of natural selection as part of the Darwinian mechanism generating species equilibrium will become important for our later analysis of interest organizations. First, and perhaps most importantly, it should be clear that in Darwinian analysis the environment is doing the selecting. Variation in phenotypes and fitness provide only the raw material. The interaction of these variables with environmental conditions results in selection. But an environment is made up of any number of "conditions." The concept of natural selection identifies only some of these as critical. Thus, Brandon (1992, 84) concludes, "From the point of view of the theory of natural selection the relevant environment is the selective environment. Selection occurs when differential adaptedness to a common selective environment leads to differential reproductive success." Or, if we were using Cooper's definition (1984) of fitness, it is the *selective environment* that leads to differences in ETE.

Second, while selection occurs at multiple levels, it means very different things at each. This too is a controversial issue in evolutionary biology. Over the course of decades, proponents of selection at the level of the genotype, phenotype, and group have competed over their particular visions of the "primary" unit of selection (D. S. Wilson 1992; Lloyd 1992; Mayr 1988, 100–103). In large part, the confusions arising from this debate result from inadequate specification of what selection is and of what is being selected for at different levels of analysis (Endler 1992; Hull 1980; Lloyd 1992). In population ecology, Mayr's view (1988, 100–103; see also Eldredge and Grene 1992, 12) that the most important unit of selection is the individual is especially useful. The individual animal, not its genes as separable units or its species as a whole, interacts directly with the environment in a manner that influences its survival. Thus, Mayr (1988, 103) notes that "Normal selection begins to operate as soon as the biased variation [in genotypes] affects the fitness of the phenotype." Selection of genotypes, then, is a consequence of selection of phenotypes, as is selection of species.

Third, natural selection is a *stochastic process*. Mayr (1988, 111) notes, "The large number of stochastic processes in populations of finite size, as well as the constraints which operate during selection, prevent selection from ever being a deterministic process. Rather, it must be remembered at all times that selection is probabilistic. . . . Each individual encounters in its environment numerous unpredictable adverse forces, such as catastrophes, epidemics, and unexpected encounters with enemies in which the outcome is largely probabilistic." The stochastic nature of selection has both advantages and disadvantages. It means that we can never predict which traits, individuals, or species will be deemed more fit in the selection process. But it also means that we can bring the very powerful tools of probability analysis to bear on questions of selection at the level of the population.

Selection is but one step in the Darwinian process of evolution and is cross-sectional in its operation. *Adaptation* adds the temporal dimension needed to link selection to the isomorphism principle. According to West-Eberhard (1992, 13), "In contemporary evolutionary biology an 'adaptation' is a characteristic of an organism whose form is the result of selection in a particular functional context. . . . Accordingly, the process of 'adaptation' is the evolutionary modification of a character under selection for efficient or advantageous (fitness-enhancing) functioning in a particular context or set of contexts." More simply, over time, selection from variations in phenotype and fitness leads to evolutionary change in the traits or characters of phenotypes—the properties of organisms (Darden 1992; Fistrup 1992). Adaptation through selection, therefore, defines evolution (Richards 1992).

For our purposes, two aspects of the biological understanding of adaptation are especially important. First, in evolutionary biology, the concept of adaptation is directly linked to selection and is not a separate process leading to evolutionary change. Adaptations arise through selection and the resulting changes in gene frequencies within populations, not through changes within single individuals as they confront the environment. We will see that the absence of such a linkage is one of the primary ways in which organization population ecology differs from population ecology in biology.

A second important aspect of adaptation—one equally evident in biological and at least some organization applications of population ecology—is that it is not an open-ended process. Adaptation is constrained in important ways. In biology, selection can only work if a variation in genotypes exists within a population and then only within the developmental limitations imposed by existing genetic endowments (Mayr 1988, 106–9; Eldredge and Grene 1992, 27).

Given the underlying assumptions of the population ecology approach and its interpretation of the concepts of traditional evolutionary biology, what is the character of interactions among individuals and species? We answer this question by looking at additional concepts central to modern ecological theory. The concept of *niche* has been employed in population ecology for many decades, but its meaning has changed greatly. Grinnell (1917) was the first to systematically employ the concept in ecological studies, viewing "ecological niche" as "roughly synonymous with habitat" (Kingsland 1991, 7). A niche was seen as a place or physical space in which an animal lived (Griesemer 1992, 233–34). In contrast, Elton (1958) saw a niche as a place in the food chain, which emphasizes the lifestyle of the organism or how it makes its living (Griesemer 1992, 234–35). While pointing to very different phenomena, Colwell (1992, 241) has noted that both concepts "identified the niche as *an attribute of the environment."* These definitions of niche said little directly about populations of animals.

Both definitions were forever displaced in the ecology literature by Hutchinson's reinterpretation (1957) of niche *"as an attribute of the population (species) in relation to its environment. . . .* [T]he Hutchinsonian niche of a population describes ecological aspects of the phenotypes of a population, including physiological characteristics and relations with other species" (Colwell 1992, 241). Hutchinson conceived of a niche as a relationship between a population and the many variables in that population's environment that bear on its survival, proposing that each variable be ordered so that "In this way an n-dimensional hypervolume is defined, every point in which corresponds to a state in the environment which would permit the species $S_1$ to exist indefinitely." The space so defined constitutes the *fundamental niche* of the species, or the space in which it *may* survive. This reinterpretation, because it includes all of the features of the environment bearing on species survival, effectively combines Grinnell's emphasis on habitat and Elton's focus on food chains and links both to populations (Real and Levin 1991, 181).

The Hutchinsonian definition of niche has become a central organizing concept of population ecology. The reason inheres in Hutchinson's definition of the fundamental niche as a potential phenomena: an n-dimensional hypervolume where a species *may* survive. Of course, the potential of all fundamental niches is rarely filled. What is filled is the *realized niche* of a species (Hutchinson 1957, 418). In accounting for the difference between fundamental and realized niches, population ecologists stress competition between species utilizing the same resources that define the n-dimensional hypervolume in question. They observed that species with overlapping fundamental niches compete over the area of overlap until only one species remains; the overlapping fundamental niche space is partitioned between the species, even to the point that one species no longer has any viable niche space at all and disappears entirely.

This finding has been codified as the *competitive exclusion principle,* which was defined by Gause (quoted by Real and Levin 1991, 180) when he noted that "as a result of competition two similar species scarcely ever occupy similar niches, but displace each other in such a manner that each takes possession of certain peculiar kinds of food and modes of life in which it has an advantage over its competition." This "principle" has received strong empirical support both in experimental laboratory settings (Park 1948) and in field observations (MacArthur 1958; Benkman 1992; Weiner 1994), and it has become another of the central ideas of modern population ecology in biology.

The reasons are not hard to understand. Most obviously, the view of competition implicit in the competitive exclusion principle represents a straightforward extension of population ecology's emphasis on intraspecific competition to interspecific competition. Both types of competition share the trait of involving conflict over common resources. More importantly, the notion of competition over common resources associated with fundamental niches and the process of niche partitioning provides a way in which to link selection, adaptation, and even speciation to the observed behavior of organisms. For example, Lack (1947) concluded on the basis of observations of Galapagos Island finches that not only do competitors partition common resources, but that partitioning can alter selection pressures of the environment from those associated with the fundamental niche to those associated with the realized niche. This will result in differential selection pressures and, thereby, adaptation over time along a different path than might otherwise have been observed. Competitive exclusion can drive character displacement and speciation (E. O. Wilson 1992, 173–76).[9] In short, the competitive exclusion principle (Gause 1934), in conjunction with niche analysis, serves as a central organizing idea for the many diverse concepts of population biology.

While quite powerful theoretically, the combination of the niche concept and the competitive exclusion principle creates two quite practical problems for ecological research. First, the competitive exclusion principle emphasizes the partitioning of resources as the primary expression of competition, rather than overt conflict. Thus, Hannan and Carroll (1992, 27) note in their study of organizational populations, "We assume that processes of intense competition may result in the *absence* of interaction across some boundary. This can be the case when two populations compete on a resource gradient and one can exclude the other through more efficient exploitation of resources or power. In such cases, the absence of interaction does not indicate that competition is lacking. Rather, the lack of observable interaction reflects the intensity of competition." While this interpretation is widely shared among population ecology scholars, by inverting our intuitive sense of competition as conflict it can make it difficult to empirically distinguish between a complete lack of competition and an outcome of very intense competition (Keller 1992a).

Second, while competition theory suggests that the overlap between two species' fundamental niches will be partitioned, it does not imply any given form of partitioning (Begon, Harper, and Townsend 1990, 269–73). If, for example, two highly generalized bird species start with overlapping niches, partitioning may entail segregating space into separate territories. But partitioning may take any number of forms: feeding at different times of the day, specializing in distinct subsets of food initially available to both, or partitioning along any of several resource dimensions shared by the species. All of these outcomes are possible. Indeed, all that competition theory suggests is that partitioning will occur along one or more shared dimensions until the two species fall below a threshold referred to as "the *limiting similarity*, which may be defined as the maximum degree of similarity that two species can have and still coexist" (Ehrlich and Roughgarden 1987, 350).

If the idea of population niche and the competitive exclusion principle are capstone concepts of population ecology's interpretation of how species interact, how are communities, or populations of populations, structured? This issue raises our level of analysis from the population level to the community level, where, again, properties emergent at only the higher level become evident. Among these properties, we are most interested in community diversity—or the mix of species found in a given spatial and temporal setting. Here, we must be especially concerned with interspecific interaction.

Population biology models generally assume that community-level traits are largely, although not exclusively, determined at the population level. Once niche spaces are partitioned via the competitive exclusion principle, such community-level traits as diversity are primarily governed by how constraints posed by the environment bear on each niche separately (Colinvaux 1978, 145), with little need to assess interspecific interactions. This might be identified as a weak interpretation of community. Thus, Taylor (1992, 54; see also Gleason 1926, 26) describes the typical approach of botanists to studying plant communities as one that "has eliminated the need for theory about ecological organization above the individual [species] level. Plant associations may display regularities, but are seen as contingent and perhaps temporary outcomes of underlying processes, such as colonization and growth." Assessing community diversity or other community-level characteristics from this perspective entails describing how each species responds to the specific constraints on its realized niche.

In part, the weak community interpretation developed in reaction to an earlier conception of communities as highly integrated biological organisms (Clements 1936; Gleason 1926; Tansley 1935). But more modern analyses of system integration deserving of being described as strong interpretations of community have survived and remain influential. Focusing on patterns of ecological succession (Watt 1947; Odum 1969) and energy transfer across trophic levels (Lindeman 1942), these models characterize communities as modestly integrated phenomena. Patterns of predation and other forms of interaction among species going beyond intraspecific competition and competition between species using similar resources can be important in characterizing some communities (Taylor 1992, 55–60; Brooks and Dodson 1965; Connell 1961; Paine 1966). The central finding of these studies concerns the importance of *keystone predators,* species whose removal brings about drastic changes in ecological communities. But Lubchenco and Real (1991, 723) also note that "Not all communities have keystone predators." Thus, the key empirical question we must address before we can describe how interspecific interactions influence community diversity is whether or not there are members of the community who can be identified as keystone predators.

## Organization Ecology

Turning to organization ecology, we find both similarities and important differences in the analysis of how systems move toward equilibrium. The key differences inhere in the absence of genetic lineages in organizations when compared to organisms and species. This means that selection and adaptation, which are closely linked in biological models through changing gene frequencies, must be viewed as distinctive processes in organization ecology models. Adaptation in biological models is dependent on selection; adaptation is a function of selection's impact on gene frequencies within populations. Instead, differential survival of organizations depends at least in part on their adaptation as individual organizations to specific environmental circumstances (Aldrich 1979, 44–46). But perhaps a more accurate statement is that in organization ecology, unlike population biology, selection and adaptation are distinctive mechanisms of enforcing isomorphism rather than a tightly connected single process leading to evolutionary change.

This difference has had the rather unfortunate effect of generating a major conflict within the literature on organizations over which process—adaptation or selection—is most influential (Carroll 1984, 73–77). Some organization ecologists argue that organizations are quite rigid, and that, therefore, adaptation is highly constrained (Hannan and Freeman 1977, 930–33). Accordingly, they view selection as a far more important device for reaching population equilibria. Others, including many traditional organization theorists, view organizations as extremely flexible (Aldrich 1979, 28; Carroll 1988a, 73; Young 1988, 8–10), which would minimize the role of selection in population responses to environmental conditions.

Despite the vigor of this debate over what in biology would be termed phenotypic plasticity (Gordon 1992), there simply is no need to hold, on an a priori basis, that one mechanism is more important than the other. Indeed, Hannan and Freeman (1977, 939), who clearly represent those giving far greater emphasis to selection, note that "Isomorphism can result either because nonoptimal forms are selected out of a community of organizations or because organization decision makers learn optimal responses and adjust organization behavior accordingly." It seems likely that both adaptation and selection are important in the construction of organization populations, that the relative importance of the two might vary depending on environmental circumstances, and that assessing the role of each is, above all, an empirical question.

Even with a disjunction between selection and adaptation, much of the biological legacy of population ecology is retained in its application to the study of organizations. Organization ecology models stress the importance of *competition* in driving adaptation and/or selection (Carroll 1984, 71; Hannan and Carroll 1992, 26–27). Thus, Aldrich (1979, 27–28), who takes the adaptationist perspective, notes that "Environmental pressures make competition for resources the central force in organization activities." But competition is especially important for those emphasizing selection. As Hannan and Freeman (1977, 940) note, "A focus on selection invites an emphasis on competition. Organization forms presumably fail to flourish in certain environmental circumstances because other forms successfully compete with them for essential resources. As long as the resources which sustain organizations are finite and populations have unlimited capacities to expand, competition must ensue."

Also similar to population biologists, organization ecologists focus on competition among those relying on common resources. For example, the most important form of competition for organization ecologists studying labor unions is that among unions, not that between unions and management (Hannan and Freeman 1988). The latter form of interaction is conceptualized in the organization ecology literature as an environmental constraint that influences the relative "fitness" of the union vis-à-vis other unions that might organize a group of workers. It is the other unions that are real competitors in the sense of relying on the shared resource defined by a common pool of members. Thus, Aldrich, Zimmer, Staber, and Beggs (1994, 234) find little evidence that the size of the labor union population influences the size of the trade association population.

What of fitness in this competition? We have seen that many biologists stress the intergenerational passage of genetic information in defining fitness. Organizations, however, do not have genes. In developing an alternative conception of fitness, organization ecologists have adopted an approach that matches well Cooper's biological conception (1984) of fitness as expected time to extinction. Thus, Hannan and Freeman (1977,

937) argue that organization fitness can "be defined as the probability that a given form of organization would persist in a certain environment."

We have noted three critical elements of the population biology understanding of selection. Each is retained in the study of organizations. First, as in the biological models, it is assumed that the environment is doing the selecting (Aldrich 1979, 29; Hannan and Freeman 1977, 939). Second, selection is assumed to operate at the level of the phenotype. It is not organization members or whole populations that are selected but the organization as an individual that confronts the environment and either perishes or survives (for an exception, see Fombrun 1988, 228–30).[10] And third, selection is assumed to be a stochastic process (Carroll 1984, 72; Aldrich 1979, 54; Singh and Lumsden 1990, 184–85). While organization traits are assumed to be associated with changes in the likelihood of an organization surviving episodes of selections, they do not influence survival in a deterministic manner. Selection within subpopulations sharing a trait is assumed to have a substantial random component.

The concepts of modern ecological theory have also been imported into organization ecology in an undiluted manner. This is especially true of the niche concept (Hannan and Carroll 1992, 28–29; Hannan and Freeman 1989, 95–97; Aldrich 1979, 28), and an extensive organization ecology literature has developed around the concept of niche width.[11] Similarly, the competitive exclusion principle has been applied in organization population ecology in an almost undiluted form. Hannan and Freeman (1977, 943) note that "According to this principle, no two populations can continuously occupy the same niche. Populations are said to occupy the same niche to the extent that they depend on identical environmental resources. . . . The broad conclusion is that the greater the similarity of two resource-limited competitors, the less feasible is it that a single environment can support both of them in equilibrium." As in population biology, organization ecologists rely on competitive exclusion to account for such diverse issues as character displacement and differential adaptations among potential competitors.[12] Finally, with the exception of cases of phenotypic diversity among subpopulations of a single larger population (e.g., craft and labor unions), organization ecologists typically ignore interspecific interactions, thereby adopting a weak interpretation of ecological communities (Singh and Lumsden 1990, 188; Aldrich et al. 1994, 234; for an exception, see Brittain and Wholey 1988). In a world without keystone predators, other forms of interspecific interaction are assumed to be captured through monitoring the environmental resource flows that directly bear on the fundamental niches of organizations (Hannan and Carroll 1992, 98).

## Environmental Constraints on Density and Diversity

Perhaps the central proposition of population ecology is that environments determine equilibria in terms of both absolute and relative numbers of individuals and species. This central idea is implicit in the isomorphism principle and in population ecology's understanding of how selection and adaptation operate to realize it. As presented until now, though, these ideas do not offer much in the way of guidance about developing specific hypotheses. They do not tell us how, when, and where the environment constrains selection and adaptation in particular ways to produce specific mixes of species at specific levels of density. In Brandon's terms (1992, 84), we need to distinguish the features of the general environment that constitute the selective environment leading to species equilibrium.

In large part, the specification of these constraints arose from the observance of empirical regularities in the distributions of species. First, analyses of the history of biodiversity noted that species diversity increased systematically as the amount of available habitat increased, especially the proportion of coastline to continental land masses as plate tectonics broke apart the single supercontinent of Pangaea (E. O. Wilson 1992, 194–95; Signor 1990). Second, population biologists observed what they identified as a "latitudinal diversity gradient" in biodiversity (E. O. Wilson 1992, 196, 401; Stevens 1989). Species density declined in a regular way as one moved from the equator to the poles. Third, research on island biogeography noted persistent regularities in species density as the size of islands varied (E. O. Wilson 1992, 205, 220–21; MacArthur and Wilson 1963).

These observations were combined by Hutchinson (1959, 150–51) to form a single theory to explain biodiversity. As E. O. Wilson (1992, 199) notes, "Enough solid analyses and theory have locked together to suggest a relatively simple solution, or at least one that can be easily understood: the Energy-Stability-Area Theory of Biodiversity, or ESA theory for short. In a nutshell, the more solar energy the greater the diversity; the more stable the climate, both from season to season and from year to year, the greater the diversity; finally, the larger the area, the greater the diversity." As this model will be the principal tool we use to understand the development of interest organization population density and diversity, it is worth considering each of its three elements in some detail.

We will start with the last element of the model, *area* (or space), because it will become one of the key features of our model of the dynamics of interest organization populations. Population ecology theory offers a very precise specification of the area-density relationship, based on work on island biogeography and historical patterns of species diversity. The area-density relationship has been found to be positive and curvilinear, with differing degrees of curvilinear responsiveness for each species. Thus, E. O. Wilson (1992, 392), basing his conclusion on the extensive work of Preston (1962; see also Real and Levin 1991, 178–80) summarizing dozens of studies of individual species, defines the area-species curve as the "relationship between the area of an island or some other discrete geographic region and the number of species living there. Approximated by the equation $S = CA^z$ where A is the area, S is the number of species, and C and z are constants that depend on the place and group of organisms (such as birds or trees) being considered." Again, the essential characteristics of this relationship are its overall positivity, its curvilinearity, and the uniqueness of the constants for each species.

But what explains this pattern? There are at least two nonobvious elements of the area-density and area-diversity relationships that merit further examination in answering this question. The first is the increase in species diversity as available space expands. This is a nonobvious issue in that while we might expect a larger area to have more individuals of the same species, we would not necessarily expect it to have more species than a smaller area. As E. O. Wilson (1992, 205) notes, "The reasons for the logarithmic increase are complicated, but two factors stand out. The larger island can support a greater overall population, say of butterflies, and so more rare species can be squeezed into the same forest. And the larger island is more likely to have additional habitats in which species can find refuge."

Of these two factors, the first is, while perhaps less intuitively obvious, probably the most important. Consider, for example, two islands identical in all respects but size, with one being twice as large as the other. Both islands may have habitat suitable to species X, but that of the smaller island may be too small to sustain a breeding population of the species. Therefore, a population of species X will survive in equilibrium only on the larger island. Further, populations of identical species that do establish themselves on our two islands will likely face very different levels of risk of extinction. The prevailing "probabilistic" model of extinction (Pimm, Jones, and Diamond 1988; Eldredge 1991; Raup 1991) holds that "the smaller the average population size of a given species through time, and the more the size fluctuates from generation to generation, the sooner will the population drift all the way down to zero and go extinct" (E. O. Wilson 1992, 227). Thus, fewer of the settling species will survive in equilibrium on the smaller island than on the larger one. In comparison to smaller areas, then, larger areas tend (1) to have more habitats absolutely; (2) to have habitats of larger size and, therefore, more habitats crossing the minimum threshold size needed to support rarer species; and (3) to have larger populations of animals within species, which reduces the probability of species extinction. In short, when it comes to species density and diversity, size matters.

The second element of the relationship meriting explanation is the curvilinear pattern (often sigmoid or logistic) of growth. Why does the increase in either population density or species diversity not continue in a linear pattern? The answer lies in competition within species for common resources and between species over overlapping elements of their respective fundamental niches. Hutchinson (1959, 149) reasoned that "Early in the history of a community, we may suppose many niches will be empty and invasion will proceed easily; as the community becomes more diversified, the process will be progressively more difficult. . . . In this way a complex community containing some highly specialized species is constructed asymptotically." Population ecologists generalize the argument by suggesting that increasing competition for resources, a separate factor discussed later in this section, interacts with space so that competition slows down the growth rate of species as an area becomes more densely settled. This is a condition of "density dependence," or as E. O. Wilson (1992, 395) defines it, "[t]he increasing severity by which factors in the environment slow down growth of a population as the organisms become more numerous and hence densely concentrated."

Indeed, space has come to be viewed as a surrogate for many variables in the environment that exhibit density-dependent effects. Thus, MacArthur (1958, 615) notes, "Any factor that can control a local population has a space distribution. Examples of such factors are food, nesting sites, and predators. Thus, all populations are limited by the amount of suitable space." MacArthur then goes on to define "suitable" by observing that "Within an environment each necessary activity requires a certain amount of space. That activity which requires the greatest amount of space is likely to be limiting." It is the limiting factor that is expected to have a curvilinear relationship with population density. And because space is a good surrogate for all limiting constraints, the area-species relationship is expected to exhibit density dependence.

The second factor cited by ESA theory is *stability*. Stability is important because broad and sharp fluctuations in the environment stress organisms and species, often to the point of extinction. The focus of much of the research on the importance of environmental stability, of course, is on episodes of mass extinction through history (Pimm, Jones, and Diamond 1988; Eldredge 1991; Raup 1991), but instabilities of lesser magnitude have also drawn the attention of biologists (Simberloff and Wilson 1969). When instabilities of either level of magnitude raise the rate of species extinction above its normal background rate, they serve to reset the clock on the building of biodiversity.

As Colinvaux (1978, 203–4) summarizes the argument in regard to the latitudinal diversity gradient, "The instability of arctic animal populations seems clearly to have something to do with a highly unstable climate. Indeed, we call upon the vagaries of the arctic weather for our best explanation of why the area is depauperate, saying that species go extinct in the arctic so quickly that a large species list cannot collect. And we explain the rich species list of the equatorial forests as being due to the fact that there is so stable a climate in the equatorial lowlands that extinction is rare, letting more and more species accumulate." In short, and relying on Mayr's claim (1988, 111) that the process of selection is in part inherently stochastic, stable environments enhance diversity and density by failing to subtract species through a lower average extinction rate than might be realized in less stable environments.

The third and final factor in the ESA model addresses *energy,* or the resources needed to sustain individuals, populations, and species. This component rests, of course, on the observed empirical regularity of the latitudinal diversity gradient. Simply put, energy in the form of sunlight falling on the ground, which directly or indirectly constitutes an essential resource for all species, increases as one moves from the poles to the equator. The implications of this for species diversity was summarized by Hutchinson (1959, 150) in answering a seemingly simple question: "If we can have one or two species of a large family adapted to the rigors of Arctic existence, why can we not have more? It is reasonable to suppose that the total biomass may be involved. If the fundamental productivity of an area is limited by a short growing season to such a degree that total biomass is less than under more favorable conditions, then the rarer species in a community may be so rare that they do not exist." Thus, more resources mean that more individuals and species can be supported within the boundaries of a given area, or as E. O. Wilson (1992, 200) so aptly puts it, "the larger the pie, the greater the number of possible slices big enough to sustain the lives of individual species."

Importantly, however, this part of the ESA model refers to all forms of energy. At progressively higher steps up the food chain, interdependent resource budgets can be created for any number of species (Hairston, Smith, and Slobodkin 1960), with the definition of resources restricted by only a few broad conceptual requirements or properties (Abrams 1992, 282–83): the item must have an "effect on survival and reproduction" and must entail "consumption or use"; and such use must entail "reduction in the resource's availability to other individuals." As resources become more abundant, so should species density and diversity. Indeed, this model implies that in discussing the density of any given species, we must be attentive to its specific pattern of resource utilization within the specific ecological community in which it exists.

In assessing the many variables summarized by the concepts of area, stability, and energy, we have highlighted space as having a density-dependent relationship with population and species density. It was the only variable identified as having a curvilinear relationship with density. In fact, any limiting factor, as MacArthur (1958, 615) suggested, might be expected to have such a relationship. Space, however, is generally treated as an indirect summary of such factors and so is usually treated in a density-dependent fashion. We should note, however, that other scholars (e.g., Davidson and Andrewartha 1948) have argued that species rarely bump against such limiting factors, or that more linear relationships are more common. Thus, the density dependence implicit in the curvilinear specification of the area-species relationship should be treated as a hypothesis to be tested in each empirical analysis of population density and species diversity.

What of population diversity? The diversity of communities—how many species there are—is analyzed using the ESA model as well. But the causal interpretation is somewhat different. Hutchinson (1959, 150) began his analysis of diversity with an assumption. "It is first obvious," he suggests, "that the processes of evolution of communities must be under various sorts of external control, and that in some cases such control limits the possible diversity." The controls, he further argued, are those specified in the ESA model as they bear on the density of each species. Diversity, then, is the cumulative product or outcome of the play of these separate density processes. In short, community diversity is an artifact of the processes governing species density.

Does the ESA model have an analogue within the population ecology literature on organizations? In fact, the model is applied with only modest changes, at least theoretically. Thus, Carroll (1984, 81), after summarizing much of the empirical literature on organization demography, notes that "most of these studies examine patterns in organization foundings over time and attempt to relate these patterns to the characteristics of the organization environment—e.g., resource abundance, organization density, and political turbulence," a list that matches well the components of the ESA model.

Of these components, "organization density" (usually measured as the number of similar organizations) is perhaps the only one that does not seem obviously equivalent to its partner in the ESA model—space.

But the way in which the two concepts are theoretically employed suggests strongly that organization density is analogous to space in the ESA model. Most organizational ecology empirical studies examine founding and disbanding rates of organizations of single populations of organizations in fixed settings (e.g., breweries or newspapers in a metropolitan area) over time. Therefore, the value of space is assumed to be fixed. Accordingly, focusing on numbers of organizations as an independent variable influencing founding and disbanding rates may provide a good surrogate measure of density within the assumed fixed space.[13] Moreover, the same curvilinear pattern is expected for "organization density" as for space in the ESA model. Thus, Hannan and Freeman (1977, 941) note that "the rate at which units are added to populations of organizations depends on how much of the fixed capacity in an environment has already been exhausted. The greater the unexhausted capacity in an environment, the faster should be the rate of growth of populations of organizations." In short, density dependence relative to space is central theoretically to both biological and organization applications of the ESA model, even if measured somewhat differently.

Later organizational ecology studies (Hannan and Freeman 1989; Hannan and Carroll 1992), however, added another factor to their version of the ESA model, one that has no counterpart in population biology models. That factor is the legitimacy of the form of organization being examined, or the degree to which it is "taken for granted" (Hannan and Freeman 1989, 34). Based on a long tradition in organization theory, population ecology scholars argue that the degree of legitimacy of an organizational form influences founding rates—with fewer foundings when legitimacy is low and more when legitimacy is high—and is influenced in turn by the density of the population—with legitimacy being low when there are few such organizations of a given type and high when there are many such organizations.[14]

Finally, because organization ecologists typically study single populations of organizations over time, they rarely address the diversity implications of the ESA model across a broad array of organizational activities. Or rather, the range of organization types examined within these populations—their diversity—tends to be extremely restrictive—for example, confined to the balance of specialist or generalist semiconductor firms or the mix of generalist, fast-food, and specialist restaurants (Hannan and Freeman 1989, 310–30). These are much narrower diversity distinctions than those addressed by Hutchinson's question (1959) in his theoretical development of the ESA model: "Why are there so many kinds of animals?" This comparative restrictiveness of organization ecology research on population diversity is not a necessary product of the ESA model, however, but of the uses to which many organization ecologists have put it (Singh and Lumsden 1990, 188; Carroll 1988b, 6).

## Population Ecology in the Study of Organizations

With some important exceptions, we have argued that biology and organization population ecology are quite similar theoretically. But some might wonder whether the concepts of population biology can be used only as metaphors in studies of organizations. In our review, we noted several specific criticisms of the application of population ecology models to the study of organizations. For the most part, these criticisms rest on an ill-informed understanding of how population ecology models are used in biology. What remains to be answered, then, are two very general criticisms bearing on the status of population ecology models in the study of human organizations.

The first concerns equating organizations to organisms. Kaufman (1985, 87), for example, argues vehemently that "while students of organizations may well have more to learn from biological metaphors than from analogies to other disciplines, they would not be justified in equating organizations and organisms. . . . [A]lthough organizations are a way of mobilizing the energies of living things (as well as other forms of energy), they are not organisms." In developing this argument, Kaufman (1985, 96–97) is especially attentive to false analogies commonly made in the traditional organization theory literature between the internal states of individual organisms and individual organizations.

Ecological models are attentive not to internal traits per se, however, but to how numbers of organizations interact with each other and with the environment. In addressing interactions, the internal characteristics of the units in question become important only in a stochastic sense. While organizations are not organisms, the importance of numbers of competitors and environmental constraints on patterns of reaction to that competition are likely to be similar for both objects of study. As Hannan and Freeman (1977, 961) have argued, "What the equations do is to model the growth path of populations that exist on finite resources in a closed system (where population growth in the absence of competition is logistic and the presence of competing populations lowers carrying capacity in that system). . . . The model is an abstraction that will lead to insight whenever the stated conditions are approximated." In a sense, then, the two sets of population ecology models are not so much theories about organizations or organisms, but about those stated conditions, which are common to both settings.

The second, related criticism suggests that inattention to the internal processes of organizations is unlikely to address some important issues of traditional concern to organization theory, such as the role of leadership and participation in decision making (Aldrich 1979, xii; Carroll 1984, 86). While some organization ecologists have extended the model to considering how environmental forces influence the internal operations of organizations (Aldrich 1979; Meyer and Scott 1983), our answer to this criticism is the same as that offered for the first. Population ecology models do not claim to be able to identify which individual animal or which individual organization will survive in a particular competitive situation. But by the same token, we cannot address population- and community-level questions with exclusive attention to internal processes as long as there is the likelihood of density-dependent relationships in interactions with the environment.

## CHAPTER 4

# Population Ecology and Organized Interests

In this chapter, we apply population ecology thinking to questions about interest organizations. We first consider the theoretical appropriateness of applying a population ecology framework to the study of organizations engaged in lobbying. We then reconsider the series of research questions raised in chapter 2, outlining how population ecology thinking can be used to generate tentative answers for each. Finally, we compare and contrast the population ecology approach to these questions with conventional models of interest organizations as well as with the way population ecology has been commonly used in organization ecology research.

## The Appropriateness of Population Ecology

### Some Essential Definitions in Population Ecology

In applying population ecology models, we place interest organizations in the position of *species*. Groups of interest organizations that are similar to each other in terms of relying on common resources are identified as members of *guilds*. And interest organizations operating in a common setting and time are members of a *population*. Are these definitions appropriate for interest organizations? We have seen in chapter 3 that even within the biology literature there is less than total agreement over the meaning of these concepts. But a number of definitions offered by population biologists are of sufficient generality that they would seem, at face value, to cover most organizations. It is on this basis that organization ecology is founded.

Still, some may be troubled by putting singular organizations in the position of species, which usually are thought to include many individuals. Indeed, the biological-species definition focuses on breeding among individuals in assigning species status. And the very general definition provided by E. O. Wilson (1992, 404; cited in chapter 3) still speaks of multiple organisms. But restricting attention only to groups raises a small problem, even for biologists, when the members of a species decline in number to a single individual. How do we identify the species of the survivor? Most of us will probably view the last 'spotted owl as a member of the spotted owl species, even after its conspecifics have disappeared.

More importantly, however, both species and interest organizations are appropriately treated as individuals when considering properties emergent at the population level (Hull 1976; 1978; 1980; 1988, 213–23). Unlike classes, species and interest organizations are individuals in that they have beginnings, endings, and a unique history between those two points. And population-level properties, such as density and diversity, are the focus of ecological analysis. Thus, single interest organizations can be treated as species for purposes of ecological analysis.

There is a more serious problem than the question of individuality, however—one that is unique to our application of ecological analysis to interest organizations. The theories of organization ecologists and population biologists focus on the life histories of the units they study, be they organizations or species. Thus, in organization ecology research (Hannan and Carroll 1992; Hannan and Freeman 1989), the concepts of organization *birth* and *death* are commonly employed. Indeed, foundings and disbandings are the raw material that organization ecologists work with to understand the dynamics of populations. Birth and death typically hold commonsense meanings in this literature; organizations are born when they are established and die when they disappear (Singh and Lumsden 1990, 163).

It is also clear, however, that birth and death may mean something quite different when we turn our attention to interest organizations. We are studying the demography of an organizational function—that of engaging in lobbying—rather than organizations per se. A function may be terminated or allowed to "die" while the larger organization continues. Moreover, lobbying may constitute the primary function of the organization or only a minor one. Therefore, we focus more appropriately on *entry* and *exit* from the active lobbying community. Entry and exit from lobbying may or may not coincide with organizational birth and death. Indeed, mapping the degree to which they overlap is one of the issues that we examine empirically.

Even with our reconceptualization of births and deaths as entry and exits, it remains at least in part an empirical question whether organization ecology models can be applied usefully to suborganizations or organizational functions. If withdrawal from lobbying coincides with the deaths of organizations, than we should be able to employ standard organization ecology models to study lobbying organizations. The life history of an organization function will be coterminous with the life history of the organization. But if withdrawal from lobbying signals only the trimming of an organization function, then we will need to consider in much greater detail the internal decision and resource allocation processes of the parent organizations.

Turning to higher levels of analysis, defining populations of organizations can be quite difficult (Zucker 1989, 543). But Hannan and Freeman (1977, 935–36) note that "a population of organizations consists of all the organizations within a particular boundary that have a common form." In our case, more than in most applications of organization ecology, boundaries are well defined via state borders, and interest organization status is well defined via lobby registration laws. As described in chapter 1, the 50 species populations we examine are the 50 collections of interest organizations registered to lobby in the American states.

Our attention will be on sets of interest organization populations that "make their living in the same way" (Ehrlich and Roughgarden 1987, 322). The most appropriate empirical referent of this definition is not self-evident, however. The literature distinguishes among interest organizations on a number of dimensions that might be used to define guilds. Two, however, strike us as most important in prior research on interest organizations. First, several of our analyses focus on species guilds as distinguished by their functional area of interest, such as farming, environmental, manufacturing, or local government interests. Second, other analyses focus on a definition of guild based on an organization's internal structure—whether it is an association, membership group, or institution. Simply put, the literature offers a number of hypotheses about how interest organizations differ on these dimensions. We will employ functional and/or internal structural definitions of guilds as these extant hypotheses relate to the research questions we examine.

## Assumptions of Population Ecology

In applying population thinking to interest organizations, we will not reexamine all of its assumptions. Most—such as resource scarcity or the stochastic nature of selection and adaptation—should not be controversial, even if they are rarely stated explicitly in the literature on interest organizations, given its inattention to population phenomena. But two others will certainly be controversial—the isomorphism principle and the assumption of equilibrium, both of which are fundamental to our understanding of the dynamics of interest organization populations.

As noted in chapter 2, most prior theories assume that the density of interest organization populations is determined solely by mobilization processes. We have argued that this is equivalent to assuming that

biological populations are determined solely by species' intrinsic reproductive rates—the rates at which species will reproduce when there are
few resource constraints. When successful reproduction takes place for a
biological species, a new individual is added to its population. When
successful mobilization takes place within an interest organization guild,
a new interest organization is added to its population.

In contrast, and following the isomorphism principle, we assume
that population density is determined by more than the rate at which
new individuals are added to populations. Species and interest organizations can and do die. Moreover, it is quite plausible that density-
dependent relationships can feed back so as to alter mobilization rates of
interest organizations just as they do reproductive rates of biological
species. Following the isomorphism principle, then, we hypothesize that
it is environmental constraints—not "intrinsic" rates of reproduction or
"intrinsic" rates of solving the disincentives of organization—that produce differential selection and generate the feedback mechanisms that
most fundamentally shape populations.

Most analyses of interest organizations—including those of Truman
(1951), Olson (1982), and Browne (1990, 503–4)—assume that the environment can support an unlimited number of interest organizations. In
contrast, a population ecology orientation leads us to assume that interest organization density is set at an equilibrium level—albeit varying
over time—by the environment. This is important. If carrying capacities
for interest organizations are infinite, then environmental constraints
need not produce the kinds of intense selection pressures or sharp
density-dependent feedbacks found for biological populations and other
organizations.

While less controversial, the competitive exclusion principle—the
idea that species relying on similar resources will partition their overlapping fundamental niches until their realized niches do not overlap—may
strike some as new. It is, however, both less new than one might imagine
and essential to our models of population density, diversity, and niche
behavior. It is less than original in that the competitive exclusion principle is highly consistent with empirical findings that interest organizations
tend to organize themselves into narrow issue niches with little competition (Browne 1990; McConnell 1966; Rose 1967; Laumann and Knoke
1987; Wilson 1973, 263–64). While we will have occasion to question the
empirical generalizability of this specific form of niche partitioning by
interest organizations, the idea of niche partitioning is not new to the
analysis of interest organization politics.

It may be less than fully appreciated, however, that the notion of niche partitioning carries with it an implicit specification of the locus of interest organization competition. The competitive exclusion principle suggests that partitioning will take place on resource dimensions that are shared among interest organizations. It is on these shared dimensions that competition takes place, competition that is then resolved by partitioning. The literature, however, tends to focus on only one of several potential dimensions of shared resources—that associated with the interface with government (Browne 1990).

In our legitimate attention to battles over public policy, we often focus on "competition" between very different types of interest organizations with very different conceptions of the public good, such as between labor unions and the companies that employ their members or between environmentalists and industries that pollute. These "competitors" do share a common resource in that they all seek space on the public agenda. So it is possible that competition and niche partitioning are conducted on this dimension.

The population ecology approach is concerned less with policy outcomes, however, than it is in understanding how populations of interest organizations are constructed. Competition for survival as organizations is likely to take place within guilds, not between guilds. Competition for such shared resources as members and financial resources will be between one union and another or between one trade association and another, not between a union and a trade association (Aldrich et al. 1994, 234). From this perspective, the primary competitors of an environmental organization are other environmental organizations, not polluters. Indeed, the presence of more polluters may actually help environmental organizations to survive by convincing their members that lobbying work remains undone.

Our interest organization population models, therefore, include no controls for interguild competition. We adopt population ecology's weak interpretation of community. Interactions of the type implicit between environmental organizations and polluters are better assessed through the energy variable in the Energy-Stability-Area density model considered in this chapter. Still, our faith in the competitive exclusion principle and in the weak interpretation of community is not founded solely on assumption. We will have occasion to assess empirically the implications of the competitive exclusion principle when we consider niche behavior on the part of interest organizations. In sum, with the possible exception of our studying an organization function rather than organizations, there is nothing intrinsic about interest organizations that should preclude our using population ecology theories and models.

## A Population Ecology Research Program

There is no single population ecology theory, although most population ecology models relate in some manner to the logic underlying the Energy-Stability-Area model of population density. Rather, population ecology research focuses on a series of questions that form a rough hierarchy, moving from demography, through population density, population diversity, and community structure, to the impact of different population configurations. We consider each issue in turn.

### Interest Organization Demography

With Truman (1951) and Schattschneider (1960) defining the poles of two conflicting interpretations, speculation about the impacts of different mixes of organized interests on democratic politics has a long tradition. Over the last decade, an economic dimension was added to the controversy through the debates engendered by Olson's theory (1982) of institutional sclerosis. That such varied perspectives can persist and even thrive over decades is in large part due to our lack of knowledge about actual populations of organized interests—how they differ from place to place and how they change over time. Indeed, we have only a handful of empirical studies that measure entries and exits from interest organization populations, studies that address basic questions of population demography.

Many might think that entry has been studied a great deal given the substantial body of work on interest organization mobilization. But because mobilization research typically focuses on how and why individuals join interest organizations, it tells us little about patterns of population change among interest organizations. As illustrated in chapter 1 by our analogy about the introduction of rabbits into Australia, these are distinct questions requiring answers at two quite different levels of analysis. And at the interest organization population level, as opposed to the individual member level, we know very little. While estimating numbers of interests represented in Washington has been a traditional pastime of social scientists (Petracca 1992b, 13), we almost never, with only a few important exceptions, examine variations in interest organization populations over time and/or over space. And the few studies that address entry patterns, most notably Schlozman and Tierney (1986), focus on a single population, often using noncomparable data from two periods to estimate entry rates, a problem we consider more fully in chapters 5 and 6.

Even worse, exit or withdrawal from lobbying by interest organizations remains virtually undefined, much less examined; perhaps only a single study (Schlozman and Tierney 1986)—again, a single-population study relying on analysis of noncomparable samples at two points in time to determine mortality rates among interest organizations—analyzes disappearances from a lobbying community. This silence might imply an assumption that interest organizations never die, a position implicit in Olson's institutional sclerosis model (1982), in which interest organizations are assumed to accumulate even until economies collapse. Or it might imply that we believe that mortality can be treated as a random process that has little systematic impact on the mix of interests in a community (Baumgartner and Jones 1993, 182). Either alternative strikes us as highly implausible.

While prolonged studies of national trade associations, using a population ecology framework (Aldrich and Staber 1988; Aldrich et al. 1990, 1994), have indicated that this population is constructed through a rich pattern of organizational formation and dissolution over time, they also report that few trade associations disappear once formed. But because these studies examine populations of associations rather than the lobbying function of associations per se, we simply do not know how patterns of entry and exit from lobbying communities interact to comprise current populations or govern their potential for change. Filling this gap in our knowledge about interest representation is important for several reasons, reasons addressing the analytic functions of description, explanation, and evaluation.

First, description has value in itself, especially given that our empirical analyses in the next seven chapters address the American states. The political systems of the states merit attention in their own right. And it does not require two hands to record the few comparative analyses of state interest organization populations—those of Zeller (1954), Morehouse (1981), Hrebenar and Thomas (1992; Thomas and Hrebenar 1990, 1992, 1995), and Hunter, Wilson, and Brunk (1991; Wilson-Gentry, Brunk, and Hunter 1991). Despite their contributions to the literature on state politics, none of these prior studies really addresses the kinds of questions about populations that interest us. The first three are reputational analyses focusing on the relative power and influence of interest organizations in the states, and only the last of these is founded on systematic quantitative research on the states. The last set of studies, while using data similar to those we employ in the following chapters, focuses on lobbyists, not interest organizations.

Systematic description of state demographic patterns is also vital to give context to prior work on interest organizations, almost all of which focuses on the single interest organization population in Washington. Indeed, it is rare for surveys of existing scholarly research on interest organizations (e.g., Cigler 1991; W. Crotty 1994) to even mention, other than in passing, studies of interest organizations outside Washington. Yet most scholars purport to conduct their research to discover generalizations about interest representation as a process. We think it unlikely that we will persuade our Washington-oriented colleagues to pack their bags and join us in the states. Instead, we propose to enhance their ability to generalize from their own research findings by providing sufficient description of state interest organization populations so that they will know when, where, and how the Washington population is similar to or differs from other interest organization populations.

Second, our ultimate goal is to explain how and why populations of interest organizations are constructed as they are. Demography provides the raw material with which to test explanations of population change. Indeed, counts of births and deaths—or foundings and disbandings, entries and exits—constitute the data typically used in most population biology (Weiner 1994) and organization ecology research (Hannan and Freeman 1989; Hannan and Carroll 1992). Schlozman and Tierney's analysis (1983, 1986) of the Washington lobbying community and other scholars' studies of national trade associations (Aldrich and Staber 1988; Aldrich et al. 1990, 1994) suggest that both populations are growing and that both are characterized by low rates of death. However, we have seen that both sets of studies are limited in terms of providing answers to our questions. The former are founded on noncomparable samples of the lobbying population at only two points in time, and the latter do not study lobbying per se.

Third, our answers to questions of explanation will almost certainly have bearing on interpretations of how the politics of interest representation either enhances or diminishes the prospects for democratic government. The central question here arises from the debate between Walker (1991) and Schlozman and Tierney (1986) about the degree of bias in interest communities. While simple description will contribute to this discussion by telling us about the dominance or lack thereof of traditional economic organizations in the 50 states, the greater contribution will be via our answers to explanatory questions. If we can account for population change, we will have a much firmer basis from which to predict how interest organization systems may be transformed as environmental constraints change.

For example, if populations of interest organizations prove to be density dependent, then it matters a great deal whether that density dependence is expressed through depressed entry rates or enhanced mortality rates. In an extreme case of the former, the composition of interest organization populations will become essentially frozen as they reach the carrying capacities of their habitat; no new entrants will be added to the population. If the latter, however, there is at least the prospect of change in the composition of populations as more interest organizations exit from the community and are replaced by a steady stream of new entrants.

The results generated by studying demographic patterns will also bear on interest organization research at other levels of analysis. Most importantly, if we find that populations of organizations are density dependent and that density dependence feeds back so as to alter mobilization rates of new interest organizations, then serious questions must be raised about our individual-level models of mobilization. Simply put, such findings will indicate that they are fundamentally misspecified due to exclusion of contextual forces that influence rates of mobilization. But if density dependence is expressed primarily through changes in mortality rates, then our individual-level models of mobilization need not account for environmental context to be valid. In this case, the processes that govern mobilization will be distinct from those that govern populations of organized interests.

### An Ecological Model of Interest Organization Density

In chapter 3, we saw that the principal tool used by population biologists and, to a lesser extent, organization ecologists to understand population density is the Energy-Stability-Area (ESA) model. Indeed, the ESA model lies at the theoretical core of much of population ecology thinking. While specific measures will be discussed in chapter 7 when we test an ESA model with state interest organization data, our present task is to interpret conceptually how the ESA concepts of energy, stability, and area might be applied to populations of interest organizations. And given the centrality of the ESA model to population ecology interpretations of population dynamics, our discussion must be somewhat more specific than for the other topics comprising the population ecology research program.

Area, or space, is the most critical of the ESA concepts; it is both a surrogate for any number of other limiting variables and, as a result, the most likely variable to exhibit density dependence. But in the world of interest organizations, what corresponds to space for biological species? Where do interest organizations live? The most appropriate analogue is the number of potential constituents the interest organization may serve, whether they be members of membership groups, patrons of social interest organizations, or corporate entities that sponsor institutional lobbying and join associations.

In all of these cases, without potential constituents, lobbyists will have insufficient "space" to survive. This interpretation is readily ap-.plied to membership organizations. But it is equally appropriate for associations and institutions that lobby. In states with no widget firms, there will be no one for the aspiring widget lobbyist to represent. In such states, there will be insufficient space for either an independent organization (in the case of associations) or a suborganizational governmental affairs division (in the case of an institution) to make a living.

The ESA model hypothesizes, first, that this relationship will be positive. As latent constituency size increases, niche spaces correspond-ing to more varied and/or increasingly precise subsets of interests be-come viable by passing the threshold number of members required for organization. If there are few commercial establishments, then only the niche typically occupied by a chamber of commerce may be viable, with too few widget firms to organize a widget trust. And as constituency number increases, a given interest organization will have more mem-bers, which affords some protection from going extinct as a result of random fluctuations in membership or the fickleness of patrons.

Second, the relationship should be curvilinear. This reflects the population ecology assumption that the number of latent constituents acts in a density-dependent manner so that as the size of the potential constituency increases, competition for patronage among interest organi-zations within guilds increases. Competition increases because as inter-est organizations become more specialized, the marginal utility of an additional, more narrowly focused organization should decline. Thus, while a widget firm might derive great utility from joining a chamber of commerce, additional utility from representation by a manufacturers' association, and still some advantage from participation in a widget trust, the marginal utility from participating in a left-handed widget combine will likely be quite small given involvement in the more general groups. In Olson's terms (1965), the probability that a group will over-come a given set of disincentives to organization and then survive in a competitive environment should decline with density.

Third, as with biological species and the organizations studied by organization ecologists, we expect the unit relationship between space and potential constituency size to vary across interest organization guilds (Aldrich et al. 1994, 224). This relationship depends on the particular interest being represented—its homogeneity across potential constitu-ents and its unique economies of scale in representation—as well as on the nature of the potential constituents, whether they are firms, patrons, or individual members. The most obvious example of such variance is the difference in levels of economic concentration across the several sectors of the economy. Equivalent proportions of a state's gross state product (GSP) may be generated by a single mining company and a thousand hardware stores. Each sector, then, will have a unique space coefficient reflecting the number of interest organizations that can survive relative to its number of latent constituents. This uniqueness means that we have to specify separate models for each interest organization guild that we examine.

Energy is the next element of the ESA model to interpret in terms of interest organizations. On what does the lobbyist sustain him or herself?[1] In deciding whether or not to lobby, the critical role is that of the lobbyist-broker who persuades his or her sponsors that they should represent their interests to elected officials. Focusing on the lobbyist as an entrepreneur is hardly unique to the population ecology approach. Indeed, this perspective is central to Salisbury's exchange theory (1969) of interest groups. From this perspective, energy should be defined in terms reflecting the stock of resources available to the lobbyist-broker for use in persuading his or her sponsors—be they members or patrons—to engage in lobbying activity.

What are those resources? While material and solidarity incentives may play an important, even critical, role in organizational maintenance, purposive benefits should be paramount when it comes to the specific decision to register to lobby. Organizations—whatever their origin and primary function and however maintained—must make a distinct decision to engage in lobbying. And for that decision to be a positive one, there must be something to lobby for. From this perspective, the appropriate analogue of energy for interest organizations should be *constituent interest,* or government goods, services, regulations, or policies—whether actually or potentially provided—that an interest organization might value (Hrebenar and Thomas 1992, 13; Salisbury 1992, 1–2; Walker 1991, 47). This conception of interest compels us to identify how active the government is now or potentially will be in the field of concern to each guild of interest organizations that we examine.

Prior studies of trade associations (Aldrich and Staber 1988, 112; Aldrich et al. 1994, 233) have found little evidence that government activity in general, as measured by the total number of regulations, is associated with population density. However, this finding may result from studying the energy variable at too high a level of aggregation. It is likely that trade associations are less concerned about regulations in general than they are about regulations bearing on their industry. Therefore, the energy variable should be measured at the guild level at least, not at the level of the entire interest organization population.

Additionally, the "energy" needed to support an interest organization should vary with the likelihood that government policy will change. If government provides a latent interest organization with some good or service and is unlikely to ever withdraw or modify it, there will be little incentive to lobby for its maintenance. The same would be true for a latent interest organization that desires a good or service not currently provided by government, if the government is unlikely to ever alter its policy. If policy change is more likely, however, we should find more interest organizations lobbying for the maintenance of desired goods or services currently provided and for desired goods or services that might be provided (Hansen 1985, 81; Hansen 1991, 17–19; Walker 1991, 154–57). Thus, we expect *interest certainty* to be another resource contributing to a polity's carrying capacity for interest organizations.[2]

Finally, stability has already been addressed for interest organization systems via Olson's hypothesis (1982) about the relationship between *interest organization system age* and the density of organized interests. If Olson's understanding of the dynamics of population density was regrettably monocausal, his observation that severe disruptions of social and political systems are likely to decimate populations of interest organizations makes a good deal of sense. If the government ceases to make decisions or is incapable of enforcing them, organizations will have little incentive to lobby, and they may themselves be caught up in the more general crisis and cease to exist in any case. Thus, this element of Olson's model is consistent with an ESA explanation of population density.

While an important part of the ESA model theoretically, stability probably is not relevant to our empirical cases—the contemporary American states. Unless one assumes either that there is a century-long time lag in reaching equilibrium or that population growth is open-ended and unconstrained, then any turbulence variable will be a constant in the cases we examine. We find the first assumption implausible, while the second directly contradicts the underlying premises of the ESA model. Still, a variable reflecting Olson's hypothesis will be included in the ESA models we test in chapter 7. We will also include in the models we test a measure reflecting the Virginia School's emphasis on the size of government as the sole determinant of the size of interest organization populations.

Some might view interest certainty, which we specify as a part of the energy component of the ESA model, as an element of the stability term of the model. *Actual* policy change, if it influences organization decision making, may constitute a source of instability. However, the *likelihood* of policy change may be quite independent of actual policy change. For example, as policies change in a competitive political system when moving from a GOP to a Democratic and then back to a GOP administration, the probability of policy change could remain constant given that the out party always stands a good chance of winning the next election. This constant uncertainty is a resource for the lobbyist rather than a liability, as would be the case if interest certainty were tapping stability.[3]

The variables of space, energy, and stability are expected to shape the contours of populations of interest organizations. But they may do so in two ways—through selection and through driving adaptation. If organizations can easily change the focus of their lobby activity as government policies change and/or if they can redefine their constituency base in response to social, economic, and demographic trends, then adaptation might constitute the primary response to environmental pressures. Some of this certainly happens. However, like Hannan and Freeman (1989), we assume that interest organizations are at least modestly rigid. If, for example, the State of Minnesota were to abandon the business of higher education, it seems unlikely that the University of Minnesota would go into the business of producing automobiles, with its lobbyist now working the legislature for lower emission standards. Given such rigidity, we expect the forces specified by the ESA model to have their primary influence on populations via selection. As the variables of space, energy, and stability change, more or fewer interest organizations will enter or withdraw from lobbying.

## An Ecological Account of Interest Organization Diversity

Both of our most common explanations of interest organization diversity point to mobilization. Truman (1951, 53) focuses on the implications of social and economic complexity. Viewing mobilization as natural, he argues that the diversity of interest organizations must reflect the diversity of interests in society. An alternative account flows from Olson's *Logic of Collective Action*. Olson assumes that while probabilistic rates of solving the incentive problems of organization vary across types of interests, they are fixed or constant for each type. It follows, then, that any observed mix of interest organizations results from the interaction of the mix of naturally occurring latent interests in society and time since the state was constituted. Thus, while often pitted against each other, both of these explanations view diversity as a causally simple, aggregate-level outcome of individual-level processes, either as the outcome of the distinctive stochastic processes governing mobilization of different types of interests or as direct reflections of the original mix of latent interests available for mobilization (Baumgartner and Jones 1993, 175–92).

But can we explain population-level attributes, such as population diversity, exclusively by understanding mobilization? A population ecology perspective answers no. The weak linkage between mobilization and the population-level attribute of diversity is implicit in two assumptions of the ESA model. Given the assumption that populations are at or near their carrying capacities, the ESA model identifies the environmental constraints defining carrying capacity as most directly shaping the contours of populations via differential mortality and/or by feeding back so as to alter reproductive rates in a density-dependent manner, rather than underlying reproductive rates per se (Lack 1954, 72–73; Colinvaux 1978, 12). And given the assumption that these relationships are unique for each species or species guild (Aldrich et al. 1994, 224), it follows that the diversity of a population is a summed function of how the environmental forces specified in the ESA model separately influence carrying capacities for each species.

The population ecology understanding of diversity, then, is not causal in the usual sense of specifying a set of variables that directly determines another variable or property. Rather, the property of diversity is an artifact generated through the separate or independent determination of the densities of all of the species or organizations comprising a community.

The population ecology perspective does not suggest, however, that the actual distributions of latent interests found in societies are irrelevant in determining the overall diversity of interest organization systems. Rather, it suggests that variations in diversity will also independently arise from the interaction of environmental constraints with the distribution of latent interests in society. Indeed, if densities of subpopulations of interest organizations respond differently to changes in the value of a given constraint, then such a change may produce a different mix of interest organizations, even if the relative distribution of latent interests in society remains unchanged. As a result, the actual mixes of represented interests in states will depend both on their given mix of latent interests and on how the subpopulations of organized interests arising from that mix are separately constrained by the environmental forces implicit in what government is doing or may do that is of concern to each type of interest, how likely it is to change its current policy, and how many organizations of a given type have already formed.

The key empirical question, then, must concern how important each of these sources of variation is to the actual determination of interest organization population diversity. In chapter 8, we answer this question by using simulations based on the results from tests of the ESA model in chapter 7. We also compare that answer to a more conventional analysis of diversity in the form of a test of Truman's complexity hypothesis (1951).

## Interest Organization Population and Community Structure

Some of the most influential work on interest organizations over the last decade has focused on the structure of the Washington interest organization community within the policy process (Laumann and Knoke 1987; Browne 1988, 1990; Heinz et al. 1993). Based on intensive analyses of issue areas, these studies map interest organization communities, identifying who interacts with whom, when, where, and how. In many respects, then, these analyses are highly compatible with a population ecology framework. So, what can a more self-conscious population ecology approach add to the study of interest organization communities?

We believe that there are several insights that can be brought to this literature using a population ecology orientation beyond our empirical application of population analysis to another set of cases—the American states. Or rather, our application is part of the contribution of taking an explicit population ecology framework. The Washington community comprises, after all, a single population of interest organizations. Despite the sophistication of previous studies, their attention to one population precludes distinguishing among alternative causal processes driving the structuring of interest organization communities.[4] As a result, they are more descriptive in orientation than they might be.

Population ecology thinking also brings with it a number of concepts that should be useful in studying community structure. When population ecologists approach questions about communities, they focus immediately on the niche concept. They attempt to identify the role of each species in the community and how each species makes its living. And in analyzing how niches are constructed and maintained, they rely on competition theory, especially the competitive exclusion principle, to search for partitioning of shared or overlapping fundamental niches of species relying on the same resources (Aldrich et al. 1990). In chapter 3, we discussed a number of important implications of the niche concept and competition theory for understanding communities and the behavior of their members.

The most important of these ideas is that an organization's niche is defined by a multidimensional space, not simply by its place of interface with the policy-making process. Indeed, Browne's niche interpretation (1990; 1995, 216–18) is highly restrictive and is more similar to Grinnell's (1917) than to Hutchinson's (1957). But multidimensionality means that there need not be one way to establish an identity for internal organizational purposes. Identity can be located within any portion of the resource dimensions defining the fundamental niche that provides an organization's minimum requirements for survival. The particular identity that an organization establishes—its realized niche—will be specified through partitioning of critical dimensions of the fundamental niche shared with competitors.

This interpretation of the niche concept is important because it may help us to answer a broader question than that encompassed by research on policy balkanization. We almost never ask why interest communities are structured as they are. An answer is far from obvious. Given sets of potential members, legislative committees, patrons, and "interests," a given community of organized interests may be quite small, with each organization representing relatively encompassing interests, or large, with each representing very discrete and precise interests. And while the very nature of the interests surely constrains how the fault lines between organized interests are drawn under either scenario, boundaries between interest groups might be demarcated in any number of ways, as indicated by the craft or industrial basis of union organization. Niche theory suggests that we can explain why interest communities are structured in one manner or another by examining how interest groups construct viable realized niches from an n-dimensional set of potential or fundamental niches.

Such an examination will entail answering a series of subsequent questions addressing issues of both internal organizational maintenance and the external interface of interests with government (Aldrich et al. 1990, 22; 1994, 226–27). What are the internal and external resource dimensions defining the fundamental niches of interest organizations? Which are most important in establishing and maintaining realized niches? How do patterns of reliance on one resource dimension, such as membership, constrain patterns of reliance on another, such as the precise interest being represented? Are the several resource dimensions independent, substitutable, or interactive? Are some realized niches more viable than others in stable or in volatile environments? Interest group scholarship addresses the first two questions, but only in a highly fragmented way, and without speaking to the general issue of community structure. And it rarely addresses the other questions.

We too are not yet ready to tackle more than the first two queries, and then in only the most preliminary way. Still, niche theory should help us to address them more comprehensively. What, then, are the resource dimensions that define the fundamental niches of interest organizations? At this time, no comprehensive list is available. Still, five resource sets have received considerable attention in the literature on interest representation, and these can serve as our initially hypothesized set of requirements for viable realized niches. While drawing sharp boundaries around these dimensions is difficult, which in itself speaks to the need for an integrated theory, the first three speak primarily to the internal relations of an organization, while the last two bear more on external interactions.

First, with the exception of institutions (Salisbury 1984), interest groups must have members.[5] If competitors secure all of an organization's potential membership, it will die. Second, and again with the exception of institutions, organizations must have access to selective benefits to mobilize potential members (Olson 1965; Moe 1980). If competitors are already providing all of the selective benefits an interest organization might provide, its ability to mobilize potential but unaffiliated members will be limited. Third, interest groups must have sufficient finances to maintain their organizations internally (Walker 1983). Fourth, a viable organization must have some access to the policy-making process on issues of concern to it. This, of course, is the dimension addressed by Browne's model (1990), which suggests that organizations require near exclusive control over a narrow issue agenda. And fifth, there must be "authoritative action or proposed action by government" that is of concern to the interest group (Salisbury 1994, 12). Without something to lobby for, legitimizing lobbying activity is difficult.

How do these resources relate to the variables in the ESA population density model? In other words, how does the density model relate to our analysis of interest niches? Clearly, access to members and government action of interest to a constituency correspond readily to variables in the ESA density model. The remaining variables—selective incentives, access to officials, and finances—address resources that will vary across individual organizations but that are less likely to vary in aggregate over state populations and/or over the time period we examine in our empirical analyses. Thus, they were not included in the density model. However, were they to vary in aggregate over time or space, they would have to be included in the density models, most likely in interaction with the model's latent constituent number and constituent interest variables.

Our resource hypotheses are presented as statements, although each has generated more than a little scholarly debate. Niche theory brings its own peculiar method of inquiry to these debates. It suggests that competitors will partition one or more of these resources until a *limiting similarity* threshold is passed. But niche theory does not require that the limiting similarity threshold be defined on any particular resource dimension or combination thereof, although the lion's share of research has been on the policy access or control dimension. Instead, specifying the resource dimensions actually used to define realized niches is an empirical question.

There are at least some reasons to suspect that policy access/control may not be as critical for all interest organizations as Browne (1990, 1995) found it to be for agricultural interests lobbying in Washington. Uncertainty over the stability of policy arenas (Baumgartner and Jones 1993; Mucciaroni 1995), the potential costs of narrow issue identification for mobilizing new members, and the identity-blurring consequences of failure to engage enemies and work with friends suggest that control of a restricted issue area may not be crucial to establishing a viable realized niche, if the limiting threshold can be exceeded through partitioning on other resource dimensions shared with competitors. Access to policy arenas is surely important to interest organizations, but narrow issue dominance and its resulting balkanization may not always be necessary or even desirable for interest organizations seeking to establish viable realized niches.

So, how can we assess which resource dimension(s) realized niches are actually based on? Niche research in population biology suggests that we should look to interactions among interest organizations in answering this question. If realized niches are established via partitioning on any or several of the dimensions we have hypothesized as defining fundamental niches, interest group leaders should indicate that their relationships with potential competitors are of a specific type. Two types of interactions would indicate that a resource dimension may not be critical to an organization's survival: cooperating/communicating with allies and engaging in overt conflict with opponents. Both would indicate an absence of partitioning to establish a limiting threshold on a critical resource dimension. The remaining interaction is competition as expressed through partitioning. While perhaps strikingly alien to political scientists, who attend almost exclusively to conflict and cooperation (for an exception, see Bath 1995), this expectation is central to the competitive exclusion principle. And studies of national trade associations by organization ecologists (Aldrich et al. 1990, 235–36) have found at least some evidence of partitioning so as to avoid conflict.

In chapter 9, we examine survey data of interest organization leaders to assess these perceptions. We examine partitioning behavior to see if the niche concept applies to the structuring of interest organization communities, and we try to determine on which dimensions the identities of interest organizations are defined. With the latter analyses, we also attempt to determine if policy balkanization is an inherent and inevitable outcome of the struggle of interest organizations to survive.

## Studying Interest Organization Impact

When we move beyond the structuring of interest organization communities to considering their impact, we move beyond a population ecology perspective per se. We saw in chapter 2, for example, that the study of interest organization impact has been a traditional part of both the political science and economics research programs on interest representation. And there is nothing specific about the population ecology framework that addresses patterns of policy processes and outcomes equivalent to what is studied in these literatures. But the population ecology approach places special emphasis on two properties of interest organization populations—their density and diversity. When we turn to the impact of interest communities, then, a population ecology perspective leads us immediately to considering the consequences of population density and population diversity.

As discussed in chapter 2, the question of influence or impact has been pursued on three quite different levels. The first is *policy,* or the ability of interest organizations to secure very specific and narrow gains, such as inclusion of a favored expenditure in an appropriations bill or revision of a regulation. While political scientists often study interest organization influence at this level (Bauer, Pool, and Dexter 1963; Rothenberg 1992), they seldom—with the important exception of Lowi's interest group liberalism model (1969)—generalize from specific cases in a way that suggests much in terms of the interest organization population traits of density and diversity.

This is not true of economists, whose traditional view of interest organization influence reflects the assumption of Stigler (1971) and Peltzman (1976) that regulations are adopted at the behest of interest organizations and serve the interest of those organizations. Their view of politicians in this process is quite different from the scheming, election-driven manipulators of the Virginia School model. Rather, politicians are assumed to rather blindly pass proposals advocated by lobbyists.[6] And this model does not consider interactions among the interest organization community or the possibility that one interest might oppose another.[7]

Given this very thin model of the political process, the implications of interest organization population density and diversity are straightforward: more interest organizations and more different types of interest organizations should be associated with more demands for narrow and specific policies benefiting their constituents. Indeed, this is Olson's hypothesis in *The Rise and Decline of Nations*. Unfortunately, however, there have been no direct tests of this hypothesis using valid and reliable measures of interest organization population density and diversity or direct measures of policies or regulations of interest to a broad range of interest organizations.

The second level of impact analyses is found in political scientists' studies of issue communities and issue networks in Washington, D.C., the same studies discussed earlier when we considered the nature of interest organization niches—those of Laumann and Knoke (1987), Browne (1988, 1990), and Heinz, Laumann, Nelson, and Salisbury (1993). Highlighting the recent expansion of interest organization populations both in size and diversity, these analysts draw attention to how these changes have altered the *process* of policy making. With more and different kinds of organizations, agendas fluctuate as uncertain structures of power respond to more and more demands. Moreover, the once simple task of coalition formation becomes a nightmare of ever-changing players from issue to issue and from year to year. As a result, there may be more policy *activity* without a concomitant increase in policy *action*. As Salisbury (1992, 359) has concluded, "the descent on Washington of so many hundreds of associations, institutions, and their agents does not mean that these private interests have acquired greater sway or even a more articulate voice in the shaping of national policy. In many ways, the opposite is true." This approach to understanding interest organization impact would lead us to expect more activity within policy systems as a result of greater density and diversity, but a lower rate of completed policy actions.

The third level of understanding the impact of interest organization populations is founded almost entirely on research on the American states and addresses the global issue of interest organization system *power*. While Belle Zeller (1954) provides the earliest example of this approach, current scholarship focuses on the typologies of interest organization system power developed by Morehouse (1981) and by Thomas and Hrebenar (1990, 1995). Developed during the late 1970s, mid-1980s, and mid-1990s, respectively, the measures rest, in the words of Thomas and Hrebenar (1990, 141), on expert assessment for each state—whether direct or from secondary sources—of "the extent to which interest groups as a whole influence public policy when compared to other components of the political system." Although separated by more than a decade and employing varied categorizations, the typologies are quite strongly related. Allowing for some variation over time, the indicators are broadly consistent and provide at least some implicit support for their authors' assumption that interest organization power is an enduring characteristic of state political systems.

It is difficult, however, to more precisely interpret what interest organization power means. On the one hand, the "power" of organized interests may be unrelated to such system-level concepts as interest organization population diversity and density (Thomas and Hrebenar 1994). Only one, two, or a few interest organizations may be extremely influential across a broad array of issues, meaning that while interest organizations might be important in that state, their political importance will be unrelated to the state's overall distribution of interests. Under this quite plausible condition, interest organization power may be unrelated to interest system density and diversity. Alternatively, the power typologies may be tapping influence derived from such population properties as the density and diversity of interests. In their interpretations of the typologies, this seems to be the position of Morehouse and of Thomas and Hrebenar. As yet, though, we lack a firm demonstration that such population traits as interest organization density and diversity are related to reputational measures of interest organization power.

In regard to all three levels of analysis of interest organization influence, it is worth keeping in mind that politics, policy making, and governance are comprised of more than a mechanistic transmission of demands to outcomes. Bureaucrats, policy experts, and perhaps occasionally even the prudential judgment of elected officials also contribute to the determination of what government does and how it does it. As Salisbury (1992, 99) has written, "the full pattern of interest representation is, or may be, significantly separate from, even largely independent of, the structure and shape of the organized group presence." While Salisbury's caution is untested, it serves as an important null hypothesis when considering each level of impact analysis.

### Relations to Other Theories

#### Does Population Ecology Tell Us Anything New?

How do the analyses offered here differ from contemporary accounts of processes of interest representation? In other words, does a population ecology perspective really tell us anything new that we cannot derive from existing theories? The most important issue here, of course, is how a population ecology interpretation relates to theories of micro- or individual-level processes of interest organization mobilization. Clearly, models of interest organization density and diversity must relate to these models in a way that does not contradict what we know about behavior at that level of analysis. But our question here focuses on a more demanding relationship than mere consistency or compatibility. We need to know whether we can get the same answers proposed here about populations if we rely strictly on knowledge about what happens through processes of individual-level mobilization.

One way to illustrate how we cannot get to population-level answers from theories of mobilization is to ask what extant knowledge about individual-level incentives governing mobilization might tell us about the central hypothesis of the ESA model—density dependence with space as measured by number of latent constituents. There is reason to expect that the rate of organization formation lags behind the growth rate of the latent members. Many older interest organizations need not be replicated as potential membership expands. Once a state chamber of commerce is established, for example, we would not expect to see another state chamber of commerce established as the number of businesses doubles. For many such membership groups, positive economies of scale may even prohibit entrance by direct competitors. Also, we have argued, there may be declining marginal utilities associated with the establishment of new interest organizations. The marginal gain in representation from the last organization representing a very narrow subpopulation is probably far less than that accrued in establishing the first interest organization representing a broader aggregation of interests. So, while new interests will be established as latent constituency expands, the rate at which they are established may be less than the rate at which potential constituency expands.

These arguments seem highly plausible. Indeed, they probably account for what happens at the individual level to produce the density dependence hypothesized by the ESA model, and we have earlier incorporated both arguments in our presentation of the ESA model. This illustrates precisely what we mean when we suggest that the individual-level behaviors implicit in population models should not contradict what we know about individual-level behaviors from mobilization theory and research. But this does not mean that the micro-level analyses could alone produce a density-dependent hypothesis.[8] Both the replication and the marginal utility arguments previously presented make reference to *other organizations* in the environment of a latent organization that might form, other organizations that may already occupy the resource dimensions required for the latent organization to establish a viable realized niche. Yet, existing micro-level theories make no reference to other organizations in the environment. Thus, the variables that make our explanations of density dependence plausible in a sense of being consistent with micro-level theories are derived from outside the theoretical framework provided by existing models of mobilization.

The case that a population ecology approach provides something quite different from prior theories of interest representation is even stronger in other areas. Until now, we have viewed diversity as a function of mobilization—either as a natural representation of the complexity of interests in society or, in a more complex manner, as a reflection of the distribution of disincentives to organization across different guilds. Instead, population ecology conceptualizes diversity not in direct causal terms, but as an artifact produced through summing the distinctive play of the ESA variables for each interest organization guild. And when we turn to representation, population ecology offers us an expanded definition of niche behavior that can both incorporate existing interpretations and provide a means to assess niche behaviors empirically via the competitive exclusion principle and the partitioning behavior it engenders.

It is also obvious, however, that population ecology interpretations are not a substitute for much of contemporary scholarship about interest organizations. The greatest proportion of research on interest representation addresses questions that bear on the life histories of specific interest organizations. Our current stock of theories addresses variables that help us to identify which latent interests will organize and which will not, which entrepreneurial strategies on the part of interest organization leaders increase the likelihood that organizations will survive and which do not, and which interest organizations are influential in the policy process and which are not. These are important questions for those concerned about the politics of interest representation. But because population ecology treats such issues as essentially stochastic processes, it provides us few direct answers to questions about the life histories of specific interest organizations.

### Similarities and Differences with Organization Ecology

While our analysis of interest organizations from a population ecology perspective shares with organization ecology research the same theoretical roots in population biology and evolutionary theory, our emphases are somewhat different. In large part, this is a function of our data. In the empirical chapters that follow, we analyze cross sections of multiple populations of interest organizations, while most organization ecology studies examine single populations of organizations over time.

By examining a single population over time, organization ecologists often assume that they can either treat many or most of the variables defining space, energy, and stability constraints as constants or control their influence through trend and period effects (Hannan and Carroll 1992, 208–9). This assumption allows them to focus more directly on density dependence in founding and mortality rates. Indeed, Aldrich and Staber (1988) and Aldrich, Zimmer, Staber, and Beggs (1990) go so far as to pit energy-based explanations attentive to government activity against ecological models, implying that such models restrict our attention to the demographic patterns defining density dependence. This narrow interpretation is not typical of most organization ecology studies (Hannan and Freeman 1989, 81–90; Hannan and Carroll 1992, 123–29, 207–31), many of which are at least theoretically attentive to energy and stability as ecological variables. But with time series data, even these researchers have not felt compelled to directly specify a broad range of environmental constraints to reach valid conclusions about density dependence (Singh and Lumsden 1990, 168–69, 178), although there is nothing about time series analysis that precludes doing so. By approaching the ESA model from a cross-sectional perspective, we cannot make similar assumptions; space and energy constraints must be measured broadly and directly in the models tested in later chapters.

Both types of analysis have long histories in the population biology tradition of ecological research. Some of the most sophisticated modeling research in population biology relies on time series data (Volterra 1926; May 1974). But while less sophisticated from a modeling perspective, some of the most insightful population biology studies have been cross-sectional in orientation, requiring direct specification of the environmental forces driving populations (MacArthur 1958; MacArthur and Pianka 1966; Lack 1947; Simberloff and Wilson 1969; Signor 1990; Stevens 1989). Our approach to population ecology, especially in terms of the models used, but also in theoretical focus, is more similar to this last set of biological studies than it is to most organization ecology research.

# CHAPTER 5

# Describing State Interest Communities

In exploring the nature of state interest organization populations, scholarly attention has been repeatedly drawn to two population-level properties: system density and system diversity (Olson 1982; Zeigler 1983; Walker 1983; Truman 1951, 60–62; Zeigler and van Dalen 1976, 95–110; Schlozman 1984; Schlozman and Tierney 1983). But while long used in the literature, the concepts have remained ill-defined and poorly measured, especially in terms of measuring *change* in density and diversity. We describe the recent evolution of state interest organizations in this chapter by exploring several measures of population density and diversity. Multiple measures of each concept are examined given competing interpretations of the meaning of each. Moreover, we examine the measures at three different periods in time. This is essential if we are to assess the temporal stability of these population properties and consider questions of change. Following presentation and discussion of the measures, we consider how they are related to each other empirically and theoretically. The latter task, especially, will influence our empirical analyses in later chapters. Though we use all of the measures in later chapters, we will see that some of the density and diversity indicators, while appropriate for descriptive purposes or as independent variables, are inappropriate objects of causal explanation. Finally in this chapter, we consider the special case of density in small states.

## Interest Organization Population Density

Each of our indicators of interest organization density, as well as those of diversity, starts with the number of organized interests operative in a state, an approach taken both by Olson (1982) in tests of his institutional sclerosis model of economic growth and by Schlozman and Tierney (1986) in their study of the Washington interest organization population. As discussed in chapter 1, we operationalize the number of state interest organizations by the number of organizations registered to lobby in state legislatures.[1] Three years of lobbying registrations are examined: 1975, 1980, and 1990. Complete data for the first two periods were not obtained for Hawaii, Rhode Island, Utah, West Virginia, Alabama, and Nevada. To facilitate valid comparisons across the three periods, the 1990 data are presented both for all 50 states and for the 44 states in the 1975 and 1980 samples. A third set of 1990 measures is also presented to facilitate valid comparison. Florida proved to be an outlier in the 1990 sample, with nearly twice as many registered interest organizations as any other state. This exception was not evident in 1975 or 1980 and does not seem to be a function of unduly strict registration laws. Given the resulting skewed distributions, however, we report the 1990 data for 49 states—excluding Florida—as well as for all 50 states.

While a raw number of interest organizations provides a starting point for measuring interest population density, it is not obvious that by itself it is an adequate indicator. Density is a relational concept. Twenty individuals in a football stadium would not be considered a dense population. The same 20 individuals in an elevator, however, would experience a high level of density. Numbers of individuals do not change as we move from one of these groups to the other, but their relationship to space does. This is also true for numbers of interest organizations. Therefore, numbers of organizations must be compared to some frame of reference to give the indicator meaning in terms of the underlying concept of density.

Specifying such a frame is difficult, however, in that interest organizations serve a mediating function in linking citizens and institutions to governments. They at one time face both society and government. So, at least two frames are appropriate in giving numbers of interest organizations meaning in terms of the concept of density—one focusing on representation, or numbers of interest organizations in relation to society, and the other focusing on governance, or numbers of interest organizations in relation to government.

Starting with the latter, the literature's discussion of density vis-à-vis the governance process usually addresses numbers of interest organizations relative to government as a unitary entity.[2] In terms of the overall governance frame, then, raw numbers of interest organizations—or rather, raw numbers divided by one—will still constitute an appropriate indicator of interest organization population density.

So, how have the number of organizations registered to lobby changed over the 15 years spanned by our three cross sections? Without question, numbers have increased sharply, as is evident in the state-by-state data reported in table 5.1. This is more easily seen in figure 5.1, which reports mean numbers for our three cross sections. The mean number of organizations registered to lobby increased 75.05 percent between 1975 and 1980, from 195.57 (s.d. = 120.48) to 342.36

**TABLE 5.1.** Number and Rank of Registered Interest Organizations in the American States, 1975, 1980, and 1990

| State | 1975 No. | 1975 Rank | 1980 No. | 1980 Rank | 1990 No. | 1990 Rank |
|-------|----------|-----------|----------|-----------|----------|-----------|
| FL | 596 | 1 | 872 | 1 | 2969 | 1 |
| CA | 559 | 2 | 774 | 3 | 1348 | 2 |
| AZ | 426 | 3 | 445 | 8 | 593 | 17 |
| MN | 355 | 4 | 687 | 5 | 954 | 7 |
| OR | 325 | 5 | 326 | 19 | 636 | 16 |
| NY | 315 | 6 | 452 | 7 | 995 | 6 |
| PA | 289 | 7 | 705 | 4 | 1180 | 3 |
| WA | 284 | 8 | 434 | 9 | 767 | 12 |
| CO | 258 | 9 | 360 | 14 | 579 | 18 |
| NJ | 252 | 10 | 423 | 10 | 746 | 13 |
| MA | 243 | 11 | 369 | 12 | 673 | 14 |
| IA | 232 | 12 | 326 | 18 | 550 | 20 |
| VA | 231 | 13 | 320 | 21 | 496 | 23 |
| MO | 228 | 14 | 308 | 22 | 557 | 19 |
| ND | 222 | 15 | 285 | 24 | 342 | 36 |
| IN | 219 | 16 | 283 | 25 | 438 | 29 |
| LA | 214 | 17 | 255 | 29 | 448 | 27 |
| IL | 209 | 19 | 389 | 11 | 906 | 9 |
| GA | 209 | 18 | 368 | 13 | 904 | 10 |
| WY | 203 | 20 | 236 | 32 | 394 | 31 |
| ME | 186 | 21 | 214 | 36 | 301 | 39 |
| KS | 180 | 22 | 336 | 17 | 518 | 21 |
| NM | 178 | 23 | 324 | 20 | 466 | 26 |
| KY | 155 | 24 | 241 | 31 | 372 | 33 |
| TX | 152 | 25 | 782 | 2 | 1166 | 4 |
| MD | 151 | 27 | 279 | 26 | 636 | 15 |
| TN | 151 | 26 | 227 | 33 | 418 | 30 |
| WI | 149 | 28 | 303 | 23 | 505 | 22 |
| MI | 145 | 29 | 353 | 15 | 1160 | 5 |
| NE | 139 | 30 | 274 | 28 | 363 | 34 |
| OH | 129 | 31 | 456 | 6 | 945 | 8 |
| ID | 110 | 32 | 220 | 34 | 263 | 41 |
| SD | 99 | 33 | 207 | 37 | 325 | 37 |
| AR | 98 | 34 | 183 | 39 | 231 | 45 |
| NC | 97 | 35 | 253 | 30 | 479 | 24 |
| MT | 96 | 36 | 277 | 27 | 345 | 35 |
| AK | 88 | 37 | 219 | 35 | 313 | 38 |
| OK | 82 | 38 | 197 | 38 | 446 | 28 |
| SC | 78 | 39 | 146 | 42 | 221 | 46 |
| NH | 76 | 40 | 149 | 41 | 194 | 49 |
| VT | 71 | 41 | 143 | 43 | 234 | 43 |
| CT | 44 | 42 | 350 | 16 | 477 | 25 |
| DE | 42 | 43 | 174 | 40 | 210 | 47 |
| MS | 40 | 44 | 140 | 44 | 107 | 50 |
| NV | -- | -- | -- | -- | 826 | 11 |
| UT | -- | -- | -- | -- | 376 | 32 |
| AL | -- | -- | -- | -- | 289 | 40 |
| WV | -- | -- | -- | -- | 262 | 42 |
| RI | -- | -- | -- | -- | 233 | 44 |
| HI | -- | -- | -- | -- | 196 | 48 |

Average Number of Interest Organizations

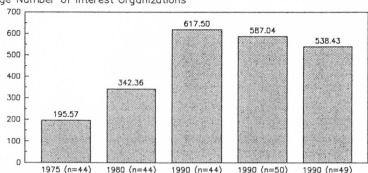

Fig. 5.1. Average number of interest organizations in 1975, 1980, and 1990 for several sample sets. The 44-state bars exclude Alabama, Hawaii, Nevada, Rhode Island, Utah, and West Virginia. The 49-state bar excludes Florida.

(s.d. = 174.23). But over the following ten years, the average number of registered organizations increased by only 71.46 percent, from 342.36 to 587.04 (s.d. = 451.43). And this most recent increase is not a product of our comparing our earlier results for 44 states to the 1990 results for 50 states. As seen in the second bar from the right in figure 5.1, restricting our 1990 sample to only the same 44 states in the 1975 and 1980 samples leads to an even greater increase in the average number of organizations—617.50 (s.d. = 466.47) instead of 587.04. And the results cannot be attributed to our inclusion of Florida's value, which—at nearly 3,000 registered organizations in 1990—far outstrips that of other states. As seen in the last bar in figure 5.1, excluding Florida modifies the average only modestly, down to 538.43 (s.d. = 299.66) interest organizations. In sum, organizations have continued to increase in number over the last decade, but at only half the rate observed between 1975 and 1980.[3]

From the perspective of representation, however, numbers of interest organizations are an inadequate measure of density. This point of view suggests that we should be concerned about density not in respect to the institutions being lobbied but in respect to the community of interests being represented. The most obvious definition of this community of interests is a state's population of citizens. A very dense interest organization system is one in which there are many interest organizations representing relatively few citizens. It is not at all clear, however, that most interest organizations represent citizens. As Schlozman (1984,

1010) has noted, many interest organizations "have no members in the ordinary sense of the word." Indeed, half of all registered interest organizations in the states in 1990 represented institutions, and fewer than a third were membership groups. Thus, measures of density founded on a population frame of reference may be missing the essential basis of who or what is being represented through the lobbying process.

Is there a valid alternative to the population frame? In assessing the Washington interest community, Schlozman (1984, 1011–15) echoes Schattschneider's assertion (1960) that the fundamental basis of organization representation is economic. This suggests that a more appropriate measure of representational density will assess numbers of organizations in relation to the size of a state's economy, or the average economic base behind interest organizations in a state. Therefore, representational economic density—GSP-BASE—is measured by the ratio of the number of organizations registered to lobby before a state's legislature and its gross state product (GSP). This identifies the GSP underlying, on average, each organization, or the average number of GSP dollars behind each organization in the state. States with high ratio values have few organizations relative to the size of the state's economy (low density), while low ratio values indicate many organizations relative to economic size (high density).[4]

State-by-state GSP-BASE values are reported in table 5.2 for 1975, 1980, and 1990. These values need to be interpreted with caution. The GSP numerators in the indicators represent somewhat different years than those reported for numbers of organizations, because of the lack of annual data on GSP prior to 1986 (Trott, Dunbar, and Friedenberg 1991). Therefore, 1975 interest organization data are matched with 1977 GSP data, 1980 organization data with 1982 GSP data, and 1990 organization data with 1989 GSP data. Importantly, the lag between the interest organization and GSP values runs in the opposite direction for the 1990 indicators than for the 1975 and 1980 measures. This will deflate the numerator of the 1990 GSP-BASE indicator relative to those for 1975 and 1980. And with a smaller numerator, the 1990 GSP-BASE values are almost certainly understated relative to those for 1975 and 1980.

With this caveat in mind, average GSP-BASE scores, an inverse measure of density, are reported in figure 5.2 for the 1975, 1980, and 1990 samples calculated for both nominal and real 1975 values of GSP. Starting with nominal GSP-BASE values, average GSP-BASE declined by 24.32 percent from 1975 to 1980, from 230.42 (s.d.=205.09) to 174.39 (s.d. = 118.98). While there was an average of $230,420,000 in GSP behind each registered organization in 1975, the average GSP behind

**TABLE 5.2. Number and Rank of GSP-BASE [GSP per Registered Interest] in the American States, 1975, 1980, and 1990**

| State | 1975 GSP-BASE | 1975 Rank | 1980 GSP-BASE | 1980 Rank | 1990 GSP-BASE | 1990 Rank |
|-------|---------------|-----------|---------------|-----------|---------------|-----------|
| TX | 869.02 | 1 | 325.46 | 4 | 291.64 | 4 |
| OH | 748.94 | 2 | 294.31 | 7 | 223.86 | 12 |
| CT | 671.52 | 3 | 134.97 | 24 | 186.29 | 16 |
| MI | 610.23 | 4 | 307.73 | 5 | 156.75 | 22 |
| IL | 552.46 | 5 | 410.74 | 3 | 283.09 | 5 |
| NY | 540.82 | 6 | 565.68 | 1 | 443.28 | 2 |
| NC | 451.07 | 7 | 273.23 | 8 | 271.58 | 9 |
| CA | 407.14 | 8 | 481.32 | 2 | 517.35 | 1 |
| MS | 394.65 | 9 | 182.41 | 20 | 356.41 | 3 |
| PA | 341.41 | 10 | 200.40 | 16 | 193.13 | 15 |
| OK | 287.65 | 11 | 247.21 | 10 | 117.35 | 28 |
| WI | 267.23 | 12 | 196.66 | 19 | 186.09 | 17 |
| NJ | 265.54 | 13 | 252.26 | 9 | 272.62 | 7 |
| SC | 252.68 | 14 | 218.77 | 14 | 272.18 | 8 |
| MD | 227.56 | 15 | 188.47 | 18 | 155.15 | 23 |
| TN | 219.84 | 16 | 228.93 | 11 | 220.73 | 13 |
| IN | 217.93 | 17 | 226.30 | 12 | 240.44 | 10 |
| MA | 201.73 | 19 | 209.12 | 15 | 215.14 | 14 |
| GA | 193.08 | 18 | 181.43 | 21 | 143.56 | 24 |
| VA | 185.63 | 20 | 219.92 | 13 | 275.20 | 6 |
| KY | 183.45 | 21 | 175.46 | 22 | 177.04 | 18 |
| MO | 181.26 | 22 | 198.79 | 17 | 179.68 | 19 |
| LA | 177.58 | 23 | 297.03 | 6 | 176.65 | 20 |
| AR | 149.64 | 24 | 128.21 | 27 | 160.82 | 21 |
| DE | 133.55 | 25 | 48.48 | 39 | 73.40 | 41 |
| WA | 123.85 | 27 | 130.75 | 25 | 125.47 | 26 |
| IA | 113.07 | 26 | 115.44 | 28 | 95.54 | 33 |
| KS | 113.01 | 28 | 99.07 | 29 | 94.26 | 34 |
| FL | 108.78 | 29 | 135.67 | 23 | 76.44 | 39 |
| MN | 100.27 | 30 | 81.40 | 32 | 98.06 | 32 |
| NE | 97.98 | 31 | 77.53 | 34 | 85.72 | 35 |
| CO | 96.02 | 32 | 125.70 | 26 | 114.30 | 29 |
| AK | 83.75 | 33 | 89.72 | 31 | 62.57 | 42 |
| NH | 82.78 | 34 | 77.89 | 33 | 126.32 | 27 |
| OR | 67.21 | 35 | 95.55 | 30 | 81.95 | 36 |
| MT | 65.80 | 36 | 39.74 | 42 | 37.98 | 46 |
| ID | 62.85 | 37 | 47.42 | 40 | 62.13 | 43 |
| NM | 56.08 | 38 | 61.80 | 36 | 54.52 | 44 |
| SD | 51.77 | 39 | 37.85 | 43 | 34.26 | 47 |
| VT | 47.87 | 40 | 41.06 | 41 | 49.15 | 45 |
| AZ | 44.59 | 41 | 75.51 | 35 | 110.13 | 30 |
| ME | 40.40 | 42 | 56.54 | 37 | 77.99 | 38 |
| WY | 26.68 | 43 | 55.32 | 38 | 28.30 | 50 |
| ND | 24.06 | 44 | 36.12 | 44 | 32.84 | 49 |
| RI | -- | -- | -- | -- | 80.71 | 37 |
| NV | -- | -- | -- | -- | 33.85 | 48 |
| UT | -- | -- | -- | -- | 74.82 | 40 |
| HI | -- | -- | -- | -- | 131.41 | 25 |
| WV | -- | -- | -- | -- | 106.58 | 31 |
| AL | -- | -- | -- | -- | 234.90 | 11 |

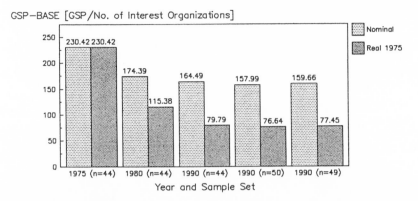

**Fig. 5.2. Average nominal and real 1975 GSP-BASE for 1975, 1980, and 1990 for several sample sets. The 44-state bars exclude Alabama, Hawaii, Nevada, Rhode Island, Utah, and West Virginia. The 49-state bar excludes Florida.**

each organization declined by 1980 to $174,390,000. Given our interpretation of GSP-BASE, this means that the interest organization system became more dense; on average more organizations were registered relative to the total amount of economic activity.

The decline in GSP-BASE, or increase in density, was much less sharp from 1980 to 1990, with average GSP-BASE declining only 9.40 percent, from 174.39 in our 1980 sample of 44 states to 157.99 (s.d. = 104.89) for our 1990 universe of 50 states.[5] But we must keep in mind our measurement caveat—that the difference in the GSP lag of the 1990 measure understates the average 1990 GSP-BASE value. Given this difference, it is likely that nominal density did not change much during the 1980s. Though the number of organizations increased sharply, it did so at the same pace as economic activity, leading to only very modest change in the overall density of state interest organization systems. Thus, the sharp increase in interest organization system density observed from 1975 to 1980 was not replicated over the course of the 1980s for nominal GSP-BASE.

GSP-BASE scores based on nominal values of GSP overstate, of course, the real economic power behind organizations in comparisons over time. This can be seen in the GSP-BASE values calculated on the basis of real 1975 values of GSP reported in figure 5.2. As expected, the decline of GSP-BASE (or increase in density) from 1975 to 1980 becomes even sharper in this comparison, dropping fully 49.03 percent, from 230.42 to 115.38. The real decline in GSP-BASE (or increase in density) was much less sharp from 1980 to 1990, with average real GSP-BASE declining only 33.54 percent, from 115.38 for our 1980 sample of 44 states to 76.64 for our 1990 universe of 50 states. In conjunction with our measurement caveat that the 1990 values are probably understated, this suggests that the rapid increase in real organization density from 1975 to 1980 slowed considerably during the 1980s but was still substantial.

Still, the averages reported in figure 5.2, whether real or nominal, are only averages. As we will see later, patterns of change in the numbers of organizations represented from 1975 to 1980 and 1990 varied across types of organizations. Moreover, the rate of GSP growth varies depending on the economic sector examined. Therefore, we also examined the average nominal GSP-BASE values of state interest organizations in 1975, 1980, and 1990 by nine categories representing major sectors of economic activity, which are more fully discussed under the topic of diversity.

Several results from this examination bear reporting. First, average GSP-BASE declined in all but one of the nine sectors from 1975 to 1990. In other words, interest organization density increased within eight of nine sectors. The exception is construction, the GSP-BASE score of which actually increased 26.04 percent, from 204.52 to 257.78. The GSP-BASE value of the finance sector hardly changed at all, declining 3.72 percent from 1975 to 1990. And with the exception of mining and manufacturing, the remaining economic sectors experience nominal GSP-BASE declines of about 25 percent.

Second, the increase in interest organization density was especially sharp for mining and manufacturing, the GSP-BASE values of which declined from 1975 to 1990 fully 54.55 and 67.01 percent, respectively. In the case of mining, this resulted almost entirely from the relatively low growth rate of GSP from mining, for, as we will see in the next section of this chapter, the actual number of mining interest organizations declined as a proportion of the total number of organized interests from 1975 to 1990.

The growth rate of GSP from manufacturing also lagged behind that of most sectors of the economy during the last 20 years, and this factor certainly contributed to the observed decline in its GSP-BASE value. Even if the number of manufacturing organizations remained constant, they would have represented a relatively smaller proportion of total GSP over time. But another contributing factor lies in the number of manufacturing interest organizations, which grew relatively faster than most other sectors since 1975, an issue we explore more fully later in this chapter. Given both factors, while manufacturing interest organizations represented on average $793,250,000 in GSP in 1975, they represented only $261,690,000 in 1990, a decline in average political/economic concentration that is stunning. While our interpretation of the magnitude of this decline might be moderated somewhat by remembering that our 1990 values likely understate the actual GSP-BASE of states relative to the 1975 and 1980 measures, this understatement is true for the other eight sectors as well. Thus, the decline of manufacturing GSP-BASE (or increase in density) relative to the other eight sectors remains undiminished.

Third, as a result of the spectacular increase in the density of manufacturing interests, the several economic sectors appear far more alike in respect to each other in 1990 than in 1975 or 1980. The manufacturing sector's 1975 GSP-BASE value of 793.25 is fully 99.39 percent larger than that of the next highest GSP-BASE value in 1975—397.83 for trade. In 1990, manufacturing still generated the highest GSP-BASE value, 261.69, but this is only 1.52 percent larger than the next highest value, 257.78 for construction. This homogenization of the density of organizations across economic sectors is better reflected in the sharply declining standard deviations of GSP-BASE for the nine sectors over the three years, which fall from 193.24 in 1975, through 126.21 in 1980, to 68.10 in 1990. In short, the political/economic concentration within the nine sectors has equalized over the course of the 1980s.

How have these changes altered the relative positions of the states? While we would not argue that density is a fixed or enduring trait, each measure exhibits considerable stability in terms of the relative positions of the states. For example, the correlation of the 1975 and 1980 GSP-BASE scores is 0.73. And consistent with the diminished rate of change in interest organization system density over the course of the 1980s, the simple correlation of the 1980 and 1990 GSP-BASE scores is even stronger—0.88. Simple correlations with similar magnitudes were generated for numbers of interest organizations (0.76 and 0.86, respectively). In short, the relative positions of high- and low-density states have been quite stable over the last two decades, irrespective of dramatic increases in the size of interest organization populations.

**Interest Organization Population Diversity**

Our indicators of interest community diversity, like our measures of density, start with the number of organizations registered to lobby state legislatures. However, we must identify how numbers of organizations are *distributed* across some relevant typology of interests. As in the case of density, diversity might be legitimately and usefully defined with respect to any number of politically interesting traits. One might, for example, be interested in the distribution of interest organizations

Economic Sector

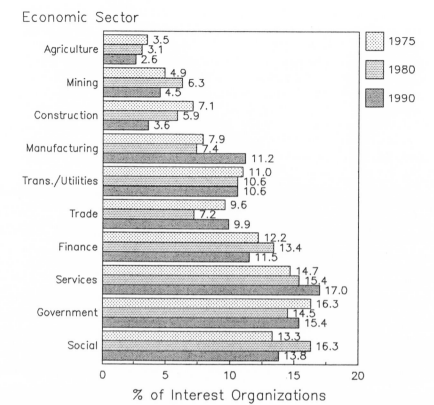

Fig. 5.3. Comparisons of elements of state interest organization populations for 1975, 1980, and 1990

across industrial and postindustrial sectors of the economy. We focus on
three politically interesting dimensions here, all of which reflect in some
manner Schlozman's assertion (1984, 1011–15) that the fundamental
basis of interest representation is economic.

Our first measure of diversity involves analyzing the distribution of
interest organizations across major economic sectors. Before we address
this diversity measure, however, we should examine how the composition of organizations has changed over the last 15 years. We should see if
the observed growth in numbers of organizations is restricted to interests
representing one or a few economic sectors. We report in figure 5.3 the
average composition of state interest organizations in 1975, 1980, and
1990 by eight categories representing major sectors of private economic
activity, a ninth representing government, and a tenth residual category

representing social (e.g., advocacy, hobby, and religious) organizations. We identify the ninth and tenth categories as not-for-profit organizations, although a few of the social organizations may be profit-making enterprises.

Clearly, some changes occurred from 1975 to 1990. The numbers of agriculture, mining, construction, transportation/utilities, and finance organizations as a percentage of the total number of organizations have declined somewhat, while the proportions of organizations representing manufacturing, trade, and services increased. With a few exceptions, however, these changes are quite modest and are hardly reflective of major alterations in the balance of interests in the states over time. Among these exceptions is the dramatic growth in the proportion of organizations representing manufacturing, which increased 49.22 percent from 1975 to 1990, from constituting only 7.87 percent of all organizations in 1975 to comprising 11.20 percent in 1990. And even this rate of growth masks the actual degree of recent change, since the proportion of organizations representing manufacturing actually declined slightly from 1975 to 1980. No other change is nearly as great.

Still, several of the more modest changes are politically interesting precisely because they are so modest. Perhaps the most striking finding reported in figure 5.3 is the decline in the proportion of social organizations, from 16.30 percent in 1980 to only 13.80 in 1990. This is surprising in light of Walker's speculation (1983) that increasing access to patronage has enabled social organizations to overcome diseconomies of organization in a manner that would allow their numbers to grow at a rate faster than those of private economic organizations. The pattern of change from 1975 to 1980 seems to support this assertion; the proportion of social organizations increased from 13.27 percent of all organizations to 16.26 percent. But nearly all of this relative growth evaporated during the 1980s leaving social organizations in the same position relative to other organizations as that they occupied in 1975. Like the findings of Schlozman (1984) and Schlozman and Tierney (1983) on the Washington interest system, these results suggest that the recent explosion in the numbers of organizations in the states has not altered the dominance of traditional economic interests.

How does this distribution of interest organizations compare to the actual distribution of these interests in society? No absolute answer can be provided given the inherent ambiguity of any definition of the "actual" distribution of societal interests. Also, representation includes much more than a count of organizations. Still, if we rely on the claim by Schlozman and Schattschneider that the basis of representation is economic, we can gain a rough impression by comparing the distribution of

**Fig. 5.4. Comparisons of distributions of 1990 interest organizations and 1989 GSP by economic sector**

interest organizations across economic sectors with their contributions to gross state product. Thus, two distributions are presented in figure 5.4—the average distribution of interest organizations in 1990 and the average distribution of GSP across nine economic sectors. The interest organization proportions reported in the first bar differ slightly from those presented in figure 5.3, given the exclusion of social interest organizations, for which there is no comparable GSP value.

The two distributions look quite similar, which provides some support for the notion that the distribution of interests is founded on economics. Indeed, the simple correlation of the two sets of proportions is 0.83. Still, some are overrepresented in terms of organizations per unit of GSP, while others are underrepresented. The overrepresented sectors, as measured by the difference in the proportions as a percent of the GSP proportion, include mining (78.55 percent more interest organizations than might be expected), government (46.12 percent), transportation/ utilities (30.00 percent), and services (13.12 percent). The underrepresented sectors include manufacturing (27.57 percent fewer organizations than might be expected), trade (−27.57 percent), finance (−19.14 percent), construction (−15.26 percent), and agriculture (−8.23 percent).

While such details are useful in developing an impression of the diversity of interest organization populations, we need a more precise measure to assess diversity across time and states. Accordingly, our first indicator of interest organization system diversity is a Herfindahl index of interest organization diversity across the ten categories of economic and social activity. Herfindahl indices, calculated by summing the squared proportions of cases distributed across categories of a nominally measured variable, are standard measures of concentration/diversity and are used frequently, for example, to measure market shares of firms in antitrust litigation. Given ten sets of interest organizations, the most concentrated interest organization system—one in which all organizations fall into one of the ten categories—would have an index value of 1.000. In contrast, an extremely diverse system in which organizations are proportionally distributed across the ten categories would have a diversity or concentration value of 0.100. Thus, high values indicate low diversity, with organizations concentrated in only one or a few categories, while low values indicate that organizations are allocated evenly across all categories.

State-by-state values of the Herfindahl index are reported in table 5.3. We can address possible concerns of those unfamiliar with Herfindahl indices in two ways. First, our indices of organization diversity for 1975, 1980, and 1990 are closely related to more familiar indicators of concentration. For example, they are correlated at greater than the 0.99 level with the simple standard deviation of the proportions of the ten categories of interest organizations.

Second, we can examine the distributions of interest organizations of those states with the highest and lowest organization diversity scores to see if we are tapping real differences in interest organization populations. Idaho and Arizona had the two lowest index scores in 1990 (indicative of high diversity): 0.110 and 0.112, respectively. As seen in figure 5.5A, interest organizations in these states were distributed very evenly across the ten categories of economic or social activity. In contrast, Colorado and Massachusetts had the two highest index values in 1990: 0.151 and 0.150, respectively. And as seen in figure 5.5B, their distributions are more concentrated, with Massachusetts having an unusually large proportion of service organizations and Colorado a relatively large

**TABLE 5.3.** Herfindahl Index (HI) of Interest Diversity—Value and Rank—in the American States, 1975, 1980, and 1990

| State | 1975 HI | 1975 Rank | 1980 HI | 1980 Rank | 1990 HI | 1990 Rank |
|-------|---------|-----------|---------|-----------|---------|-----------|
| WI | 0.1542 | 1 | 0.1325 | 10 | 0.1300 | 29 |
| CO | 0.1536 | 2 | 0.1274 | 20 | 0.1509 | 1 |
| CT | 0.1531 | 3 | 0.1315 | 13 | 0.1405 | 6 |
| WA | 0.1469 | 4 | 0.1174 | 39 | 0.1175 | 46 |
| SC | 0.1467 | 5 | 0.1194 | 34 | 0.1330 | 16 |
| FL | 0.1460 | 6 | 0.1480 | 2 | 0.1474 | 3 |
| NH | 0.1429 | 7 | 0.1390 | 4 | 0.1335 | 14 |
| NY | 0.1417 | 8 | 0.1322 | 11 | 0.1324 | 20 |
| WY | 0.1392 | 9 | 0.1303 | 16 | 0.1386 | 10 |
| DE | 0.1350 | 10 | 0.1380 | 5 | 0.1272 | 34 |
| MI | 0.1321 | 11 | 0.1261 | 24 | 0.1404 | 7 |
| MA | 0.1320 | 12 | 0.1260 | 25 | 0.1497 | 2 |
| NE | 0.1309 | 13 | 0.1236 | 28 | 0.1300 | 26 |
| IA | 0.1286 | 14 | 0.1342 | 8 | 0.1327 | 17 |
| ND | 0.1265 | 15 | 0.1362 | 6 | 0.1217 | 41 |
| MD | 0.1259 | 16 | 0.1216 | 30 | 0.1274 | 33 |
| SD | 0.1258 | 17 | 0.1157 | 40 | 0.1301 | 27 |
| AK | 0.1248 | 19 | 0.1397 | 3 | 0.1450 | 4 |
| KY | 0.1244 | 18 | 0.1148 | 44 | 0.1169 | 48 |
| VT | 0.1232 | 20 | 0.1302 | 17 | 0.1206 | 43 |
| MT | 0.1232 | 21 | 0.1151 | 43 | 0.1320 | 21 |
| TX | 0.1224 | 22 | 0.1218 | 29 | 0.1208 | 42 |
| AR | 0.1218 | 23 | 0.1320 | 12 | 0.1229 | 40 |
| NM | 0.1192 | 24 | 0.1290 | 19 | 0.1300 | 28 |
| OH | 0.1190 | 25 | 0.1343 | 7 | 0.1413 | 5 |
| ID | 0.1190 | 27 | 0.1258 | 27 | 0.1102 | 50 |
| VA | 0.1188 | 26 | 0.1212 | 32 | 0.1170 | 47 |
| IL | 0.1188 | 28 | 0.1215 | 31 | 0.1393 | 9 |
| CA | 0.1186 | 29 | 0.1189 | 35 | 0.1401 | 8 |
| IN | 0.1186 | 30 | 0.1156 | 41 | 0.1281 | 31 |
| TN | 0.1186 | 31 | 0.1184 | 36 | 0.1339 | 12 |
| GA | 0.1183 | 32 | 0.1306 | 15 | 0.1339 | 13 |
| MN | 0.1173 | 33 | 0.1261 | 23 | 0.1275 | 32 |
| MO | 0.1170 | 34 | 0.1340 | 9 | 0.1312 | 22 |
| KS | 0.1165 | 35 | 0.1238 | 26 | 0.1254 | 37 |
| LA | 0.1157 | 36 | 0.1153 | 42 | 0.1229 | 39 |
| NJ | 0.1156 | 37 | 0.1263 | 22 | 0.1335 | 15 |
| OR | 0.1153 | 38 | 0.1267 | 21 | 0.1306 | 25 |
| AZ | 0.1145 | 39 | 0.1307 | 14 | 0.1120 | 49 |
| NC | 0.1141 | 40 | 0.1208 | 33 | 0.1291 | 30 |
| OK | 0.1139 | 41 | 0.1282 | 18 | 0.1204 | 44 |
| PA | 0.1136 | 42 | 0.1702 | 1 | 0.1339 | 11 |
| ME | 0.1113 | 43 | 0.1180 | 37 | 0.1259 | 35 |
| MS | 0.1113 | 44 | 0.1176 | 38 | 0.1192 | 45 |
| RI | -- | -- | -- | -- | 0.1327 | 19 |
| AL | -- | -- | -- | -- | 0.1250 | 38 |
| UT | -- | -- | -- | -- | 0.1310 | 24 |
| HI | -- | -- | -- | -- | 0.1310 | 23 |
| WV | -- | -- | -- | -- | 0.1254 | 36 |
| NV | -- | -- | -- | -- | 0.1325 | 18 |

Economic Sector

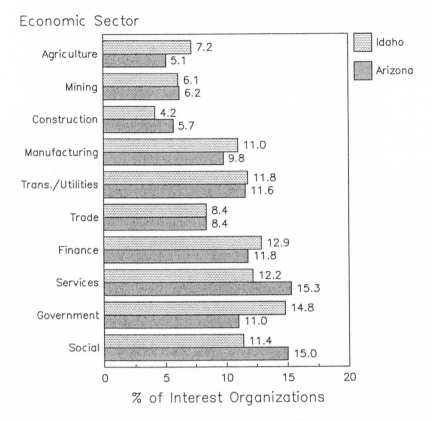

Fig. 5.5. *A,* **Elements of interest organization populations, two highest diversity states, 1990**

proportion of social and government interests. Although the range of these index values—from 0.110 for Idaho to 0.151 for Colorado—may not be very large, the patterns represented in figure 5.5A are quite different from those evident in figure 5.5B. Thus, we are confident that our measure taps real variation in organization diversity.

Has the average diversity of state interest organization systems—as measured by the Herfindahl indices—changed over time? Truman (1951) would lead us to expect that it has. He argued that growth of interest organization populations can be driven by countermobilization, which enhances diversity of representation. But as seen in figure 5.6, and despite rapid change in the density of interest organizations from 1975 to 1980 and a more modest increase during the 1980s, the average diversity of state interest organization systems remained very stable.

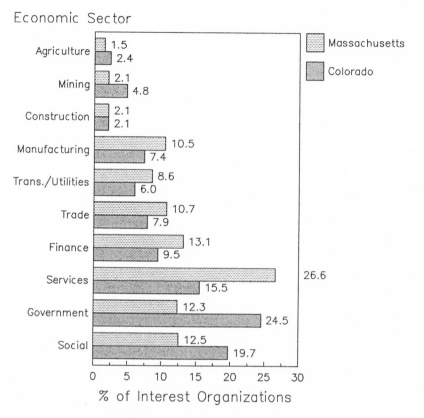

Fig. 5.5. *B*, Elements of interest organization populations, two lowest diversity states, 1990

Mean diversity across the 44 states in 1975 (mean = 0.126, s.d. = 0.012) is hardly different from 1980 (mean = 0.127, s.d. = 0.010), which in turn is similar to the 50-state average in 1990 (mean = 0.130, s.d. = 0.009). More importantly, however, all of these values are close to the minimum computational value of a Herfindahl index of 0.100 for a distribution with ten nominal values, indicating that, on average, state interest organization systems are quite diverse.

Perhaps because of the general similarity of the states in regard to the diversity of their interest organization systems, this measure is far less stable than is interest organization system density. The simple correlation between the 1975 and 1980 diversity scores is only 0.156. And again consistent with the diminished rate of change in interest organization systems over the course of the 1980s, the relationship between 1980

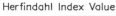

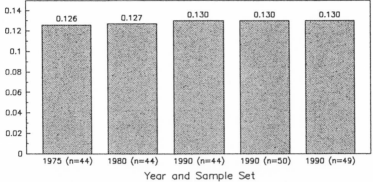

Year and Sample Set

**Fig. 5.6. Average Herfindahl index of diversity for 1975, 1980, and 1990 for several sample sets. The 44-state bars exclude Alabama, Hawaii, Nevada, Rhode Island, Utah, and West Virginia. The 49-state bar excludes Florida.**

and 1990 density is modestly stronger ($r = 0.29$). But this is still much weaker than the strong relationships between our 1975, 1980, and 1990 density measures. Diversity across the categories of economic activity clearly is not a fixed or enduring trait of interest systems when it is measured in terms of the relative positions of the states.

Surprisingly, this fluidity does not arise from changes in the economic concentration of the states. This fact can be demonstrated by comparing the simple correlation between Herfindahl indices of economic concentration for 1980 and 1990 using the proportions of GSP arising from each of the nine categories of economic activity reported in figure 5.4, which is a robust 0.70, with the far weaker relationship previously reported for the 1980 and 1990 measures of interest organization diversity ($r = 0.29$). Despite wrenching changes in state economies over the two decades, relative levels of economic diversity in 1990 remained similar to those of 1980. Since we cannot say the same about interest organization system diversity, we will have to look elsewhere for an explanation of how interest organization population diversity evolves over time.

Our second measure of diversity builds on our first indicator by focusing narrowly on the balance of profit and not-for-profit sector interests within state interest organization communities. It is this balance, rather than diversity across numerous sectors of economic activity, that motivates much of the debate in the literature over the diversity of interest organization populations (Schattschneider 1960; Schlozman and Tierney 1986; Schlozman 1984; Walker 1991). We measure this more

**TABLE 5.4. Percentage of Not-for-Profit [NFP%] Interest Organizations in the American States, 1975, 1980, and 1990**

| State | 1975 NFP% | 1975 Rank | 1980 NFP% | 1980 Rank | 1990 NFP% | 1990 Rank |
|-------|-----------|-----------|-----------|-----------|-----------|-----------|
| CO | 46.90 | 1 | 35.20 | 7 | 44.21 | 1 |
| WA | 46.50 | 2 | 32.10 | 20 | 27.12 | 28 |
| FL | 43.50 | 3 | 40.20 | 2 | 40.08 | 4 |
| WY | 41.10 | 4 | 36.30 | 6 | 41.62 | 2 |
| DE | 35.80 | 5 | 36.70 | 5 | 27.14 | 26 |
| WI | 34.90 | 6 | 33.40 | 13 | 28.63 | 22 |
| CA | 33.10 | 7 | 32.30 | 17 | 36.57 | 7 |
| IA | 32.70 | 8 | 37.40 | 3 | 34.00 | 12 |
| MI | 32.50 | 9 | 31.60 | 23 | 26.12 | 32 |
| MN | 32.10 | 11 | 34.50 | 8 | 32.60 | 14 |
| IN | 32.10 | 10 | 27.20 | 33 | 22.37 | 45 |
| CT | 31.90 | 12 | 34.20 | 9 | 27.88 | 23 |
| AR | 30.50 | 13 | 32.70 | 15 | 24.68 | 38 |
| MS | 30.00 | 14 | 23.40 | 38 | 20.56 | 49 |
| IL | 28.60 | 15 | 27.20 | 32 | 32.89 | 13 |
| OR | 28.30 | 16 | 33.60 | 11 | 35.69 | 10 |
| AK | 28.30 | 17 | 41.70 | 1 | 40.89 | 3 |
| AZ | 27.90 | 19 | 24.00 | 36 | 25.97 | 33 |
| ND | 27.30 | 18 | 17.50 | 43 | 26.90 | 29 |
| ID | 27.20 | 20 | 31.50 | 24 | 26.24 | 31 |
| PA | 27.00 | 21 | 23.90 | 37 | 24.75 | 37 |
| NE | 26.50 | 22 | 33.20 | 14 | 31.68 | 17 |
| TX | 26.40 | 23 | 31.70 | 21 | 23.50 | 43 |
| KY | 26.30 | 24 | 28.40 | 30 | 23.12 | 44 |
| NH | 26.20 | 25 | 30.10 | 26 | 25.77 | 34 |
| OH | 25.70 | 27 | 36.70 | 4 | 31.22 | 18 |
| OK | 25.70 | 26 | 31.70 | 22 | 21.30 | 47 |
| MA | 25.40 | 28 | 27.20 | 31 | 24.81 | 36 |
| ME | 25.20 | 29 | 29.40 | 29 | 27.24 | 27 |
| SD | 25.20 | 31 | 29.80 | 28 | 36.00 | 8 |
| VT | 25.20 | 30 | 32.20 | 18 | 27.78 | 24 |
| GA | 24.90 | 32 | 34.00 | 10 | 34.85 | 11 |
| NJ | 24.80 | 35 | 33.50 | 12 | 23.99 | 42 |
| MT | 24.80 | 33 | 30.20 | 27 | 36.81 | 6 |
| VA | 24.80 | 34 | 20.30 | 41 | 25.00 | 35 |
| NM | 24.00 | 36 | 32.30 | 19 | 35.84 | 9 |
| TN | 23.30 | 37 | 18.60 | 42 | 24.16 | 41 |
| NC | 22.60 | 38 | 27.00 | 34 | 24.22 | 40 |
| MD | 22.60 | 39 | 26.90 | 35 | 29.87 | 21 |
| NY | 21.80 | 40 | 23.10 | 39 | 27.44 | 25 |
| KS | 20.30 | 41 | 32.60 | 16 | 32.43 | 15 |
| MO | 19.30 | 42 | 31.10 | 25 | 32.12 | 16 |
| LA | 17.40 | 43 | 22.10 | 40 | 24.55 | 39 |
| SC | 14.20 | 44 | 15.80 | 44 | 20.81 | 48 |
| UT | -- | -- | -- | -- | 31.65 | 19 |
| AL | -- | -- | -- | -- | 26.64 | 30 |
| RI | -- | -- | -- | -- | 30.90 | 20 |
| WV | -- | -- | -- | -- | 22.14 | 46 |
| NV | -- | -- | -- | -- | 38.38 | 5 |
| HI | -- | -- | -- | -- | 16.84 | 50 |

% Not—for—Profit Interests

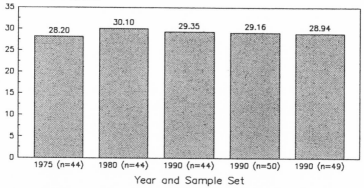

**Fig. 5.7. Average proportion of not-for-profit interest organizations in 1975, 1980, and 1990 for several sample sets. The 44-state bars exclude Alabama, Hawaii, Nevada, Rhode Island, Utah, and West Virginia. The 49-state bar excludes Florida.**

narrowly focused conception of diversity by the proportion of interest organizations falling in the not-for-profit government and social categories of interests as reported earlier in figure 5.3 (for a similar measure, see Baumgartner and Jones 1993, 180). Proportions of not-for-profit interests for 1975, 1980, and 1990 are reported for each state in table 5.4.

As seen in figure 5.7, on average, just under a third of registered organizations represent not-for-profit interests in each of our three samples: 28.20 percent (s.d. = 6.76) in 1975, 30.10 percent (s.d. = 5.74) in 1980, and 29.16 percent (s.d. = 6.09) in 1990. In the debate between Schlozman and Tierney (1986) and Walker (1991) over recent changes in interest organization systems, these results seem much more supportive of Schlozman and Tierney's position that the explosion of interest organization numbers has done little to alter the balance of traditional profit and not-for-profit interest organizations. However, nearly a third of all interest organizations in each period—hardly a negligible proportion—represent something other than private economic interests.

The final point worth noting about this measure of diversity is that it too indicates that interest organization systems are very fluid. The simple correlation of the 1975 and 1990 proportions is only 0.52, while that between the 1980 and 1990 proportions is 0.61. While these values are higher than those observed for the Herfindahl indices, they are still weaker than those observed for the density measures. Overall, then, diversity appears to be a very fluid property, with the relative positions of the states changing greatly over the course of the 15 years separating our samples. However, mean levels of diversity, using either measure no matter how temporally fluid they are, have changed hardly at all over the same period, despite the dramatic growth in the size of interest organization populations.

Our third and final measure of diversity concerns the form interests organizations can take—whether they are institutions, membership groups, or associations. The latter two types of interest organizations have members, either individuals or other organizations. Institutional interest organizations represent, instead, public or private corporate entities. This property of institutional interest organizations is politically interesting for three reasons (Salisbury 1984). First, as noted earlier, institutions face few of the collective action problems inhibiting the mobilization of associations and membership groups. Second, their internal management decisions about entering the political process are more hierarchical than democratic; leaders have no "members" to answer to. And third, their interests are likely to be far more narrow and precise than those of associations and membership groups, reflecting those of a unitary actor rather than those of a community. In Olson's terms, then, institutions are far less likely to reflect encompassing interests than are associations or membership organizations.

Unfortunately, only the 1990 data could be coded by organizational type for all 50 states, although we use 1980 data on 6 states that were coded by organizational type in chapter 6. The 1990 percent and rank of each of the three types of interest organizations are presented in table 5.5. We might use the data presented in the table to measure diversity in organizational form in several different ways. But given the several reasons for expecting that institutions will behave differently than other types of interest organizations (Salisbury 1984), we focus on the percent of institutional interests in a state's interest organization community as our indicator of diversity. In states with high percentages of institutional interests, we expect a narrower form of policy advocacy, one more focused on the specific concerns of institutions than on collective interests. In this sense, such states can be identified as having less diverse interest organization communities. In total, institutional interests accounted for 49.02 percent of all interest organizations in the states in 1990. The average for the states was somewhat lower—46.24 percent (s.d. = 7.79). As seen in table 5.5, however, there is considerable variation in the dominance of institutions, ranging from a high of 64.91 percent in Arizona to a low of only 30.00 percent in Rhode Island.

**TABLE 5.5. 1990 Institutions, Membership Groups, and Associations—Percentage and Rank—in the American States**

| State | Total No.[a] | Institutions % | Institutions Rank | Memb. Groups % | Memb. Groups Rank | Associations % | Associations Rank |
|-------|------|--------|------|--------|------|--------|------|
| AZ | 587  | 64.91 | 1  | 16.70 | 47 | 18.40 | 49 |
| PA | 1155 | 60.52 | 2  | 17.06 | 46 | 22.42 | 47 |
| TX | 1159 | 59.45 | 3  | 15.88 | 49 | 24.68 | 41 |
| MI | 1157 | 58.34 | 4  | 16.59 | 48 | 25.06 | 40 |
| FL | 2965 | 58.04 | 5  | 21.08 | 35 | 20.88 | 48 |
| AK | 306  | 55.88 | 6  | 20.26 | 39 | 23.86 | 44 |
| OH | 944  | 55.51 | 7  | 21.61 | 31 | 22.88 | 46 |
| NV | 801  | 54.81 | 8  | 27.59 | 12 | 17.60 | 50 |
| LA | 444  | 54.73 | 9  | 20.72 | 37 | 24.55 | 42 |
| NM | 457  | 54.27 | 10 | 21.88 | 29 | 23.85 | 45 |
| UT | 375  | 53.60 | 11 | 22.13 | 26 | 24.27 | 43 |
| IL | 901  | 53.27 | 12 | 20.31 | 38 | 26.42 | 36 |
| CA | 1343 | 52.64 | 13 | 19.88 | 42 | 27.48 | 33 |
| HI | 189  | 51.32 | 14 | 10.58 | 50 | 38.10 | 4  |
| TN | 416  | 50.72 | 15 | 18.99 | 45 | 30.29 | 28 |
| MA | 670  | 50.60 | 16 | 20.75 | 36 | 28.66 | 32 |
| OK | 438  | 49.32 | 17 | 25.11 | 17 | 25.57 | 38 |
| AR | 229  | 48.47 | 18 | 20.09 | 41 | 31.44 | 25 |
| ME | 304  | 48.36 | 19 | 19.41 | 44 | 32.24 | 21 |
| AL | 282  | 48.23 | 20 | 21.99 | 28 | 29.79 | 30 |
| NJ | 741  | 48.18 | 21 | 20.24 | 40 | 31.58 | 23 |
| WY | 378  | 48.15 | 22 | 25.13 | 16 | 26.72 | 35 |
| MO | 550  | 47.82 | 23 | 25.82 | 14 | 26.36 | 37 |
| WV | 259  | 45.17 | 24 | 25.48 | 15 | 29.34 | 31 |
| MS | 111  | 45.05 | 25 | 19.82 | 43 | 35.14 | 11 |
| KY | 371  | 44.47 | 26 | 22.10 | 27 | 33.42 | 17 |
| MD | 627  | 44.02 | 27 | 22.81 | 23 | 33.17 | 19 |
| MN | 950  | 43.79 | 28 | 23.89 | 20 | 32.32 | 20 |
| GA | 899  | 43.72 | 29 | 31.15 | 2  | 25.14 | 39 |
| NY | 980  | 43.27 | 30 | 21.12 | 34 | 35.61 | 9  |
| DE | 206  | 43.20 | 31 | 22.33 | 25 | 34.47 | 14 |
| NC | 480  | 42.92 | 32 | 22.71 | 24 | 34.38 | 15 |
| IN | 439  | 42.60 | 33 | 24.15 | 19 | 33.26 | 18 |
| OR | 633  | 42.50 | 34 | 30.33 | 5  | 27.17 | 34 |
| VA | 491  | 41.75 | 35 | 23.63 | 22 | 34.62 | 13 |
| SC | 216  | 41.20 | 36 | 21.76 | 30 | 37.04 | 5  |
| KS | 508  | 40.75 | 37 | 23.82 | 21 | 35.43 | 10 |
| CT | 472  | 40.68 | 38 | 24.58 | 18 | 34.75 | 12 |
| NE | 358  | 40.50 | 39 | 29.61 | 8  | 29.89 | 29 |
| WA | 723  | 39.70 | 40 | 29.05 | 9  | 31.26 | 26 |
| VT | 233  | 39.48 | 41 | 21.46 | 32 | 39.06 | 3  |
| ID | 286  | 38.11 | 42 | 30.07 | 6  | 31.82 | 22 |
| WI | 501  | 37.72 | 43 | 26.55 | 13 | 35.73 | 8  |
| CO | 553  | 37.61 | 44 | 30.92 | 3  | 31.46 | 24 |
| IA | 541  | 37.15 | 45 | 28.84 | 10 | 34.01 | 16 |
| ND | 322  | 36.65 | 46 | 32.92 | 1  | 30.43 | 27 |
| NH | 189  | 34.92 | 47 | 21.16 | 33 | 43.92 | 1  |
| SD | 321  | 34.58 | 48 | 28.66 | 11 | 36.76 | 6  |
| MT | 341  | 33.43 | 49 | 30.50 | 4  | 36.07 | 7  |
| RI | 230  | 30.00 | 50 | 30.00 | 7  | 40.00 | 2  |

[a] Excludes cases that could not be coded by type of interest organization (3.05 percent of all cases).

**TABLE 5.6.    Correlations of Measures of Density and Diversity**

| 1975 Sample (44 States) | GSP-BASE | Herfindahl | Not-for-Profit % | Institutions % |
|---|---|---|---|---|
| No. | -0.105 | -0.122 | 0.331 | --[a] |
| GSP-BASE | | 0.023 | -0.010 | -- |
| Herfindahl | | | 0.489 | -- |

| 1980 Sample (44 States) | GSP-BASE | Herfindahl | Not-for-Profit % | Institutions % |
|---|---|---|---|---|
| No. | 0.370 | 0.321 | 0.207 | -- |
| GSP-BASE | | -0.128 | -0.274 | -- |
| Herfindahl | | | 0.260 | -- |

| 1990 Sample (50 States) | GSP-BASE | Herfindahl | Not-for-Profit % | Institutions % |
|---|---|---|---|---|
| No. | 0.260 | 0.400 | 0.321 | 0.460 |
| GSP-BASE | | 0.077 | -0.353 | 0.194 |
| Herfindahl | | | 0.521 | 0.139 |
| Not-for-Profit % | | | | -0.050 |

[a]Institutions percentage not available for 1975 and 1980 samples.

### Relations among the Measures

How are our measures of interest organization population density and diversity related to each other? Simple correlations are presented in table 5.6 for each pair of measures for each of our three samples. If we keep in mind that GSP-BASE and the Herfindahl index are *inverse* measures of their concepts, the correlations in table 5.6 offer a few surprises.

First, the density measures are not strongly correlated. Indeed, the positive correlations, albeit weak, between GSP-BASE and number of interest organizations in the 1980 and 1990 samples indicate that as number of registrations increases, density relative to the size of the economy declines. More to the point, density vis-à-vis governance and density vis-à-vis the representative function of interest organizations appear to be distinct and independent properties for our populations, precluding our making easy inferences about one based on measures of the other.

Second, the correlations between our Herfindahl index measure of diversity for a number of major sectors of the economy and diversity as measured by the proportion of interest organizations representing not-for-profit interests are modestly correlated: 0.50 for 1975, 0.26 in 1980, and 0.52 in 1990. But more importantly, the correlations are uniformly positive. If we keep in mind the inverse nature of the Herfindahl measure, this means that as diversity declines across the ten economic sectors as a whole, the proportion of the population comprised of not-for-profit interests increases. Again, these represent distinct, although related, dimensions on which to assess the diversity of state interest organization populations. This generalization is especially applicable to diversity as measured by the proportion of institutional interests, which is very weakly related to both the Herfindahl index ($r = 0.14$) and diversity as measured by the proportion of not-for-profit interests ($-0.05$).

Most of the density measures are only weakly and inconsistently related to the measures of diversity. GSP-BASE, especially, is only weakly related to the Herfindahl index measure of diversity. The major exception to this pattern is the consistent, modest, negative relationship between the GSP-BASE measure of density and diversity as measured by the proportion of not-for-profit interest organizations. Given the inverse measurement of the density measure, this indicates that the proportion of not-for-profit interests increases as density relative to the economy increases. Still, the relationship is not strong. The more general message, we think, is that density and diversity represent distinct properties, and that each is better viewed as a bundle of only partially related properties than as a one-dimensional concept.

Given the weak relationships among our indicators, which measure should we be most attentive to? The answer depends, of course, on our purpose. We believe that they all represent valid *descriptive* indicators of the very specific concepts they were designed to measure. Therefore, we will use all of these measures as we explore the nature of interest organization populations in the chapters that follow. Indeed, at one point or another, all of the measures will be used as independent variables in our empirical analyses.

When our attention turns to *explanation*, however, we focus exclusively on interest organization numbers. Simply put, the units underlying the GSP-BASE indicator of density and the Herfindahl, not-for-profit proportion, and institutional interest proportion measures of diversity are not natural entities that act or are acted on directly. They are products or artifacts of what happens to numbers of interest organizations in relation to something else. However, interest organizations are natural units—they are born, live, and occasionally die. Only they act and are acted on. Therefore, when our discussion shifts to explanation, especially of our use of the Energy-Stability-Area model of interest organization population density and population diversity, attention will be given exclusively to interest organization numbers.

### The Special Case of Small, Dense States

In exploring the relationships among the density measures, one curious pattern emerged in all three samples.[6] The residuals produced from regressing the GSP-BASE measure of density on GSP and its squared value are heteroskedastic with respect to GSP. In each sample, it is obvious that the ten or so smallest states with the most dense interest populations relative to economic size (Vermont, South Dakota, Delaware, North Dakota, Idaho, Montana, New Hampshire, Maine, Wyoming, and Alaska) have very small residuals, or that their densities are very well predicted merely by the size of their economies.

What are we to make of these patterns? These states tend to have few interest organizations, but they also have tiny economies. Therefore, their interest organization populations are very dense when measured using GSP-BASE. These results, taken together with those presented in chapter 7 do not indicate that the processes governing interest organization populations in these state are different in any fundamental way. Interest organization numbers still respond, as we will see in chapter 7, to the environmental constraints specified in the ESA model, but they may do so in a particularly strict manner.

The most plausible reason for this strict response derives from an unusual analog of organization ecology's legitimacy hypothesis. We assume that there is a class of organizations that can be described as "natural interests," or interests that must be actively represented in any state, irrespective of state size or complexity. Just as every state must have a department of revenue—whether it collects taxes from many or a few—certain interest organizations will be part of the interest system of every state. Every state will have groups representing such basic interests as teachers, bankers, and farmers. And every state's legislature can be expected to be lobbied by its chamber of commerce and its liquor interest. In short, these interest organizations have high legitimacy in the organization ecology sense of "taken-for-grantedness" (Hannan and Carroll 1992, 34). The view of a lobbyist from Arkansas (phone interview, 11 May 1994)—a state with one of the smallest and slowest growing interest populations—is typical: "I don't see much change in the basic structure over twenty years. You have the same basic lineup: business, which is basically united; medical, which has some competition within it; the workers—labor's influence has decreased; and the splinter groups, the single issue people who are in and out."

These states are so small that the environmental constraints specified by the ESA model may operate so that few other "discretionary" organizations can form. Indeed, the variance in the numbers of interest organizations is substantially smaller in these states than in others. In our 1990 sample, for example, the mean number of interest organizations in all states (excluding the unusual case of Florida) was 538.43, with a standard deviation of 299.66. For the ten states with the smallest economies, the mean number of interests was only 296.00, with a relatively tiny standard deviation of 56.19 organizations. Even the next ten smallest states produced a standard deviation that was substantially larger—199.49, with a mean of 353.90 organizations.

Given interest organization populations largely restricted to a constant number of natural interest organizations, variation in GSP-BASE will depend solely on variation in the size of GSP. Thus, it is not surprising that economic size predicts so well the densities of small dense states relative to the sizes of their economies. In sum, the interest organization populations of small states with dense interest organization systems may be qualitatively different from those of large states in that their composition is heavily biased toward "natural" interest organizations with great legitimacy, the implications of which we explore more fully in chapter 6.

CHAPTER 6

# Population Entry and Exit

To this point, our empirical analysis has been entirely descriptive, focusing on static cross sections for the years 1975, 1980, and 1990. But populations change over time as entry and exit—or founding and mortality in the language of organization ecology (Hannan and Freeman 1989; Hannan and Carroll 1992)—renew their composition. Mortality, especially, is a central topic for population ecology theories, given their emphasis on the role of selection as a result of environmental pressures. Despite a few studies on founding and mortality rates among interest organizations in the Washington interest organization community, most notably that of Schlozman and Tierney (1986), and on national trade associations by Aldrich and his colleagues (Aldrich and Staber 1988; Aldrich et al. 1990, 1994), we still know little about how patterns of entry into and exit from *lobbying communities* interact to comprise contemporary populations or to govern their potential for change.[1]

We address this opportunity in this chapter by asking a series of quite simple questions about the demography of interest organization populations. Along the way, we review and critique the tiny handful of prior studies that have examined patterns of interest organization population entry and exit. We then develop some tentative answers to our questions, using data on 1980 and 1990 interest organizations communities of six American states. Finally, we consider the implications of our answers for further study of interest organization populations.

## Questions about Populations

Given the limited attention to interest organization populations, in part as a result of the difficulties of measuring population-level phenomena (Salisbury 1992, 2), we must start by asking some basic demographic questions. The first of these is the simple descriptive question of whether or not interest organizations cease to engage in lobbying once it is initiated. It does not seem surprising that few leaders of lobbying organizations doubt the long-term survival of their organizations. In our survey of interest organization leaders in six states (described more fully in chapter 9), 67.37 percent of the respondents answered "not very likely" (254 of 377 complete responses) when asked how likely it is that their "organization will face a serious challenge to its existence" over the next five years. Only 13.79 percent answered "very likely," while 18.83 percent indicated that survival was "somewhat likely." When given an assumption that their organization will continue in operation, 85.52 percent of the respondents (319 of 373 complete responses) indicated that it is "very likely" that it will continue to register to lobby. Another 8.04 percent indicated that continued registration was "somewhat likely," while only 6.43 percent indicated that continued lobbying was "not very likely." Are these expectations supported by the actual experiences of interest organizations?

The best evidence we have is Schlozman and Tierney's analysis of the Washington interest organization system (1986, 78) and Aldrich and his colleagues' work on national trade associations (Aldrich and Staber 1988; Aldrich et al. 1990, 1994), both of which suggest that exits are rare. Fully 79 percent of the organizations in Schlozman and Tierney's 1960 sample were still active in 1980. Unfortunately, the authors employed two very different cross sections—one from the 1960 *Congressional Quarterly Almanac* and the other from *Washington Representatives–1981*—in tracking organizations over time. This provides a snapshot of organizational exiting, but one of unknown bias (Schlozman and Tierney 1986, 78). This may account for why they were able to track only 69.50 percent of the 1960 organizations. In contrast, Aldrich and his coauthors examined the universe of national trade associations over decades, but they did not focus on lobbying per se. As a result, their report of a low mortality rate among associations may or may not bear on exiting from the lobbying function.

If we find that organizations do allow the lobbying function to lapse, our second question must be about variations in exiting. Exiting is especially interesting if different types of organizations allow the lobby function to lapse at different rates. Assuming common entry patterns, this would, over time, alter distributions of the several types of interest organizations in populations. We might expect such differences for two reasons, reasons with somewhat contradictory implications.

First, we have long-standing expectations about the kinds of collective action problems different types of organizations face. Here, we use Schlozman and Tierney's definitions (1986) of three distinct types of interest organizations. *Institutions* are organizations, including business firms and local governments, that have an identifiable and separate corporate identity distinct from that of the individuals representing the organization. While they face no internal collective action problems of the type described by Olson (1965), they do have opportunities for free riding if competitors within their industry actively lobby for policy and regulatory changes that are beneficial to the industry as a whole. *Associations* are confederations of organizations, such as the businesses and governments comprising trade and local government organizations. Their collective action problems include some aspects of Olson's disincentives of organization as well as the difficulties inherent in encouraging what are often competitors to cooperate in joint pursuit of common interests (Aldrich and Staber 1988, 112–13). And finally, *membership organizations*— including unions, professional associations, and hobby organizations— are composed of autonomous individuals. Membership organizations are the classic kinds of organizations addressed by Olson (1965) and Walker (1991), and they are the focus of mobilization studies.

Different collective action problems may produce different levels of vulnerability to environmental stresses. Thus, Salisbury (1984, 75) argued that institutions would be far more "durable and persistent," while membership organizations are riven with "weakness and fragility." This assumes, of course, that organizations having the least probability of forming will consequently have the most difficult time surviving. But while this expectation is highly plausible in terms of organizational mortality, it is not at all clear that it is valid for the mortality of organizational functions, such as lobbying.

Second, lobbying might be an organization's primary or even sole activity, or it might be only a minor or peripheral one. It seems likely that the primary business of most institutions is not lobbying. And while many associations and membership organizations engage in other activities, interest representation is probably a core function for many of them (Sabatier 1992, 109–10). For this reason, we might expect that institutions may more readily allow the lobby function to lapse while continuing their broader functions and retaining the organizational capacity to reenter the political market when threats or opportunities develop. For many associations and membership organizations, termination of the lobbying function may entail organizational death, something that an organization leader would not undertake lightly. In a twist on Salisbury's analysis, then, we might expect that the unique strengths of institutions may actually produce higher lobbying exit rates than those observed for associations and membership organizations. Institutions can exit with lower costs than associations and membership organizations.

Evidence of such differences would have important implications. Democratic theorists worry about the balance of representation among different types of interests, especially if the dominance of traditional economic institutions and associations biases policy agendas and outcomes (Schattschneider 1960; Schlozman and Tierney 1983, 1986). Indeed, Walker (1991) saw the explosion in numbers of citizens organizations as redressing balance among different types of interests.[2] If lobbying function exit rates vary by type of organization, then changes in their distribution resulting from variations in entry rates may be canceled, reversed, or perhaps enhanced. Exit patterns would contribute directly, thereby, to determining the contours of interest communities.

Again, the best available evidence is Schlozman and Tierney's (1986, 79), although it somewhat confounds terminations of lobbying and organizational mortality. We reconstructed their data by collapsing their interest categories into institutions, associations, and membership organizations, focusing, as they do, on only the 363 organizations tracked through 1980. The resulting survival rates are all high, with institutions having the highest rate at 88.73 percent, followed by associations (79.22) and membership organizations (66.48). The higher survival rate of institutions seems to support Salisbury's expectations. Again, though, the comparability of the 1960 and 1980 samples is questionable. Therefore, our second question remains less than fully answered.

Our conflicting expectations on the second question hinge fundamentally on the meaning of exiting from lobbying. As previously noted, it is critical to distinguish between termination of an organizational function, such as lobbying, and death of the organization as a whole. Disappearance from lobby registration rolls may indicate either phenomenon, and each has quite different implications for an organization's capacity to reenter the political market. Therefore, our third question must address variations in the meaning that withdrawal from lobbying holds for our three types of organizations. Does withdrawal from lobbying signal the same thing for institutions, associations, and membership-based interest organizations? To date, no one has developed the kind of autopsies of terminated lobbying efforts needed to answer this question.

Our fourth set of questions concerns the balance of entry and exit rates. How do patterns of entry and exit from the lobbying function among different types of organizations produce observed lobbying communities? Are the presumed advantages of institutions in overcoming collective action problems *and* weathering environmental stresses reinforcing as suggested by Salisbury (1984) and Schlozman and Tierney (1986, 79)? Or do higher rates of entry of some types of organizations compensate for relatively lower rates of survival? And which mechanism, entry or exit, most strongly influences population demographics?

Again, answers to these questions have important implications for the prospects of change within interest organization communities. If, for example, organizations of a given type are more likely to withdraw from lobbying but this pattern is balanced by a relatively higher rate of entry, then the community of interests might be highly stable. Alternatively, different mixes of entry and exit rates may promote very rapid shifts among the balance of interest organizations. Prospects for large-scale shifts in the composition of interest communities depend, therefore, on variations in entry and exit rates and on how each rate is influencing population demographics.

At present, we can answer none of these questions. The detailed analyses of exit patterns provided by Aldrich and his colleagues (Aldrich and Staber 1988; Aldrich et al. 1990, 1994) examine only one type of organization: associations. And even if we were confident about the exit findings of Schlozman and Tierney (1986, 78–79), their entry data are highly questionable. Schlozman and Tierney (1983, 1986) analyze the founding dates of organizations listed in *Washington Representatives– 1981*. But as an indicator of entry, the measure is hopelessly contaminated by exits; many organizations founded even in the recent past surely withdrew from lobbying prior to 1980 and remain uncounted. At best, they have a measure of *net* entry over some unknown period. Moreover, lack of comparability across the two samples means that the entry and exit findings cannot be linked.

To this point, our questions have concerned variations across types of interest organizations. This is appropriate given the importance accorded such differences in the theoretical literature. But we are also interested in variation in rates of entry and exit *across lobbying communities*. Given its almost exclusive attention to isolated interest organization populations, the literature is all too silent on this issue.

The population ecology literature on organizations suggests that such variations are important. More to the point, organization ecology research and theory (Hannan and Freeman 1989; Hannan and Carroll 1992) suggests that entry and/or exit rates should vary by level of contemporary density. This is the *density dependence hypothesis,* which suggests that, as competition for resources among organizations increases as interest systems become more dense, the rate of expansion of the carrying capacity of the system for organizations slows (Hannan and Freeman 1989, 11). Strong evidence of density dependence has been found in studies of national trade associations (Aldrich and Staber 1988; Aldrich et al. 1990, 1994). And while not designed to test this hypothesis, Conybeare and Squire's analysis (1994) of Political Action Committees (PACs) reports evidence of such density dependence for this subpopulation of interest organizations.

If further evidence of density dependence is found (see chapter 7), then we will need to account for which of two processes, if not both, accounts for it. High density may feed back onto entry rates so that fewer new interest organizations are added to populations. Alternatively, increasing competition for a fixed pool of resources may enhance exit rates as interest systems become more dense. Evidence of both processes has been found for other populations studied by organizational ecologists (Hannan and Carroll 1992), although studies of national trade associations have concluded that founding rates are a far more powerful influence on populations than mortality (Aldrich et al. 1990, 41; 1994, 230).

Our fifth set of questions, then, addresses the impacts of density dependence on interest community entry and exit rates. These impacts also influence the prospects of change for interest organization communities. If density dependence is expressed through lowered entry rates, then the composition of communities of interest organizations may become frozen as they become more crowded. If, however, density dependence is expressed primarily through increased exit, then there exists the potential for rapid turnover in interest communities, if patterns of entry change so as to reconstitute populations.

**Data on Interest Organization Populations**

To answer our questions, we turn to demographic data derived from lists of registered interest organizations for 1980 and 1990. Measures built on these data provide us with precise operational definitions of entry and exit. Entry occurs when an interest organization registers to lobby, and its exit is recorded when it no longer does so.

Since tracking thousands of interests across time is exceptionally time consuming, we analyze six states: Arkansas, South Dakota, Pennsylvania, North Carolina, Michigan, and Minnesota. They constitute a broad cross section in terms of size, economic complexity, and region. And in their aggregate mix of organizational types—institutions, associations, and membership organizations—they are almost identical to patterns observed for all 50 states.[3]

At the same time, these states do not comprise a random sample. Instead, they were purposively selected on the basis of several criteria. The most important of these criteria is the density of the states' interest organization communities, which is the focus of one of our questions. We will see (in figures 6.6A through 6.6D) that the six states represent most of the range of density observed among the states. This is especially important in regard to South Dakota, which is one of the handful of very small states with few interest organizations but high levels of density relative to the size of their economies. Indeed, South Dakota had the fourth most dense interest organization population in 1990 if we use the GSP-BASE measure of density. Such states are interesting because their interest populations are far less variable in respect to density as a function of economic size than those of states with larger economies. In contrast, Arkansas is one of the few small states evidencing low density relative to economic size, ranking as only the thirty-first most dense state in 1990, using GSP-BASE. And in contrast to both of these small states, North Carolina has one of the relatively least dense interest organization communities, with only eight other states having higher GSP-BASE values in 1990.

**TABLE 6.1.   The Distribution of Interest Organizations for Six States for 1980 and 1990, by Type of Organization**

| State | 1980 Organizations | % of Total | 1990 Organizations | % of Total | % Change 1980-1990 |
|---|---|---|---|---|---|
| Arkansas | | | | | |
| Institutions | 88 | 49.16 | 109 | 47.81 | 23.86 |
| Membership Groups | 39 | 21.79 | 49 | 21.49 | 25.64 |
| Associations | 52 | 29.05 | 70 | 30.70 | 34.62 |
| Total | 179 | 100.00 | 228 | 100.00 | 27.37 |
| South Dakota | | | | | |
| Institutions | 52 | 27.51 | 112 | 34.46 | 115.38 |
| Membership Groups | 56 | 29.63 | 94 | 28.92 | 67.86 |
| Associations | 81 | 42.86 | 119 | 36.62 | 46.91 |
| Total | 189 | 100.00 | 325 | 100.00 | 71.96 |
| North Carolina | | | | | |
| Institutions | 64 | 26.12 | 206 | 42.56 | 221.88 |
| Membership Groups | 72 | 29.39 | 111 | 22.93 | 54.17 |
| Associations | 109 | 44.49 | 167 | 34.50 | 53.21 |
| Total | 245 | 100.00 | 484 | 100.00 | 97.55 |
| Pennsylvania | | | | | |
| Institutions | 399 | 56.44 | 712 | 60.14 | 78.45 |
| Membership Groups | 122 | 17.26 | 210 | 17.74 | 72.13 |
| Associations | 186 | 26.31 | 262 | 22.13 | 40.86 |
| Total | 707 | 100.00 | 1184 | 100.00 | 67.47 |
| Michigan | | | | | |
| Institutions | 143 | 41.21 | 659 | 56.62 | 360.84 |
| Membership Groups | 83 | 23.92 | 209 | 17.96 | 151.81 |
| Associations | 121 | 34.87 | 296 | 25.43 | 144.63 |
| Total | 347 | 100.00 | 1164 | 100.00 | 235.45 |
| Minnesota | | | | | |
| Institutions | 259 | 40.34 | 409 | 43.23 | 57.92 |
| Membership Groups | 158 | 24.61 | 237 | 25.05 | 50.00 |
| Associations | 225 | 35.05 | 300 | 31.71 | 33.33 |
| Total | 642 | 100.00 | 946 | 100.00 | 47.35 |

A second criterion was the rapidity of growth of interest organization communities from 1980 to 1990. To validly assess the impact of patterns of exit and entry on population size, we selected states with a broad range of growth rates. As seen in the last column of table 6.1, Michigan had one of the fastest growing populations, increasing in number 235.45 percent in ten years. In contrast, Arkansas had one of the slowest growing populations, with an increase in numbers of interest organizations of only 27.37 percent. Thus, our sample was selected purposively to insure variation on variables we believe to be important in understanding patterns of entry and exit.

The 1980 and 1990 data on interest organization registrations were

**TABLE 6.2.   Interest Organization Demographics from 1980 to 1990 for Six States, by Type of Organization**

| State | 1980 Organizations | Survived to 1990 | Died by 1990 | 1990 Organizations | New since 1980 |
|---|---|---|---|---|---|
| Arkansas | | | | | |
| Institutions | 88 | 22 | 66 | 109 | 87 |
| Membership Groups | 39 | 18 | 21 | 49 | 31 |
| Associations | 52 | 24 | 28 | 70 | 46 |
| Total | 179 | 64 | 115 | 228 | 164 |
| South Dakota | | | | | |
| Institutions | 52 | 15 | 37 | 112 | 97 |
| Membership Groups | 56 | 32 | 24 | 94 | 62 |
| Associations | 81 | 46 | 35 | 119 | 73 |
| Total | 189 | 93 | 96 | 325 | 232 |
| North Carolina | | | | | |
| Institutions | 64 | 30 | 34 | 206 | 176 |
| Membership Groups | 72 | 43 | 29 | 111 | 68 |
| Associations | 109 | 66 | 43 | 167 | 101 |
| Total | 245 | 139 | 106 | 484 | 345 |
| Pennsylvania | | | | | |
| Institutions | 399 | 170 | 229 | 712 | 542 |
| Membership Groups | 122 | 69 | 53 | 210 | 141 |
| Associations | 186 | 101 | 85 | 262 | 161 |
| Total | 707 | 340 | 367 | 1184 | 844 |
| Michigan | | | | | |
| Institutions | 143 | 69 | 74 | 659 | 590 |
| Membership Groups | 83 | 43 | 40 | 209 | 166 |
| Associations | 121 | 76 | 45 | 296 | 220 |
| Total | 347 | 188 | 159 | 1164 | 976 |
| Minnesota | | | | | |
| Institutions | 259 | 81 | 178 | 409 | 328 |
| Membership Groups | 158 | 66 | 92 | 237 | 171 |
| Associations | 225 | 88 | 137 | 300 | 212 |
| Total | 642 | 235 | 407 | 946 | 711 |

State

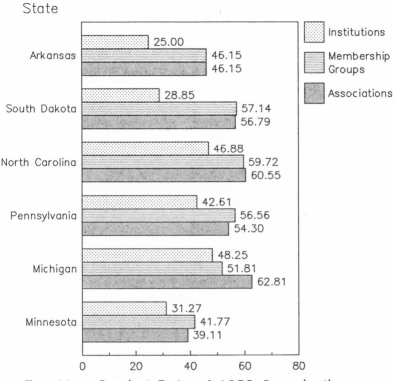

Fig. 6.1. Ten-year survival rate of organized interests by type from 1980 to 1990—six states. Survival rate is calculated as a percentage of 1980 organizations still registered in 1990.

coded by type of organized interest: membership group, institution, or association, as reported in chapter 1. The data used to construct our measures of interest organization entry and exit rates are presented in tables 6.1 and 6.2. Table 6.1 presents, by mode of organization, the number of 1980 and 1990 registered organizations. Table 6.2 reports the same information but breaks it down into the numbers of organizations in the 1980 populations that had either survived (continued to register) or exited (no longer registered) by 1990 and the number of interest organizations in the 1990 populations that had entered the six populations (registered) since 1980.

Exit rates were calculated on the basis of observed survival from 1980 to 1990. Thus, as seen in figure 6.1, the ten-year survival rate of

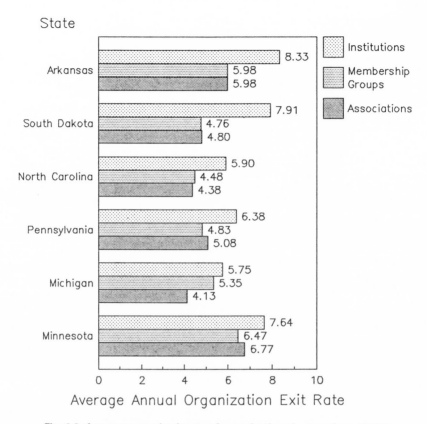

Fig. 6.2. Average annual exit rate of organizations by type from 1980 to 1990—six states. Annual rate is calculated as an average percentage loss of 1980 organizations to produce observed survival pattern.

each of three sets of interest organizations for each of the states is the proportion of 1980 organizations still registered in 1990. These values are translated in figure 6.2 into annual exit rates, or the average annual percentage decline in the number of 1980 interest organizations calculated as necessary to produce the observed ten-year survival rate.

Organization entry rates were more difficult to calculate. The firmest data we have are net entry rates, or the simple percentage increase in organization numbers from 1980 to 1990, which are presented in table 6.1 and figure 6.3 by mode of organization for each state. This measure represents an improvement over the rates calculated by Schlozman and Tierney (1983, 1986), because we use comparable data for 1980 and 1990; but it is still very limited. It is reasonable to expect that many other

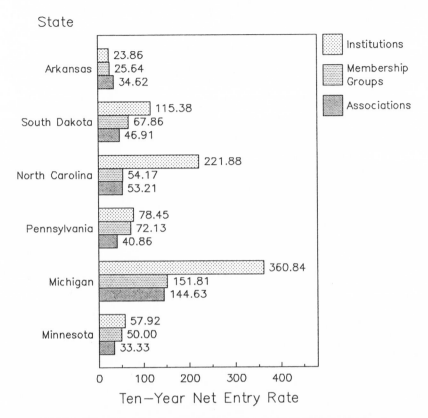

Fig. 6.3. Net entry rate of organizations by type from 1980 to 1990—six states. Net entry is a simple percentage increase in organization number from 1980 to 1990.

organizations entering after 1980 exited before 1990 and, therefore, remain untallied by measures of net mobilization.

To construct a more valid measure of the annual entry rate, we employ plausible, yet conservative, assumptions. First, we assume that numbers of organizations increased in a simple linear manner from 1980 to 1990. With this assumption, we can calculate by category the number of organizations expected to be registered each year. Second, we assume that exits from the 1980 population are distributed evenly over the 1980s. This, of course, is the annualized exit rate already discussed and reported in figure 6.2. Third, we assume that the annual exit rate of organized interests entering after 1980 is the same as that observed for organizations in the 1980 sample.

How valid are these assumptions? The first two should not be troubling. While numbers of organized interests continued to grow steadily throughout the 1980s, the rate of growth slowed considerably from the explosive pattern of the 1970s. Assumption three is more troubling, however. The exit rate of the 1980 population is likely to provide a conservative estimate for organizations entering after 1980, since the latter population by definition excludes well-established and entrenched organizations that would be expected to persist over time. Moreover, Hannan and Freeman (1989, 85–86) report finding a consistent "liability of newness" among young organizations, whereby the greatest risk of death occurs just after an organization's founding. Still, the 1980 annual exiting rate is the best estimate that we have. And if it errs, it will do so in a conservative direction, by underestimating exits.

With these assumptions, average annual entry rates were estimated for each of our sets of organized interests. In 1981, for example, the estimate of the number of entrants is the expected number of extant organizations in 1981 minus the number of observed 1980 organizations discounted for those expected to exit given the observed annual exit rate. Each succeeding year's estimate of new organizations is similarly calculated by discounting the number of organizations operative in the prior year and subtracting the resulting total from the expected total number of interest organizations for the current year. Each year's estimate was then represented as a proportion of the prior year's total number of interest organizations, with the average of these proportions constituting the annual entry rate for each type of organization. These values are reported in figure 6.4 by mode of organization for each state. Their interpretation is straightforward; the first value in the figure, for example, indicates that, on average, numbers of institutions in Arkansas increased 13.84 percent per year.

### Analysis of the Demographic Estimates

Similar to Schlozman and Tierney's findings (1986, 49) and Salisbury's expectations (1984), institutions typically dominate our six organized interest systems, and they became much more dominant over the course of the 1980s. As seen in table 6.1, institutions comprised the largest proportion of interest organizations in 1980 in four states, with associations dominating in South Dakota (42.86 percent) and North Carolina (44.49 percent). But by 1990, with their numbers increased by 221.88 percent, institutions became the most numerous type in North Carolina, at 42.56 percent. As seen in the last column, the average pattern of relatively fast growth among institutions and slower growth among asso-

State

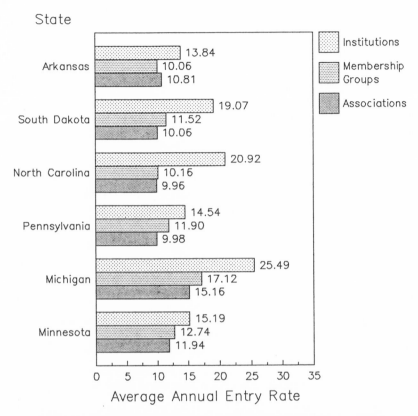

Fig. 6.4. Annual rate of entry for organizations by type from 1980 to 1990—six states. Annual rate is a percentage of the average gross increase of organization number from prior year.

ciations is replicated in five of our states. The exception is Arkansas, where the institutional growth rate of 23.86 percent is actually lower than that of both associations (34.62 percent) and membership organizations (25.64 percent). Overall, the organization population of Arkansas grew the least, only 27.37 percent, while Michigan's exhibited the most rapid expansion—235.45 percent. The remaining states produced overall population increases of between 47.35 and 97.55 percent.

Against this broad outline, we are interested in how entry and exit from the lobbying community determine the distribution of the different types of organized interests. The raw data we use to assess such patterns are presented in table 6.2. Numbers of organizations by type and state are reported in the first and fourth columns for 1980 and 1990, respectively. The second and third columns report, respectively, numbers of 1980 organizations that survived until 1990 and numbers that died during the 1980s. The final column is the difference between numbers of survivors and the total number of 1990 interest organizations, or the numbers of organized interests entering since 1980.

The key finding of table 6.2 is that organized interests do withdraw from lobbying. Even in North Carolina and Michigan, which experienced the lowest exit rates among our six states, many interest organizations exited—43.27 and 45.82 percent, respectively. In South Dakota (50.79 percent) and Pennsylvania (51.91 percent), a majority did not survive the 1980s. And in Arkansas and Minnesota, a whopping 64.25 and 63.40 percent of all 1980 interest organizations joined the true "heavenly chorus" by 1990. For each state, then, the interest organization exit rate over ten years far exceeded the 21 percent reported by Schlozman and Tierney (1986, 78) for the Washington interest population or the low mortality rate found for national trade associations (Aldrich et al. 1990, 1994).

Importantly, exiting of the lobbying function is not random. Contrary to both Schlozman and Tierney's findings (1986, 79) and Salisbury's expectations (1984, 75), institutions were far more likely to exit than were associations and membership organizations. As seen in figure 6.1, the ten-year survival rate of institutions is uniformly lower in all six states, and in most by very large margins. In three states—Arkansas, South Dakota, and Minnesota—fewer than one of three institutions registered in 1980 were still registered in 1990. The differences between associations and membership organizations are far less dramatic; with one tie, membership organizations had a slight advantage, with modestly higher survival rates in three states. Using the assumptions outlined in the discussion of our measures, the ten-year survival rates in figure 6.1 are reported as annualized exit rates in figure 6. 2. The resulting patterns are the inverse of those in figure 6.1.

This brings us back, of course, to the meaning of *exit* when speaking of an organizational function, such as lobbying, as opposed to organizational mortality. Making determinations about the nature of organizations' withdrawals from lobbying is, however, very difficult; tracking organizations that may have been defunct for a decade or more requires detailed knowledge of an interest community over a considerable period. For this reason, we are confident only about the fates of organizations that withdrew over the 1980s from the Minnesota lobbying community. Relying on a number of directories of companies, organizations, and groups, as well as on familiarity with the state's lobbying scene, we sought to identify whether the 407 exits reported among organizations

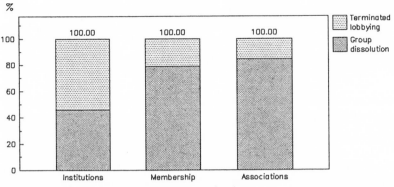

Fig. 6.5. Percentage of Minnesota interest organizations exiting from
1980 to 1990—by source of exit. Total institutions = 166; total membership Groups = 86; total associations = 109.

registered in Minnesota in 1980 resulted from dissolution (whether absolute or via merger) or simple withdrawal from lobbying activity. Answers were developed for 88.70 percent of the 407 organizations (93.26
percent for institutions, 93.48 percent for membership organizations,
and 79.56 percent for associations).

As seen in figure 6.5, these results indicate that withdrawal from
registration lists carries different meaning for the three types of organizations. Fully 54.22 percent of the exiting institutions merely withdrew
from lobbying, while 45.78 percent dissolved or merged so that organizational identity was lost. In contrast, for 79.07 percent of the membership
organizations and 84.40 percent of the associations no longer registered
in 1990, withdrawal from lobbying signaled dissolution. For the latter
two types of organizations, death of the lobbying function typically coin-
cided with death of the organization that supported it. This is consistent
with our hypothesis that lobbying often is a central activity for these
organizations. In contrast, institutions can enter and leave the political
arena as salient issues wax and wane. Thus, institutions that withdraw
from lobbying retain a Lazarus-like capacity to resurrect that function
when new circumstances arise.

Net entry rates, or the simple percentage increase in numbers of
organized interests, are reported by type and by state in figure 6.3.
These results raise an important conundrum for us. In every state but
Arkansas, institutions exhibited the highest net increase in numbers
over the 1980s. In South Dakota, North Carolina, and Michigan, net
growth rates of institutions far outpaced those of associations and

membership organizations. How can we reconcile this higher net growth among institutions with their much higher exit rates?

The answer is that institutions have much higher rates of entry than other types of organized interests. Annual entry rates by organizational type and by state are reported in figure 6.4. Given our assumptions, these values represent the average percentage increase in numbers from the prior year, uncontaminated by intervening exits. In all six states, the annual percentage increase is highest for institutions. And while the differences between membership organizations and associations is again more modest, membership organizations' entry rates exceeded those of associations in five of six states.

We can now take advantage of our use of two comparable populations. The values reported in figures 6.2 and 6.4—representing, respectively, annual exit and entry rates—are directly comparable. The first values in the two figures indicate, respectively, that, on average, 8.33 percent of all Arkansas institutions exited each year, while 13.84 percent more entered. Two conclusions emerge from such comparisons.

First, annual entry rates exceed annual exit rates in all cases. Beyond indicating that these organized interest systems are growing, this means that entry has been, at least potentially, a more powerful source of population change over this period than has been mortality. In Arkansas and Minnesota, overall annual exit rates are about half the size of annual entry rates—59.20 and 52.34 percent, respectively. Thus, patterns of entry are exercising nearly twice the influence of exit in shaping the organized interest systems of these states. Overall annual entry and exit rates are even less balanced in the other states—Pennsylvania, 44.86; South Dakota, 44.05; and North Carolina, 35.68 percent. And in Michigan, the annual exit rate is only 25.00 percent the size of the overall annual entry rate. While patterns of exit were clearly important in shaping the 1990 organized interest systems of these states, entry was much more influential.[4]

Second, the patterns in figures 6.2 and 6.4 are quite similar across states. In all six, institutions exit *and* enter at a faster rate. This means that withdrawal from lobbying acts in a conservative manner by dampening the strong trends toward increased dominance of institutions. Evidence of the size of this effect is presented in table 6.3, where the values in the first column reflect the actual 1990 distributions of organized interests by states and those in the second are predicted distributions for 1990 if none of the 1980 interest organizations and none of those born after 1980 had exited. In 1990, for example, institutions would have comprised 53.90 percent of all organizations in Arkansas if the exit rate had been zero compared to the actual proportion of 47.81.

In North Carolina, Pennsylvania, Michigan, and Minnesota, the institution's proportion of all organizations would have been, respectively, 6.30, 5.84, 3.74, and 6.36 percent higher than actually observed. And in South Dakota, institutions would have comprised 42.29 percent of the population, 22.72 percent higher than the actual 1990 value of 34.46 percent.

Still, the influence of exiting rates on distributions of interest organizations by type is far less than that of entry rates. The last column in table 6.3 presents predicted distributions for 1990 assuming that the entry rates of all organized interests had dropped to zero while exit rates remained as observed. The resulting organized interest communities are

TABLE 6.3. Actual Percentage of 1990 Organizations and Percentage Projected Assuming Zero Entry and Zero Exit since 1980, by Type of Organization

| State | Actual 1990 % of Organizations | Projected % with Zero Exit | Projected % with Zero Entry |
|---|---|---|---|
| **Arkansas** | | | |
| Institutions | 47.81 | 53.90 | 34.38 |
| Membership Groups | 21.49 | 19.07 | 28.13 |
| Associations | 30.70 | 27.03 | 37.50 |
| Total | 100.00 | 100.00 | 100.00 |
| **South Dakota** | | | |
| Institutions | 34.46 | 42.29 | 16.13 |
| Membership Groups | 28.92 | 25.26 | 34.41 |
| Associations | 36.62 | 32.45 | 49.46 |
| Total | 100.00 | 100.00 | 100.00 |
| **North Carolina** | | | |
| Institutions | 42.56 | 45.24 | 21.58 |
| Membership Groups | 22.93 | 22.01 | 30.94 |
| Associations | 34.50 | 32.76 | 47.48 |
| Total | 100.00 | 100.00 | 100.00 |
| **Pennsylvania** | | | |
| Institutions | 60.14 | 63.65 | 50.00 |
| Membership Groups | 17.74 | 15.78 | 20.29 |
| Associations | 22.13 | 20.58 | 29.71 |
| Total | 100.00 | 100.00 | 100.00 |
| **Michigan** | | | |
| Institutions | 56.62 | 58.75 | 36.70 |
| Membership Groups | 17.96 | 18.32 | 22.87 |
| Associations | 25.43 | 22.94 | 40.43 |
| Total | 100.00 | 100.00 | 100.00 |
| **Minnesota** | | | |
| Institutions | 43.23 | 45.98 | 34.47 |
| Membership Groups | 25.05 | 23.13 | 28.09 |
| Associations | 31.71 | 30.89 | 37.45 |
| Total | 100.00 | 100.00 | 100.00 |

sharply different from those actually observed, and the differences are much greater than those resulting under our scenario of zero exiting. Without the addition of new organizations, associations would have become the largest category of interest organizations in all states but Pennsylvania.

Exiting clearly influences the makeup of populations of organized interest communities. But does it influence their overall size? Given that entry rates exceed exit rates by large margins, might we not be able to ignore exits in explaining the growth of organized interest systems? We can answer this question by using the first set of regression results presented in table 6.4.[5] The dependent variable is the net entry rate for our six states as reported in figure 6.3, which reflects the 1990 outcome of entries and exits over the 1980s. The entry and exit rates are those reported in figures 6.2 and 6.4. In part, these regressions are trivial, given that, except for rounding error and averaging, entry and exit rates should relate to net entry in the manner of an accounting identity. As expected, the R-square values are very high, and both coefficients are of the expected sign and highly significant. As the annual exit rate increases, ten-year net entry declines, the opposite of what we observe for annualized entry rates.

Importantly, and as seen in the second set of results, high R-square values and significant coefficients are produced when ten-year net entry rates are regressed on annual entry alone. But unlike the previous results, which are insensitive to case selection, these estimates depend heavily on Michigan's very high rates of net and annual entry. When Michigan is excluded, as seen in the last set of results, a large proportion of the variance in ten-year net entry remains unaccounted for. And worse, entry has a negative estimate in the associations model. This suggests that we must account for exiting if we are to explain variations in net entry into interest organization populations. Our first set of results are trivial in that they define an accounting identity. But no element of that identity is trivial.

Our final question concerns the expression of density dependence in interest organization populations. We have hypothesized that, as systems become more dense, their growth rates slow, a hypothesis we test in chapter 7. Is density dependence the result of greater exiting, less entry, or both? The relationships between annual entry rates and interest system density are assessed via the regression analyses presented in table 6.5. The independent variable—the average of 1980 and 1990 ratios of gross state product and total numbers of organizations (GSP-BASE)—is an *inverse* measure of system density. The first set of results indicates that there is little relationship between system density and annual entry rates. And this is not a function of the outlying of Michigan, as seen in the second set of regressions, which reports equally weak results. Both sets of results suggest that the increasing density of interest organization populations does not feed back to reduce the rate at which new interest organizations are added to populations.

Very different results emerge, however, for exit rates. As seen at the top of table 6.6, interest organization density produces estimated

**TABLE 6.4. Entry and Exit Rate Components of Net Ten-Year Entry—Six States**

| Ten-Year Net Entry | Model | Intercept | Exit Rate | Entry Rate | $R^2$ |
|---|---|---|---|---|---|
| *Six-State Sample* | | | | | |
| All organized interests | 4-1 | -- | -28.208*** (2.149) | 18.224*** (.889) | .988 |
| Institutions | 4-2 | -- | -34.640*** (3.205) | 21.199*** (1.213) | .983 |
| Membership Groups | 4-3 | -- | -23.377*** (1.738) | 15.895*** (.746) | .990 |
| Associations | 4-4 | -- | -22.856*** (.588) | 15.699*** (.271) | .998 |
| *Six-State Sample* | | | | | |
| All organized interests | 4-5 | 246.255 | -- | 23.736*** (2.853) | .945 |
| Institutions | 4-6 | -350.470 | -- | 27.154*** (3.223) | .947 |
| Membership Groups | 4-7 | -118.202 | -- | 15.385*** (3.131) | .858 |
| Associations | 4-8 | -145.648 | -- | 18.075** (5.346) | .741 |
| *Five-State Sample (excluding Michigan)* | | | | | |
| All organized interests | 4-9 | -358.839 | -- | 32.420* (18.880) | .496 |
| Institutions | 4-10 | -281.416 | -- | 22.790*** (5.173) | .866 |
| Membership Groups | 4-11 | -37.530 | -- | 8.113 (7.883) | .261 |
| Associations | 4-12 | 122.701 | -- | -7.660 (3.534) | .611 |

*Note:* Figures in parentheses are standard errors.
* = $p < .10$; ** = $p < .05$; *** = $p < .01$, one-tailed test

**TABLE 6.5.  Density Dependence in Entry Rates**

| Entry Rate | Model | Intercept | Interest System Density [GSP-BASE] | $R^2$ |
|---|---|---|---|---|
| | | Six-State Sample | | |
| All organized interests | 5-1 | 14.630 | .023 (.023) | .185 |
| Institutions | 5-2 | 11.459 | .005 (.014) | .028 |
| Membership Groups | 5-3 | 10.520 | .005 (.011) | .047 |
| Associations | 5-4 | 11.984 | .014 (.016) | .162 |
| | | Five-State Sample (excluding Michigan) | | |
| All organized interests | 5-5 | 15.608 | .007 (.019) | .049 |
| Institutions | 5-6 | 12.225 | -.006 (.006) | .262 |
| Membership Groups | 5-7 | 11.111 | -.004 (.005) | .167 |
| Associations | 5-8 | 12.859 | -.001 (.004) | .019 |

*Note:* Figures in parentheses are standard errors.
* = $p < .10$; ** = $p < .05$; *** = $p < .01$, one-tailed test

slope coefficients of the expected sign for all four dependent variables, although only two are significant. However, the associated bivariate plots, as seen in figures 6.6A through 6.6D, suggest that there is a strong linear relationship between density and mortality rates for five of the six states. Only South Dakota's mortality rate falls outside the pattern. This discrepancy is reflected in the second set of regressions; with South Dakota excluded, R-square values are high, and all estimates are significant. These results suggest that density dependence expresses itself through increasing exiting behavior. For associations and membership organizations, where withdrawal from lobbying usually signals organizational death, our results suggest that the increasing competition for scarce resources associated with high levels of density leads to greater organizational mortality.

Beyond answering our puzzle over which of two mechanisms carries the burden of expressing density dependence, this finding suggests that the causal forces that increase the probability that new organizations will

**TABLE 6.6.   Density Dependence in Exit Rates**

| Exit Rate | Model | Intercept | Interest System Density [GSP-BASE] | $R^2$ |
|---|---|---|---|---|
| | | Six-State Sample | | |
| All organized interests | 6.1 | 7.015 | -.007* (.004) | .377 |
| Institutions | 6.2 | 8.677 | -.010*** (.003) | .703 |
| Membership Groups | 6.3 | 5.849 | -.003 (.004) | .145 |
| Associations | 6.4 | 6.159 | -.006 (.005) | .302 |
| | | Five-State Sample (excluding South Dakota) | | |
| All organized interests | 6.5 | 8.633 | -.014*** (.003) | .897 |
| Institutions | 6.6 | 9.287 | -.013** (.005) | .712 |
| Membership Groups | 6.7 | 7.367 | -.010*** (.003) | .843 |
| Associations | 6.8 | 8.030 | -.015*** (.002) | .924 |

*Note:* Figures in parentheses are standard errors.
* $= p < .10$; ** $= p < .05$; *** $= p < .01$, one-tailed test

form are unrelated to those governing survival as a lobbying organization. Thus, it is unlikely that we will be able to explain interest organization exiting by reference to the kinds of causal processes used to explain entry. The relationship between density dependence and exit points to where we must look. As interest systems become more dense, free-riding opportunities among institutions and resource competition among associations and membership organizations increase. While these consequences of system density must be further explored, they represent the kinds of relationships that are most likely to enable us to explain variation in exit and/or mortality rates.

Now, let us consider the special case of South Dakota, which was included in our sample because it is one of ten or so very small states with both very dense and highly invariant interest organization systems. We have argued that only "natural" interests are likely to overcome disincentives of organization in such states. Just as all states will have a department of revenue irrespective of size, they will all have a number

Interest Organization Annual Exit Rate

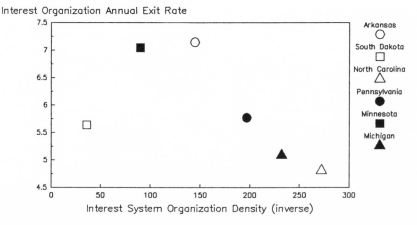

Fig. 6.6. **A, Relation of annual exit rate and interest system density—six states**

Institutions Annual Exit Rate

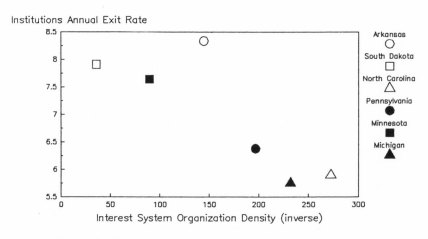

Fig. 6.6. **B, Relation of annual exit rate and interest system density—institutions**

of very basic organized interests, such as a chamber of commerce or a teachers association. Such "natural" organizations would, by their very nature, have great legitimacy and a high survival potential.[6] This assumption is consistent with our finding in figure 6.6A that South Dakota's population has a much lower exit rate than we would expect given its level of interest organization density.

In such a small state, however, more specialized associations and

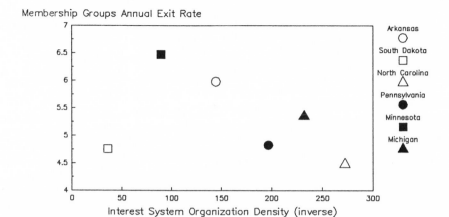

Fig. 6.6. **C, Relation of annual exit rate and interest system density—membership groups**

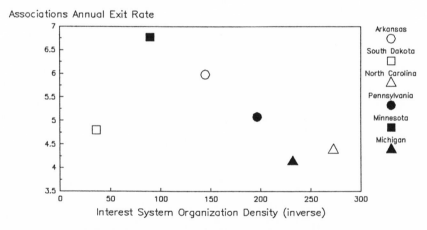

Fig. 6.6. **D, Relation of annual exit rate and interest system density—associations**

membership organizations that might potentially form will lack the numbers of constituents needed to construct viable realized niches. That the problem lies in the need to secure members is evident in the results presented in figure 6.6B, which indicate that South Dakota's institutions are not unusual in regard to the relationship between density and annual exit rates. Institutions do not have to worry about securing members as do membership groups or associations. It is not surprising, therefore, that

South Dakota fits the linear pattern of the institutions scattergram as well as any other state. At high levels of density (inversely scored in the figure), we should expect South Dakota institutions to follow the common pattern by having higher than average exit or mortality rates. In contrast, the South Dakota case on the scattergrams for all interest organizations (figure 6.6A), membership organizations (figure 6.6C), and associations (figure 6.6D) diverges sharply from the linear density-exit rate pattern defined by the other states. South Dakota, and by extension other very small, dense states, are special—and interesting—cases.[7]

### Implications of Exit and Entry

Our findings point to several conclusions. First, in contrast to the often reported permanence and stability of interest organization populations, state interest organizations frequently withdraw from lobbying. Second, and in contrast to the standard assumption that institutions are especially permanent members of interest organizations communities, institutions withdraw at higher rates than associations or membership organizations. Third, however, withdrawal from lobbying is far more likely to indicate organizational death for associations and membership organizations than for institutions. Fourth, at least for the period from 1980 to 1990, patterns of exit greatly influence the diversity and density of organized interest systems, although not to as great a degree as do patterns of entry. And fifth, density dependence in interest communities is expressed primarily through increased mortality, not reduced mobilization; greater density is associated with higher exit or mortality rates.

More generally, these findings have two implications for the study of communities of organized interests. First, they substantively suggest that—with both high entry and high exit rates—interest organization populations are, at least potentially, highly fluid. This is especially the case for high-density populations where rates of exit increase while rates of entry remain unchanged. On such fluidity, Walker (1991) rested his hopes for greater balance among interests. But such fluidity remains only a potential. Indeed, our results indicate that the dominance of institutions actually increased over the 1980s, an outcome that is more supportive of Schlozman and Tierney's position than of Walker's. Fluidity by itself is not enough.

Second, because our results indicate that density dependence is primarily expressed through enhanced mortality rates rather than through depressed entry rates, they suggest that mobilization can be studied as a self-contained process that is not greatly influenced by environmental pressures. This is good news for the mobilization literature. If our results had indicated that density dependence was expressed through depressed entry rates, then our standard mobilization models—based directly or indirectly on Olson's work (1965)—would be misspecified through exclusion of relevant contextual variables, like those included in the ESA model of population density.

These findings point to several avenues of research. Most importantly, they suggest that we need to balance our long-standing attention to the entry of new interest organizations with greater concern for exiting from interest organization communities. Even in the rapidly growing interest organization populations of the states, exiting plays a substantial role in shaping the observed contours in interest organization populations. Exiting would likely play an even more prominent role in political systems with populations of interest organizations that are growing more slowly.

We should, for example, examine what happens to organizations that withdraw from lobbying but do not dissolve as organizations. It seems implausible, for instance, to expect that they remain totally inactive politically. Do they monitor legislation so as to be ready to enter the fray when appropriate? If so, how? When not engaged in lobbying, do they remain active in other ways, such as supporting political action committees? Given that only a third of our survey respondents reported that their organizations sponsored a PAC, activity on one dimension is only weakly related to activity on the other. In general, then, we need more information about the mix of political activities that organizations engage in and how they select among them.

Also, given the close relationship between withdrawal from lobbying and organizational death for associations and membership organizations, we should study death processes both at the level of the individual interest organization and at the level of the community. The most obvious questions must concern cause of death. Exiting need not indicate absolute mortality, although we have employed it here to mean loss of organization identity. Identity could be lost through disbanding or through merger (Aldrich and Staber, 1988). Indeed, in our survey of interest organization leaders discussed in chapter 9, 12.95 percent of association, 18.95 percent of institution, and 16.67 percent of membership group respondents reported that their organizations were born through merger with another organization. In short, autopsies of withdrawals from lobbying are needed.[8]

More importantly, though, identifying the causes of death is essential if we wish to understand the nature of selection in populations of interest organizations. Ideally, we would like to know what it is about survivors that enables them to survive. Is the focus of selection pressures the organizations' size, their access to a particular kind of funding, the strategies of their leaders, or some other trait? Answering such questions will link the population thinking inherent in an ecological perspective directly to the kinds of issues studied within the interest organization maintenance literature (Aldrich et al. 1990).

And given the link between density dependence and mortality, we need to examine how the sizes of organized interest communities shape competition for resources and enhance opportunities for free riding among organizations. For example, biology's competitive exclusion principle might be useful in explaining how interest systems evolve. It holds both that potential competitors will partition niche spaces even until one competitor perishes and that more specialized interest organizations tend to displace more general interests as organizational populations increase in size. Indeed, our finding that institutions are rapidly supplanting associations as the most common type of organization is consistent with this expectation.

CHAPTER 7

# The ESA Model of Population Density

Throughout our discussion of state interest organization populations, much of our attention has been focused on the central population-level properties of density and diversity. From both representational and governance points of view, we have seen that these are among the central properties used by scholars and citizens to assess interest organization systems. Several measures of each were developed and evaluated in chapter 5. Ultimately, though, we need to move beyond simple description to provide a plausible theoretical and empirically founded account of population density and diversity. The central theoretical tool employed by population ecologists in explaining density and diversity is the Energy-Stability-Area (ESA) model presented in chapter 3 and applied to populations of organized interests in chapter 4. In this chapter, we test the ESA model of state interest organization population density. In the following chapter, the diversity implications of these tests are explored.

To make our test more rigorous, the ESA population density model is contrasted to the two major alternative theoretical accounts of density found in the literature: (1) Mancur Olson's explanation of population density as developed in *The Rise and Decline of Nations,* which accounts for increasing numbers of interest organizations as a simple function of time since a polity was constituted, and (2) the Virginia School model (Mueller and Murrell 1986; Coughlin, Mueller, and Murrell 1990; Mitchell and Munger 1991), which explains the growth of interest organization populations as a function of the increasing size of government. Two sets of density models are examined, the first for the total number of interest organizations in the 44 states for which we have complete data for 1975 and 1980 and in all 50 states in 1990. The second set of tests examines six subpopulations of interest organizations in all 50 states, using 1990 data. Finally, we discuss the implications of both sets of density findings for our understanding of state interest systems.

### Testing the ESA Model of Population Density

Prior to testing the ESA model of interest organization density, we must consider just what it is that we are trying to explain. Two measures of density were developed in chapter 5: numbers of interest organizations and numbers of interest organizations relative to size of the economy (GSP-BASE). But while the latter measure has value as a descriptive indicator of density, it should be obvious that its use in tests of an explanatory model is inappropriate. Simply put, it is interest organizations, not some artificial ratio of interest organizations to GSP, that form, register with state legislatures, engage in lobbying, and, perhaps, disband. Moreover, the inherently *relational* nature of the concept of density is captured in the ESA model through its attention to space as a density-dependent explanatory variable. Therefore, we employ numbers of registered organizations as our dependent variables.

We consider two sets of tests of the ESA model: one for the total number of interest organizations and the other for six subsets of interest organizations. The first set is considered because we are interested in the overall density of state communities of organized interests. Unfortunately, however, we have good reason to suspect that such tests will not be very precise. We saw in chapters 3 and 4 that one of the distinguishing features of the ESA model is its specification of unique functional relationships between different species and the explanatory variables of energy, stability, and area. Also, niche theory suggests that each species will come to depend, through the competitive exclusion principle, on a unique combination of resources. Tests of the ESA model for total numbers of interest organizations will necessarily submerge these differences in global measures of energy, stability, and area that only indirectly reflect the underlying processes governing the densities of subsets of interest organizations. In contrast, we have stronger expectations about our tests for six subpopulations, or species guilds, where we can be far more precise in our measurements of energy and space.

## Data and Operationalizations

Our dependent variables are numbers of organized interests registered to lobby state legislatures.[1] In the first set of tests, total numbers for 1975, 1980, and 1990 serve as our dependent measures. In the second, we examine 1990 numbers of six interest organization guilds: three sets of organizations in the profit sector—construction, agriculture, and manufacturing—and three in the not-for-profit sector—local government, welfare, and environmental interests. The six guilds represent a range of types along dimensions thought to be important in the literature and constitute about one-third of all registered interests in the states in 1990.

As noted earlier, one state—Florida—proved to be an outlier in the

1990 census, with nearly twice as many registered interest organizations as any other state. Given the resulting skewed distributions, however, we report the results for analyses using all 50 states for 1990, but with a dummy variable for Florida.[2]

Measures designed to tap two competing explanations are included in the estimation models comprising our tests. Olson's *interest organization system age* is measured by the number of years prior to 1975, 1980, or 1990 that a state joined the Union or, in the case of the Confederate states, the number of years since 1865. This is the same measure used by Olson (1982) in his tests of the institutional sclerosis explanation. For the Virginia School explanation, *size of government* is measured by the 1977, 1982, or 1989 proportion of gross state product (GSP) from state and local governments. Both state and local governments are examined to control for differing patterns of fiscal centralization and to recognize that local government spending is influenced greatly by decisions made in state capitols. Positive and significant coefficients would indicate support for these alternative explanations.

Turning to the ESA explanatory variables, we have interpreted the ESA concept of area, or space, as *size of latent constituency,* or constituency number. It is not obvious how we should measure this variable for total numbers of interest organizations. The latent constituencies of membership groups are individuals, those of associations are other organizations, and those of institutions are the unitary institutions being represented. Any general measure, then, will necessarily be indirect. But in our earlier analysis of measures of density, we indicated broad agreement with Schattschneider's observation (1960) that the primary basis of representation is economic. Therefore, in tests using total numbers of interest organizations, the total size of a state's economy, as measured by GSP, is employed as an indicator of latent constituency size. In an analogous test, Aldrich, Zimmer, Staber, and Beggs (1994, 230–31) report that gross national product is strongly and positively associated with the expansion of the national trade association population. To tap the density-dependent relationship between size and interest organization population number, the squared value of GSP is also included in our specification. The ESA model leads us to expect that the nominal value of GSP will generate a positive coefficient, while the estimate for its squared value should be negative, indicating density dependence.

We can be far more precise in our measurement of size of latent constituencies in our tests with six subpopulations or guilds. In developing these measures, we generally follow Walker's observation (1991, 187) that the most familiar "organizational formula is to base an association upon a tightly knit commercial or occupational community in the profit sector." Therefore, the size of the profit-sector latent constituencies are measured by the number of construction firms with payrolls operative in a state in 1989, the number of farms with more than $10,000 in sales in 1987, and the number of manufacturing establishments in a state in 1987. Again, squared values of each are also included in our estimating models to tap density dependence.

Turning to governments, both local governments and their associated professions might be expected to represent their interests. We measure both with one indicator: the total number of local governments in a state in 1987 (including counties, townships, municipalities, school districts, and special governments). While clearly appropriate for governments as governments, the measure should also be appropriate for professional groups. As Walker (1991, 11) notes, public professional associations arise as informal vehicles of professional communication *across* governments. Within highly centralized states like Hawaii, such informal vehicles are needed far less, because information can be processed internally, through bureaucratic means. Thus, numbers of public professional groups should increase with numbers of local governments.

At least two latent constituencies can be noted for welfare interest organizations: the poor and welfare bureaucrats. The poor, perhaps most closely analogous to the constituents of profit-sector interest organizations, face the kinds of barriers to organization that have been identified by Olson (1965). Recognizing this, Walker (1991, 13) looked to welfare professionals as a surrogate. Number of poor is measured by the number of households in a state using food stamps in 1989. Because this program employs nationwide eligibility standards, this indicator should be independent of our measure of interest. Welfare bureaucrats are measured by the 1988 number of state and local full-time-equivalent welfare workers.[3]

Walker (1991, 61–62) argues that environmental organizations are typical of citizens groups and face, therefore, many of the same disincentives to organization as the poor. But because environmentalism is often conceptualized as a middle-class issue (Kemp 1981), there is no obvious national entitlement program that can be used to assess the size of the potential constituency of environmental interest organizations as was done for welfare organizations. Therefore, we follow Williams and Matheny (1984, 447) by measuring potential environmental constituency size with 1989 state membership in the Sierra Club. We expect Sierra Club membership to covary with the size of the potential constituency of all members of the environmental guild. For each of the six subpopulations, we expect the coefficient of constituency number to be positive, while the estimate of its squared value should be negative, indicating that the relationship between number and size is density dependent.

Two concepts were discussed in chapter 4 as reflecting the energy term of the ESA model: constituency interest and interest certainty.[4] Turning to constituent interest, we again face severe difficulties of measurement for the models in which we use total numbers of interest organizations as our dependent variables. Our task would be simplified greatly if all interest organizations consistently sought more government spending, as suggested by the Virginia School model. If this assertion were valid, we could use the proportion of GSP devoted to government as a population-wide measure of constituent interest.[5]

The plausibility of such a simple characterization of interests is very questionable, however. Political scientists have noted that government size and interest organization density might be related, but they tend to reverse the causal relationship specified by the Virginia School interpretation. Thus, Salisbury (1992, 85–86) argues that an expanding government *attracts* interest organization attention because interest organizations are affected by public policies. A causal pattern of the type suggested by the Virginia School also is questionable because many economic interest organizations, while supportive of spending in their own, narrow domain, nevertheless oppose greater spending in general. Other organizations, such as taxpayer unions, lobby against spending as their primary mission. And still others may not be interested in the public fisc at all, but in symbolic or regulatory governmental actions or nonactions that have few implications for the budget. Therefore, while we will examine the estimate for the proportion of GSP devoted to state and local government variable in terms of constituency interest, as well as its primary function of testing the Virginia School explanation, we do not have strong expectations that it validly measures the underlying concept of interest.

Nor do we see any alternative measure of constituent interest as likely to solve our problem as long as we examine the entire population of interest organizations.[6] Two possible alternatives—the overall level of regulatory activity and major political events—were examined by Aldrich and his colleagues (Aldrich and Staber 1988; Aldrich et al. 1994) in their analysis of the national trade association population, but neither was found to be strongly related to population growth. Simply put, if any specific policy is desired by all interest organizations, it is likely to have been easily adopted some time ago and to not be the object of contemporary lobbying. Interest organizations are more likely to be energized not by global policy issues but by concerns quite specific to their members. As a North Carolina contract lobbyist (phone interview, 26 April 1994) put it, "There are a lot of different reasons, but mostly numbers increase because more groups are aware that government may adversely impact them. Some groups have a specific goal in mind to accomplish, like environmentalists." Given that only specific interests matter, we may be able to test the constituent interest term of the ESA model only when our attention turns to specific interest organization guilds.

To make our review of the issues associated with measuring constituent interest for the six interest organization guilds more concrete, we first present the indicators. Constituency interest of construction interest organizations is measured by the 1986–87 proportion of state and local spending on construction. Constituency interest of agricultural interest organizations is measured by an index of the standardized values of the proportion of farms that were irrigated in a state in 1987 and the 1989 ratio of state farm debt to farm assets. And the constituency interest of manufacturing interests is an index of the standardized values of a state's 1989 average weekly unemployment benefits and its 1988 proportion of unionized manufacturing employees.

Turning to the not-for-profit sector, constituency interest of government interest organizations is measured by the proportion of state expenditures in 1988 allocated as intergovernmental aid. Only state spending is used for this measure, given that local governments are claimants to state government providers on this indicator. Welfare constituent interest is measured by the 1989 average monthly AFDC payment in a state. And environmental constituent interest is measured by an additive index of the standardized values of a state's 1988 per capita tons of airborne toxic releases, 1990 per capita number of toxic waste sites, and 1990 score on an Environmental Protection Agency index of its groundwater vulnerability to pesticide contamination.

Now let us consider the difficulties associated with our measures. First, constituent *interest* must be measured so that it remains distinct from constituent *number*. For example, using total state AFDC spending (instead of average AFDC payments) as an indicator of constituency interest would render it collinear with the size of the welfare population. Therefore, all of the constituency interest measures are expressed as proportions, per capita values, or rankings on absolute scales.

Second, our six guilds represent many diverse interests. For example, not all farmers are interested in the same farm programs. Capturing the specific policy interest of each interest organization at the state level is obviously difficult (see Laumann and Knoke 1987, 109–51, for the same effort at the national level). Our task, then, is to find either relatively encompassing interests or sets of smaller, narrower interests that can serve as markers for a broader array of policy concerns to the guild.

In some cases, however, the disjunction between the two types of measures may not be great. While construction interest organizations may be interested in broad labor or tax legislation, most construction interests lobby the state in pursuit of higher levels of state construction spending. And while local governments may be interested in other enabling legislation, securing and then protecting high levels of aid is clearly paramount.

In other cases, our indicators are more clearly markers for general state involvement with issues of concern to the guilds. Thus, high ratios of farm debt to assets and high proportions of irrigation should indicate that farmers are highly dependent on state decisions more generally, not just on decisions about finance and water. We expect high AFDC payments to be indicative of more extensive state action on welfare issues, just as high levels of unemployment benefits and large proportions of unionized workers should signal that a state supports a broader array of policies usually opposed by manufacturing. And the items in our environmental constituency interest index should tap environmental degradation generally, even if the index does not include every form of pollution.

Third, while high levels of constituency interest should promote interest organization formation, it is not always clear when constituent interest should be high. For example, are environmental interests mobilized to restore degraded environments or to protect pristine ones? Answers may even change over time, depending on whether threats to current policy or opportunities for program expansion are more salient. During the 1980s, a time of fiscal scarcity, health care and corrections gobbled up ever larger proportions of state spending, and voters evidenced opposition to higher taxes. In such conditions, the most vulnerable interests should be those in states with the highest benefit levels. For our four types of organizations that are consumers of state benefits, therefore, we expect constituency interest to be heightened when benefit levels are high.

Our measures of manufacturing and environmental constituency interests operate differently given that they do not reflect government benefits. But the states were under great pressure to protect manufacturing during the 1980s, and many were compelled to step back from policies favorable to labor, especially those setting national ceilings (Gray and Lowery 1990; Lowery and Gray 1992). Thus, we expect the constituent interest of manufacturing interest organizations to be highest among states with strong labor movements and public policies traditionally perceived as favorable to labor. And with such crises as Love Canal, the 1980s saw increased environmental activism at the local level (Walker

1991, 154). Therefore, environmental constituency interest should increase as the level of environmental threat increases.

Fourth, while we expect constituency interest to enhance the size of populations of lobbying organizations, reverse causality may be likely. Traditional interest group liberalism (Lowi 1969) and traditional public choice theory (Bush and Denzau 1977) might argue that greater numbers of construction, government, agriculture, and welfare interest organizations generate higher levels of construction, agricultural, intergovernmental, and welfare spending through their lobbying efforts. However, constituency interest for one guild in the profit sector (manufacturing) and one in the not-for-profit sector (environmental) has been defined so that reverse causality is implausible. Having more environmental interest organizations should not increase numbers of toxic waste sites, and having more manufacturing interest organizations should not lead to greater unionization. Thus, these guilds serve as controls for the possibility of reversed causality. If the ESA model works only for the other cases, reverse causality may be likely. We also conducted additional tests for one guild in the profit sector and one in the not-for-profit sector. These tests, presented with the ESA model results, assess whether having more interest organizations early on is associated with changes in benefit levels. We also present a comparable test for the models employing total numbers of interest organizations and the government proportion of GSP.

We have defined interest certainty as another important resource that might influence interest organization density.[7] Expectations that policy may change can arise from many sources—program innovations that are sweeping neighboring states, fiscal scarcity that may be driving tough budget decisions, or court decisions that unsettle long-standing administrative practices. In explaining the growth in lobbying activity, for example, an Arkansas contract lobbyist (phone interview, 21 April 1994) suggested that, "legislative activity became more high profile due to budget difficulties." In answer to the same question, another Arkansas lobbyist (phone interview, 19 April 1994) noted that "legislative turnover creates uncertainty." Uncertainty, then, can arise from a variety of factors.

But while all of these factors are likely to have some importance, state politics scholars have looked to party competition as the most general source of issue *un*certainty for interest organizations (Walker 1991, 10, 154). In highly competitive states, the out party stands a good chance of suddenly becoming the in party. Not only will this entail turnover in personnel, but it may initiate a broad range of policy reversals with associated budgetary consequences. Party competition—or party hegemony, given the inverse scoring of the measure relative to our theoretical concept of issue certainty—is measured with a folded Ranney index of party competition for the period 1974–1980 or 1981–88.[8] It should produce a negative coefficient in estimations of the ESA model.

How do we apply the stability term of the ESA model? A measure capable of tapping this concept has already been addressed for interest organization systems via Olson's hypothesis (1982) about the relationship between the age of a political system or the time since the last major disruption of the political system and the size of interest organization populations. But as noted in chapter 4, we doubt that Olson's hypothesis applies empirically to the American states. While we find Olson's hypothesis plausible theoretically (although not as a sole determinant of the size of interest organization populations), it does not have value in the case of the American states in the contemporary setting unless one assumes either that there is a century-long time lag in reaching equilibrium or that population growth is open-ended and unconstrained. If neither assumption is valid, then any turbulence variable will be a constant for the cases examined here.[9]

We test our models with OLS regression analysis, with density dependence assessed through the polynomial space variables. In prior organization ecology studies using time series data on single populations (Hannan and Freeman 1989; Hannan and Carroll 1992), density dependence is usually assessed with logistic, rather than polynomial, models. But as Carroll (1984, 85) notes, "This misspecification is probably insignificant . . . because researchers rarely have data on the beginning of organizational populations, i.e., the point where the models diverge the most." This is especially likely with cross-sectional data, such as our data from lobby registration rolls in the American states.

We saw in chapter 5 that small states with dense interest organization systems may be different. They may have both a disproportionate number of "natural" interest organizations with high legitimacy and low entry rates of "discretionary" interest organizations. The low mortality rate observed for South Dakota in chapter 6 supports the former expectation. However, the entry rate for South Dakota in the results presented in chapter 6 did not provide strong evidence of low entry. Still, the presence of such states might undermine OLS tests of a polynomial model if number of interest organizations is a near constant for small, dense states. To assess this potential, we tested the models by excluding the ten smallest states with dense populations of interest organizations.

The results from these tests were not even marginally different from those drawn from our complete sets of states. Therefore, we present only the latter set of test results.

### Findings for Total Numbers of Interest Organizations

The 1975, 1980, and 1990 estimates for the model for total numbers of interest organizations are presented in table 7.1. Clearly, the model

**TABLE 7.1.  Population OLS Regression Results, 1975, 1980, and 1990**

| Independent Variable | Total No. of Interest Organizations | | |
| --- | --- | --- | --- |
| | 1975 | 1980 | 1990 |
| Years since statehood/CW | -0.631 (0.411) [-1.535] | -0.701 (0.457) [-1.534] | -1.602 (0.701) [-2.285] |
| Size of government | 13.118 (16.797) [0.781] | 9.422 (16.747) [0.563] | -16.130 (11.214) [-1.438] |
| No. of constituents [GSP] | 0.020** (0.011) [1.734] | 0.034*** (0.008) [4.419] | 0.077*** (0.009) [8.259] |
| No. of constituents$^2$ [GSP$^2$] | -0.002 (0.006) [-0.422] | -0.005** (0.002) [-2.182] | -0.004*** (0.001) [-4.369] |
| Interest certainty | -145.074 (145.279) [-0.999] | -152.992 164.567) [-0.930] | -601.972*** (226.027) [-2.663] |
| Florida dummy | --- | --- | 2056.944*** (162.140) [12.686] |
| Constant | .192.965 | 284.839 | 1054.557 |
| $R^2$ | 0.325 | 0.592 | 0.902 (0.774) |
| n | 44 | 44 | 50 |

*Notes:* Figures in parentheses are standard errors; figures in brackets are *t*-values; the values in parentheses under the 1990 $R^2$ is the $R^2$ generated by the same model but run for 49 states (excluding Florida) and dropping the dummy variable for Florida. *Measures:* "Years since statehood/CW" is the number of years prior to 1975, 1980, or 1990 that a state was admitted to the Union or, if a Confederate state, since 1865; "size of government" is the proportion of 1977, 1982, or 1989 gross state product generated from government; "GSP" and "GSP$^2$" are surrogates for "no. of constituents" and are 1977, 1982, and 1990 total gross state products; and "interest certainty" is a folded Ranney index of state party competition for 1974–80 for the 1975 and 1980 models and for 1981–88 for the 1990 models, where low values indicate high levels of party competitiveness.

\* = $p < .10$; ** = $p < .05$; *** = $p < .01$, one-tailed tests

provides little support for Olson's expectation that numbers of interest organizations are a simple function of time since a polity was formed or since upheaval, such as the Civil War. For all three samples, the estimates across the first row of table 7.1 carry the wrong sign. Indeed, if two-tailed tests had been employed, two of the coefficients (that for 1975 and that for 1980) would have approached the standard criterion values of statistical significance, and the 1990 estimate would have exceeded them.

Only somewhat more positive results were obtained for the estimates for the size of government variable, which test the Virginia School's explanation of interest organization population density and provide a very crude—and perhaps not very valid—indicator of the constituent interest term of the ESA model. Two of the three estimates in the second row of table 7.1 (again, that for 1975 and that for 1980) carry the expected sign but do not exceed in magnitude their standard errors. The 1990 estimate in column three is greater in magnitude but carries the wrong sign. These results provide little support for the hypothesis that the size of interest organization populations is a function of government size, and they are consistent with prior findings on national trade associations (Aldrich and Staber 1988; Aldrich et al. 1994).

As noted earlier, however, even this weak relationship could represent reverse causality. Traditional interest group liberalism theory and traditional public choice theory, especially, would argue that greater spending—our measure of constituent interest—is a function of many interest organizations, not the reverse as suggested by Mueller and Murrell (1986) as well as our model. We assessed the reverse causality hypothesis (running from number of interest organizations to constituent interest) by regressing the percentage change in the proportion of GSP devoted to state and local government from 1982 to 1989 on two sets of variables: (1) the total number of interest organizations in 1980 and (2) that variable plus total GSP in 1982 and the percentage change in GSP from 1982 to 1990 as controls. If causality runs from number of interest organizations to constituent interest, then more interest organizations in 1980 should be associated with an increase in the size of government over the 1980s. The first model generated an R-square value of only 0.030 and a slope coefficient that was of the wrong sign and insignificant. In the second model, the R-square value climbed to 0.331, but the estimate for numbers of interest organizations in 1980 was again wrongly signed and of tiny magnitude ($t = 0.352$). Thus, the reverse causality hypothesis has little support.

These results provide little support for the Olson and Virginia

School explanations, and their support of the ESA model is only partial. The strongest support is for the space term of the model, conceptualized as constituent number and measured here by GSP and its
squared value. As expected, and consistent with the findings reported
by Aldrich and his colleagues (Aldrich et al. 1994), the GSP coefficients are uniformly signed positive, while those of its squared value
are negatively signed. This is consistent with the ESA expectation that
population size has a density-dependent relationship with space, or that
numbers of interest organizations increase as economies become larger,
but at a declining rate. Given the results presented in chapter 6, this
pattern results from increasing rates of mortality, among associations
and membership groups especially, as interest organization populations
become more dense.

The estimates for the interest certainty term of the model, as measured by levels of party competition, were far weaker, even if all three
coefficients are correctly signed. Only the 1990 estimate is statistically
discernible, indicating that the increasing policy uncertainty associated
with high levels of party competition is associated with expansion of
interest organization populations. Two explanations might account for
the weakness of the 1975 and 1980 estimates in comparison with the 1990
coefficient.

First, we have argued that these variables are likely to have different and unique bearing on the size of each guild of interest organizations, even if the direction of impact is expected to be similar for all or
most guilds. If party competition influences different types of interest
organizations to greater or lesser degrees, then weak estimates might be
expected as a function of "noise." But while we find this general argument to be plausible, it is also true that such differences were not so
great as to wash out the population-wide impact of party competition in
the 1990 sample.

Second, and more plausibly, these mixed results could be a function
of the changing meaning of party competition for the likelihood of policy
change. Many scholars have observed that policy differences between
the parties have sharpened over the 1980s, as evidenced by the very
different levels of policy partisanship of two Republican governors of
Michigan—William Milliken in the 1970s and John Engler in the 1990s.
If this observation is true, then a given level of party competition may
produce greater policy uncertainty in the 1990s than it did during prior
decades. As a result, party competition might be expected to have
greater impact on interest organization population size in our 1990 results than in the results of earlier years.

Finally, it is worth noting that the variance explained by the model increases as we move from 1975 (R-square = 0.325), through 1980 (0.592), to 1990 (0.774). This may indicate that rapid population growth over the last two decades is both cause and effect of the nationalization of the processes governing state interest organization systems (Lowery and Gray 1994a). As historically founded differences in the interest organization communities of the 50 states have disappeared, our model produces sharper results.

### Findings for Six Subpopulations, 1990

The 1990 construction guild estimates are presented in the first two columns of table 7.2A. Column one provides little support for the expectations of the Virginia School or Olson models. Their coefficients carry the expected positive sign, but with minuscule t-values. All four of the ecological model estimates carry the expected sign, and three are significant (the exception being constituent interest, which has a t-value greater than one). When the ESA variables are tested alone, as seen in column two, the R-square value remains the same, and all four estimates are significant at the 0.10 level or better.

Again, these relationships could represent reverse causality for our measure of constituent interest. High levels of spending for construction could be a function of many interest organizations, not the reverse as suggested by our model. We assessed the reverse causality hypothesis (running from number of interest organizations to constituent interest) by regressing change in the proportion of state and local expenditures on construction from 1977 to 1987 on two sets of variables: (1) the number of construction organizations in 1975 and (2) that variable plus total and per capita GSP and the proportion of state and local spending on construction in 1977 as controls. If causality runs from number of organizations to constituent interest, then more organizations in 1975 should be associated with an increase in the proportion of construction spending from 1977 to 1987. The first model generated an R-square value of only 0.013 and a slope coefficient that, while positive, was not significant. In the four variable model, the R-square value climbed to 0.151, and the estimated coefficient for number of organizations was positive but again insignificant. Given these results, the reverse causality hypothesis has little support.

The results for agricultural interest organizations are presented in the last two columns of table 7.2A. They also provide little support for the Olson and Virginia School models. In both sets of results, neither coefficient approaches discernible size; and the Olson estimate is wrongly

**TABLE 7.2A.  Profit-Sector OLS Regression Results—Construction and Agriculture**

| Independent Variable | No. of Construct. Interests Model 1-1 | No. of Construct. Interests Model 1-2 | No. of Agricult. Interest Model 2-1 | No. of Agricult. Interest Model 2-2 |
|---|---|---|---|---|
| Years since statehood/CW | 0.002 (0.045) [0.044] | --- | -0.005 (0.038) [-0.030] | -0.008 (0.038) [-0.231] |
| Size of government | 0.077 (0.621) [0.124] | --- | 0.241 (0.608) [0.396] | 0.192 (0.603) [0.318] |
| No. of constituents | 0.015$^{***}$ (0.003) [4.717] | 0.015$^{***}$ (0.003) [5.320] | 0.084 (0.162) [0.521] | 0.210$^{***}$ (0.057) [3.709] |
| No. of constituents$^2$ | -0.015$^{***}$ (0.006) [-2.420] | -0.015$^{***}$ (0.006) [-2.666] | 0.193 (0.233) [0.828] | --- |
| Constituent interest | 0.624 (0.523) [1.193] | 0.639$^{*}$ (0.399) [1.603] | 6.170$^{***}$ (1.716) [3.596] | 5.840$^{***}$ (1.663) [3.512] |
| Interest certainty | -31.414$^{***}$ (12.434) [-2.526] | -31.024$^{***}$ (11.706) [-2.650] | -17.680$^{*}$ (11.049) [-1.600] | -17.564$^{*}$ (11.008) [-1.600] |
| Florida dummy | 83.231$^{***}$ (9.389) [8.865] | 83.135$^{***}$ (9.144) [9.094] | 53.730$^{***}$ (7.608) [7.062] | 53.301$^{***}$ (7.563) [7.048] |
| Constant | 20.162 | 20.989 | 19.274 | 19.213 |
| $R^2$ | 0.841 (0.614) | 0.841 (0.614) | 0.675 (0.489) | 0.676 (0.480) |

*Notes:* Figures in parentheses are standard errors; figures in brackets are *t*-values; the values in parentheses under the $R^2$ values are the $R^2$ values generated by the same model but run for 49 states (excluding Florida) and dropping the dummy variable for Florida. *Measures:* "Years since statehood/CW" is the number of years prior to 1990 that a state was admitted to the Union or, if a Confederate state, since 1865; "size of government" is the proportion of 1989 gross state product generated from government; and "interest certainty" is a folded Ranney index of state party competition for 1981–88, where low values indicate high levels of party competitiveness. For the construction interest models, "no. of constituents" is the 1989 number of contruction establishments with payrolls divided by 10; "no. of constituents sq." is the squared value of constituents divided by 10,000; and "constituent interest" is the 1986–87 proportion of state and local expenditures devoted to construction. For the agriculture interest models, "no. of constituents" is the 1987 number of farms in thousands with sales of $10,000 or more; "no. of constituents sq." is the squared value of constituents divided by 1,000; "constituent interest" is the average of the *z*-scores for the 1987 proportion of all farms that were irrigated and the 1989 percent of farm debt to farm assets.

\* = $p < .10$; \*\* = $p < .05$; \*\*\* = $p < .01$, one-tailed tests signed. In contrast, two ESA variables—constituent interest and interest certainty—generated significant coefficients of the expected sign. Two others—those for number of constituents and its squared value—failed to approach our criterion levels, although they were signed as expected. But when either was dropped from the model, as seen in column four, the other proved to be highly significant. Thus, while size of potential constituency clearly matters, density dependence is not a very powerful check on numbers of agricultural interests.

The manufacturing results are presented in table 7.2B and proved difficult to assess. There was no difficulty, however, with the Olson and Virginia School variables. In all versions of the model, both estimates carry the wrong sign, and neither is significant. Also as expected, the coefficients of both number of constituents and its squared value in the model presented in the first column are signed as expected and significant. But while correctly signed, the coefficients of neither constituent interest nor interest certainty approached the one-tailed 1.30 significance criterion at the 0.10 level. Yet, when other ESA variables were deleted, as seen in columns two and three, the remaining coefficients were signed correctly and generated significant *t*-values, with only modest change in the R-square values of the models. This appears to be a result of collinearity.[10] And we have long-standing theoretical expectations that levels of manufacturing, party competition, unionization, and policies favorable to labor are closely interrelated (Morehouse 1981). Thus, the most plausible account for these results is that while the ESA variables work as expected, their collinearity makes it difficult to sort out independent impacts.

The government guild results are presented in column one of table 7.3 and are very similar to those reported for agriculture. The Olson and Virginia School estimates again failed to generate *t*-values greater than 1, and all of the ESA variables were signed as expected. But as in the case of agricultural interest organizations, neither constituent number nor its squared value generated significant coefficients when *both* were in the model. Again, however, each was significant when the other was excluded, as seen in column two. As in the case of agricultural interest organizations, while potential constituency size matters, density dependence does not act to check the growth of government-oriented lobbying organizations.

Our most complicated results are those for welfare interest organizations as reported in the third column of table 7.3. We should note first, however, that the Virginia School and Olson coefficients were not significant, and the Olson variable was again wrongly signed. Turning to the ESA variables, tests in which both constituency measures were included

**TABLE 7.2B.    Profit-Sector OLS Regression Results—Manufacturing**

| Independent Variable | No. of Manufacturing Interests | | |
|---|---|---|---|
| | Model 3-1 | Model 3-2 | Model 3-3 |
| Years since statehood/CW | -0.082 (0.097) [-0.849] | -0.056 (0.107) [-0.525] | -0.078 (0.094) [-0.826] |
| Size of government | -0.119 (1.602) [-0.074] | -1.161 (1.742) [-0.666] | -0.021 (1.535) [-0.014] |
| No. of constituents | 0.075$^{***}$ (0.011) [6.798] | 0.041$^{***}$ (0.004) [9.738] | 0.077$^{***}$ (0.009) [8.259] |
| No. of constituents$^2$ | -0.008$^{***}$ (0.002) [-3.300] | --- | -0.008$^{***}$ (0.002) [-3.908] |
| Constituent interest | 1.244 (5.000) [0.249] | 8.951$^{**}$ (4.898) [1.827] | --- |
| Interest certainty | -37.626 (33.181) [-1.134] | -17.116 (36.149) [-0.473] | -40.560$^{*}$ (30.679) [-1.322] |
| Florida dummy | 120.137$^{***}$ (22.671) [5.299] | 142.691$^{***}$ (23.974) [5.952] | 118.893$^{***}$ (21.872) [5.436] |
| Constant | 3.847 | 66.793 | 55.995 |
| $R^2$ | 0.858 (0.816) | 0.821 (0.768) | 0.857 (0.816) |

*Note:* Figures in parentheses are standard errors; figures in brackets are $t$-values; the values in parentheses under the $R^2$ values are the $R^2$ values generated by the same model but run for 49 states (excluding Florida) and dropping the dummy variable for Florida. *Measures:* "Years since statehood/ CW," "size of government," and "interest certainty" are measured as in table 7.2A; "no. of constituents" is the 1987 number of manufacturing establishments in tens; "no. of constituents sq." is the squared value of constituents divided by 10,000; "constituent interest" is the average of the $z$-scores for the 1989 average weekly unemployment benefits and the 1988 percentage of manufacturing employees that are unionized.
$* = p < .10; ** = p < .05; *** = p < .01$, one-tailed tests

produced few significant estimates, although all were signed as expected. Not surprisingly, there was evidence of marked collinearity, with auxiliary R-square values exceeding 0.963 for all of the constituency measures. Where there are poor people, there are welfare bureaucrats. Rather than drop either constituency, we examined forms of these variables that were less collinear, eventually including the number of house-

**TABLE 7.3.  OLS Regression Results for Not-for-Profit Sector**

| Independent Variable | No. of Gov't Interests Model 4-1 | No. of Gov't Interests Model 4-2 | No. of Welfare Interests Model 5-1 | No. of Environmental Interests Model 6-1 |
|---|---|---|---|---|
| Years since statehood/CW | 0.020 (0.167) [0.118] | 0.374 (0.167) [0.224] | -0.009 (0.039) [-0.233] | -0.467 (0.024) [-1.999] |
| Size of government | 2.240 (2.934) [0.763] | 2.630 (2.934) [0.897] | 0.041 (0.624) [0.066] | -0.470 (0.373) [-1.258] |
| No. of constituents | 0.020 (0.120) [0.167] | 0.168*** (0.042) [3.703] | 0.044*** (0.012) [3.786] | 0.078*** (0.013) [5.885] |
| No. of constituents$^2$ | 0.002 (0.002) [1.223] | --- | -0.021*** (0.007) [-3.075] | -0.041*** (0.007) [-5.678] |
| Proportion of welfare bureaucrats | --- | --- | -27.822*** (11.212) [-2.520] | --- |
| Constituent interest | 2.978*** (0.737) [4.041] | 2.738*** (0.714) [3.832] | 0.038*** (0.012) [3.177] | 1.604* (0.999) [1.606] |
| Interest certainty | -105.593** (55.968) [-1.887] | -98.443** (55.983) [-1.759] | -49.720*** (15.100) [-3.497] | -11.858* (7.593) [-1.562] |
| Florida dummy | 461.316*** (37.945) [12.162] | 462.791*** (38.135) [12.156] | 76.211*** (8.736) [8.724] | 45.902*** (5.456) [8.413] |
| Constant | -0.050 | -15.611 | 38.666 | 26.072 |
| $R^2$ | 0.837 (0.575) | 0.831 (0.560) | 0.767 (0.468) | 0.800 (0.540) |

*Notes:* Figures in parentheses are standard errors; figures in brackets are *t*-values; the values in parentheses under the $R^2$ values are the $R^2$ values generated by the same model but run for 49 states (excluding Florida) and dropping the dummy variable for Florida. *Measures:* "Years since statehood/ CW" is the number of years prior to 1990 that a state was admitted to the Union or, if a Confederate state, since 1865; "size of government" is the proportion of 1989 gross state product generated from government; and "interest certainty" is a folded Ranney index of state party competition for 1981–88, where low values indicate high levels of party competitiveness. For the government interests, "no. of constituents" is the 1987 total number of local governments including counties, municipalities, townships, school districts, and special districts divided by 10; "no. of constituents sq." is the squared value of constituents divided by 1,000; "constituent interest" is the 1988 percentage of state general expenditures devoted to intergovernmental expenditures. For the welfare interests, "no. of constituents" is the 1989 number of households in hundreds of thousands participating in the food stamp program; "no. of constituents sq." is the squared value of constituents divided by 1,000; "proportion of welfare bureau-

(*Continued*)

**TABLE 7.3.  Continued**

crats," also a measure of constituency size, is the 1988 number of state and local FTE public welfare employees as a proportion of a state's labor force; and "constituent interest" is the 1989 state average monthly AFDC payment. For the environmental interests, "no. of constituents" is the 1989 number of Sierra Club members in a state in hundreds; "no. of constituents sq." is the squared value of constituents divided by 10,000; and constituent interest is the average of the $z$-scores for the 1988 per capitized tons of toxic releases in a state from the EPA's Toxic Release Inventory, the 1990 per capitized number of Superfund Hazardous Waste Sites on the EPA's National Priority List in a state, and the GAO's 1991 DRASTIC score of relative state vulnerability to pesticide contamination of groundwater.
* = $p < .10$; ** = $p < .05$; *** = $p < .01$, one-tailed tests

holds receiving food stamps, its squared value, and the number of FTE welfare employees *as a proportion* of a state's labor force, which produced an auxiliary R-square value of only 0.381.

In this specification, all of the ESA coefficients but one are signed as expected and significant. But the exception is interesting; the estimate for number of welfare bureaucrats *as a proportion* of the labor force is reported as significant too, although it is incorrectly signed. Given collinearity between numbers of welfare employees and numbers of households receiving food stamps, we should not conclude that number of bureaucrats is negatively related to numbers of welfare interest organizations. More plausibly, a high proportion of welfare bureaucrat participation in the labor force acts as a surrogate or alternative for direct representation of interests of the poor. Therefore, once we account for the impact of the number of poor people on number of interest organizations, number of bureaucrats depresses the formation of welfare interest organizations.

As with construction interest organizations, additional tests were conducted for the welfare interest organizations to assess the reverse causality hypothesis. In this case, change in average AFDC benefits from 1980 to 1989 was regressed on two sets of variables: (1) number of welfare interest organizations in 1980 and (2) that variable plus total and per capita GSP and the 1980 AFDC benefit level as controls. If causality runs from number of interest organizations to interest, then more organizations in 1980 should be associated with an increase in AFDC benefits from 1980 to 1989. The first model generated an R-square value of less than 0.001 and a slope coefficient that, while positive, was not significant. The four-variable model produced an R-square value of 0.043 and a coefficient for the number of 1980 welfare organizations that was incorrectly signed, albeit close to zero.

Our final set of empirical results in table 7.3 are for environmental interest organizations. The Virginia School and Olson coefficients are incorrectly signed once again, and the former would be significant if a two-tailed test were employed.[11] In contrast, all four ESA estimates are significant at least at the 0.10 level and are correctly signed. Indeed, the environmental interest organization results are among the most supportive of our empirical findings.

### Implications of the ESA Model Findings

Starting with our alternative models, there obviously was no support found for the Olson and Virginia School models.[12] In contrast, our expectations for the ESA model in our tests using the six subpopulations—the tests most appropriate given our population ecology interpretation—were disconfirmed for only 2 of 24 hypothesized relationships—for the squared value of local government and agriculture constituency number. But the curvilinearity of the area-density relationship, we have seen, has always been the most theoretically and empirically controversial part of the ESA model. In 18 other cases, as seen in table 7.4, there is strong support in the form of correctly signed and significant coefficients. And in the 4 remaining cases, support, while partial, is still incomplete. High collinearity precludes our cleanly sorting out the distinct impacts of the ESA variables in the manufacturing model especially. Still, the pattern of results is quite strong, especially given our rough indicators of constituent interest and interest certainty and in comparison to previous efforts to explain interest organization population density (Olson 1982; Gray and Lowery 1988; Hunter et al. 1991).

**TABLE 7.4.   Confirmatory Support Provided Hypotheses by Empirical Tests**

| Type of Interest Organization | Olson Model Time since State/CW | VA. Model Size of Gov't | ESA Model No. of Constit. | No. of Constit.$^2$ | Constit. Interest | Interest Certainty |
|---|---|---|---|---|---|---|
| Construction | No | No | Yes | Yes | Yes | Yes |
| Agriculture | No | No | Yes | No | Yes | Yes |
| Manufacturing | No | No | Yes/? | Yes/? | Yes/? | Yes/? |
| Government | No | No | Yes | No | Yes | Yes |
| Welfare | No | No | Yes | Yes | Yes | Yes |
| Environment | No | No | Yes | Yes | Yes | Yes |

*Notes:* A "no" indicates that the final models failed to produce a significant coefficient of the correct sign for this hypothesis. A "yes" indicates that the final models produced a significant coefficient of the correct sign. The "question marks" indicate that the manufacturing results, while generally supportive of the population ecological model hypotheses, were likely characterized by high levels of collinearity that precluded definitively sorting out the individual impacts of the several variables.

The density findings have several implications. First, they indicate that interest organization density and other population-level attributes are unlikely to be explained solely by reference to mobilization. Mobilization, while an important subject in its own right, is not important in understanding population-level attributes, except in the trivial sense of adding more interest organizations to the hopper. The environmental constraints facing interest organizations then determine the ultimate contours of populations by bringing selective pressures to bear so that not all interest organizations survive and/or by feeding back onto mobilization processes in the case of density-dependent relationships so as to dampen rates of entry. And given our results in chapter 6, it appears that the former is a far more powerful response to density dependence than the latter, even if high founding rates continue to have tremendous impact on the shape of interest organization populations.

Second, our findings suggest that interest organization population density is understandable in a manner quite congenial with Salisbury's conception (1994, 12–13) of interest: "I hold the view that an interest arises from the conjunction between some private value . . . and some authoritative action or proposed action by government. Neither private value nor governmental action (actual or potential) can by itself generate the interest. Likelihoods and propensities may abound, but unless the conjunction occurs there is no interest." The population ecology variables that dominate our results—constituent number and the resources of constituent interest and interest certainty—reflect well those two requirements.

At the same time, the population ecology framework in which we have set these variables ensures that we are providing something more than old wine in a new bottle. The isomorphism principle, its attendant assumption of equilibrium, and the concept of density dependence should lead us to modify assumptions about the natural emergence of interests as well as interpretations of Olson's model of the disincentives of organization *via greater attention to context.* And population ecology's attention to competition, selection, and adaptation, and especially its competitive exclusion principle, should provide us new opportunities to theoretically link micro- and institutional-level analyses of interest organizations. The population ecology model is broadly consistent with traditional views of interest organization politics while simultaneously enhancing their analytic depth and potential for theoretical integration.

Third, our findings indicate that populations of organized interests are unlikely to grow in an unlimited fashion. The carrying capacity of political systems may change, and dramatically so, as constituent number, constituent interest, and interest certainty change. But at any given level of these variables, there exist limits to how many interest organizations can survive, irrespective of how many membership groups, associations, and institutions may overcome the incentive problems of organization. This suggests that predictions of inevitable hyper interest organization politics attendant to the continuing explosion of interest organization populations may be unfounded.

Fourth, our models suggest that the likely sources of recent growth of interest organization populations are long-term changes in the sizes of latent constituencies and the resources of government activity and interest certainty. Temporal variation in these variables cannot be tapped via the data employed here, except in a very general manner by using our three samples of total numbers of interest organizations. But temporal change can certainly be accommodated by our theory. More to the point, our analysis is consistent with the idea that the explosion of interest organizations in the states since 1975 resulted from economic-driven changes in the relative mix of constituent numbers, declining interest certainty associated with increased party competition and heightened policy differences between the parties, and increasing constituent interest arising from fiscal scarcity (Hrebenar and Thomas 1992, 13). Expansion of interest communities was likely influenced as well by the Reagan-era devolution of responsibilities from the federal government to the states, which further accentuated policy uncertainty. Should these conditions reverse, the ESA model would lead us to expect a decline in state interest organization populations.

# CHAPTER 8

# The ESA Model of Population Diversity

The standard state politics interpretation of interest organization diversity starts with Truman's hypothesis (1951, 53) that it is a product of complex societies and economies. State politics scholars have followed Truman's lead by testing the link between diversity and economic complexity, albeit indirectly. The conceptualization of diversity underlying this approach is inappropriate, however, from a population ecology perspective. Simply put, there is a causal gap between such societal-level variables as economic complexity and the diversity of interest organization systems. It is not at all clear how or through what agency the variables specified as the causal forces in this interpretation act on the outcome of diversity. As a result, existing analyses of interest organization diversity are ultimately unsatisfying.

Our alternative population ecology interpretation of diversity clearly does not reject the notion that societal-level environmental variables matter. But instead of acting directly on the population-level trait of diversity, the ESA model suggests that they condition the founding rates and, especially, the death rates of interest organizations, and that they do so in a unique manner for each guild of interest organizations. Given the ESA model, then, interest organization community diversity is a cumulative or additive outcome of the play of the ESA density processes for each interest organization guild. Direct causal linkages between the environmental constraint variables of the ESA model, or any other variables for that matter, and interest organization community diversity are implausible from an ecological perspective. As a baseline against which to evaluate the ESA model, however, we test the complexity hypothesis using a standard regression format. We will see not only that the complexity hypothesis is unsatisfying theoretically but that it is founded on only the weakest of empirical evidence.

As an alternative, we then use a series of simulations, based on the results of our tests of the ESA density model for six interest organization guilds in 1990 (presented in chapter 7), to tease out the implications of the ESA interpretation of community diversity. Following our presentation of the results from testing the conventional complexity hypothesis, we discuss how the alternative population ecology simulations were constructed. The results of the simulations are presented in the third section of this chapter and are followed by consideration of their implications using two measures of interest organization diversity developed in chapter 5. Finally, we discuss how the findings bear on our understanding of diversity and speculate about the substantive meaning of our results.

### A Test of the Complexity Model

We must first define economic complexity if we are to adequately assess its association with interest organization population diversity. While Truman (1951, 52) noted the ambiguity of the concept, the state politics literature suggests that it has at least three dimensions. The first is *economic diversity,* the degree to which economic activity is concentrated or dispersed across multiple categories of economic and social activity. Surprisingly, given its face validity, this aspect of economic complexity is rarely considered in a systematic matter. Yet it is precisely this dimension of complexity that best underlies the many anecdotal accounts of interest organization diversity (e.g., Zeigler and van Dalen 1976, 95–110), including those offered by Morehouse (1981). The other two dimensions are *economic size* and *economic wealth,* both of which derive from Truman's implicit argument (1951; also see Aldrich et al. 1994, 230–31) that size and wealth create opportunities for greater specialization, both in the demand for new products and in our capacity to meet that demand.

Our dependent variables are two of the measures of interest organization diversity presented and discussed in chapter 5: the Herfindahl index of interest organization diversity across a number of economic sectors, and the proportion of interest organizations representing not-for-profit (i.e., government and social) interests.[1] Economic diversity is measured by a Herfindahl index of economic concentration and is the sum of the squared proportions of gross state product (GSP) across the economic sectors (minus one for social interest organizations, for which there is no comparable GSP category) used to construct the Herfindahl index of interest organization diversity. Both measures are inverse indicators, with high values indicating greater concentration and low values greater diversity. Economic size is measured by GSP, and economic wealth is measured by per capita GSP for 1977, 1982, and 1990.

The first three columns of table 8.1 present the results of testing the complexity model with the Herfindahl index of interest organization diversity. Note, first, the weakness of the estimates—only the 1990 results account for more than 6 percent of the variance in diversity, and the

R-square value of 0.287 for the 1990 sample is nothing to write home about given the strong expectations about this model in the state politics literature. Second, note that all of the economic wealth and economic size coefficients, except the latter for 1975, are incorrectly signed. Given the inverse nature of the dependent measure, the estimates suggest that diversity in representation declines as size and wealth increase. It is also true, however, that their t-values—with the exception of the incorrectly signed wealth variable for 1990—are quite small. The only real support provided for the complexity model by these results is found in the economic diversity coefficients. They are signed as expected and approach or barely exceed the standard criterion values for statistical significance. In general, however, these results are quite weak given the very strong expectations of conventional interpretations of interest organization diversity.

The results for the same model with the proportion of not-for-profit interest organizations substituted as the dependent variable are presented in the last three columns of table 8.1 and are even weaker than those

TABLE 8.1.   Tests of the Complexity Model with Two Measures of Diversity

| Independent Variable | Herfindahl Index of Organization Diversity | | | Not-for-Profit Interest Organizations (%) | | |
|---|---|---|---|---|---|---|
| | 1975 | 1980 | 1990 | 1975 | 1980 | 1990 |
| Economic diversity | 0.110* (0.084) [1.319] | 0.110* (0.081) [1.366] | 0.179** (0.084) [2.139] | -0.067 (46.347) [-0.001] | 5.800 (44.612) [0.130] | -76.575 (66.041) [-1.160] |
| Economic size | -0.024 (0.042) [-0.582] | 0.007 (0.021) [0.320] | 0.010 (0.009) [1.029] | -0.978 (23.034) [-0.042] | -2.239 (11.524) [-1.194] | 0.376 (7.443) [0.050] |
| Economic wealth | 0.697 (0.861) [0.810] | 0.035 (0.313) [0.112] | 0.651 (0.315) [2.068] | 0.716* (0.477) [1.501] | 0.336** (0.173) [1.943] | 0.372* (0.248) [1.500] |
| Constant | 0.103 | 0.109 | 0.088 | 21.730 | 24.539 | 33.517 |
| $R^2$ | 0.053 | 0.010 | 0.287 | 0.054 | 0.135 | 0.057 |
| n | 44 | 44 | 50 | 44 | 44 | 50 |

*Notes:* Figures in parentheses are standard errors; figures in brackets are *t*-values. *Measures:* "Herfindahl index of organization diversity" and "% not-for-profit interest organizations" are presented and discussed in chapter 5; "economic diversity" is a Herfindahl index of economic concentration constructed for 1977, 1982, and 1989 with GSP using the same economic sectors (minus social) used to construct the index of interest organization diversity; "economic size" is 1977, 1982, and 1989 GSP (divided by millions for ease of presentation); and "economic wealth" is per capita GSP for the same years (divided by thousands).
* = $p < .10$; ** = $p < .05$; *** = $p < .01$, one-tailed tests

presented for the Herfindahl index. The variance in the proportion of not-for-profit organizations explained is very modest, exceeding 13 percent in the 1980 model only. None of the economic complexity or economic size coefficients are discernible statistically. Even worse, the estimates for economic complexity are incorrectly signed in the 1980 and 1990 results, while the estimates for economic size are incorrectly signed for 1975 and 1980. Only the economic wealth coefficients support the complexity model. All are signed as hypothesized, indicating that the proportion of government and social interest organizations increases as wealth increases; and all three approach or exceed standard criteria for statistical significance. In general, however, the pattern of results is quite weak. Not only is the complexity interpretation dissatisfying theoretically; it also does not work empirically.[2]

## Assumptions Underlying the Simulations

The weak results of our tests of the complexity model are not surprising from a population ecology perspective, which suggests that diversity is an artifact resulting from the play of the causal forces separately governing each of the interest organization guilds in a community. In the remainder of this chapter, we explore the diversity implications of the ESA model, using simulations based on the empirical results presented in chapter 7.

We employ simulations for the simple reason that they allow us to assess the range of impact the variables specified in the ESA models have on the mix of interest organizations. By systematically manipulating the environmental constraints governing the densities of each of the several types or guilds of interest organizations in a community, we assess the magnitude of their impact on the overall diversity of the community. Simply put, it is not obvious a priori how the overall diversity of a population of interests will change as values of the independent variables change, because the number of each type of interest organization is a distinct product of the values of the specific independent variables in each of the six models. Of course, results generated from simulations of this type are only as strong as the underlying models used to produce them. Still, the results presented in the last chapter provided strong support for the six guild-level ESA models.

The stylized political community in our simulations consists of only the six subpopulations of interest organizations examined in the 1990 tests of the ESA model in chapter 7: the three profit-sector sets of interest organizations representing construction, agriculture, and manufacturing; and the three not-for-profit sets of interest organizations representing local government, welfare, and environmental interests. As seen in the first column of table 8.2, our community of interest organizations is nearly evenly divided between the two sectors, with means of 95.87 (49.83 percent) organizations in the profit sector and 96.54 (50.17 percent) in the not-for-profit sector.

Perhaps the most important assumption underlying our simulations is that the community-level mix of interest organizations is solely a

**TABLE 8.2.  Actual and Predicted Mean Number of Interest Organizations, by Interest Organization Type, for Three Scenarios of Constituency Number**

| Type of Organization | Actual Mean No. of Orgs. | Pred. Scen.1-1[a] (Avg. No.) No. | Pred. Scen.1-2[b] (High No.) No. | % Increase | Pred. Scen.1-3[c] (Low No.) No. | % Increase |
|---|---|---|---|---|---|---|
| | | Profit Sector Organizations | | | | |
| Construction | 19.47 | 21.72 | 33.42 | 53.87 | 9.18 | -72.53 |
| Agriculture | 13.32 | 12.55 | 17.19 | 36.97 | 10.25 | -40.37 |
| Manufacturing | 63.08 | 68.85 | 113.63 | 65.04 | 24.74 | -78.23 |
| Subtotal | 95.87 | 103.12 | 164.24 | 59.27 | 44.17 | -73.11 |
| | | Not-for-Profit Organizations | | | | |
| Local gov't | 67.91 | 65.12 | 91.72 | 40.85 | 43.09 | -53.02 |
| Welfare | 17.87 | 21.63 | 29.29 | 35.41 | 10.44 | -64.36 |
| Environment | 10.76 | 13.19 | 19.72 | 49.51 | 7.08 | -64.10 |
| Subtotal | 96.54 | 99.94 | 140.73 | 40.81 | 60.61 | -56.93 |
| TOTAL | 192.41 | 203.06 | 304.97 | 50.19 | 104.78 | -65.64 |

[a]The number of organizations predictions for each of the six types of interests in scenario 1-1 were generated using models from chapter 7 (modified by dropping Florida and the Olson and Virginia School variables), with the mean population values of the independent variables used in those models. The manufacturing model including constituent number squared was used.

[b]The number of organizations predictions in scenario 1-2 were generated with the same models used to produce the scenario 1-1 predictions, while holding interest certainty and constituent interest at their actual mean values but increasing constituent number 108.60 percent over the observed 49-state mean, equivalent to an increase in a state's population by one standard deviation over the actual mean. The percentage increase values reported for scenario 1-2 are the percentage increase in number of organizations from the figures reported for scenario 1-1.

[c]The number of organizations predictions in scenario 1-3 were generated with the same models used to produce the scenario 1-1 predictions, while holding interest certainty and constituent interest at their actual mean values but decreasing constituent number 89.96 percent from its observed mean, equivalent to a 0.828 percent of a standard deviation reduction in population below the mean. The percentage increase values reported for scenario 1-3 are the percentage increase in number of organizations from the figures reported for scenario 1-1.

product of the dynamics governing the responsiveness of the separate sets of interest organizations to their own unique environmental conditions. Indeed, as outlined in chapter 4, the ESA model assumes that competition takes place largely *within* the six types or guilds of interest organizations, given their reliance on common resources of membership and sources of financing. This is population ecology's weak interpretation of community.

What do we make of competition *among* the six types of interest organizations? Specifying such interactions would complicate our task. But the weak interpretation of community suggests that they are rare except for communities with keystone predators (Colinvaux 1978, 145; Taylor 1992, 54). Yet, some scholars follow Truman (1951, 59, 503–16) in asserting that interest organizations mobilize in response to perturbations created by other interest organizations. This countermobilization hypothesis suggests that such interspecific or interguild interactions are quite important and should not be ignored when simulating interest organization responses to changing environmental conditions.

Still, three reasons lead us to do just that. First, as noted in our development of the ESA model, such interactions are best conceptualized as part of the energy or resources term of the ESA model, as measured by the constituent interest variables of our estimating models (Hannan and Carroll 1992, 98). If manufacturers are successful, for example, in persuading legislatures to avoid regulating pollution, the degradation of the environment will directly spur the mobilization of environmental interest organizations. Second, we will see in chapter 9 that the most important resources of interest organizations in the securing and protection of viable niches are those vital to internal maintenance of interest organizations—their membership and financial support—rather than resources reflecting external relations of the organization, such as control of a narrow policy domain. Competition over the former is primarily intraguild rather than interguild. And third, despite the long survival of Truman's countermobilization hypothesis (1951, 59, 503–16), and its recent resurrection by Becker (1983, 1985), little in the way of systematic empirical evidence has ever been presented in its support. Indeed, in one of the few systematic tests of the countermobilization hypothesis, Aldrich and his colleagues (Aldrich et al. 1994, 234) found little evidence that union activity influences the size of the national trade association population. For these reasons, we do not model competitive interactions among our interest organization subpopulations. Thus, the predicted size of our organization community as a whole is the sum of the predicted totals of each of the six sets of organized interests.

The baseline simulations—scenarios 1–1, 2–1, and 3–1—use the estimates from modified versions of the 1990 ESA density models in chapter 7 (modified by dropping Florida and the Olson and Virginia School variables) to predict numbers of interest organizations, with the values of the ESA model variables set at their actual mean population values. These baseline predictions are reported in the second column of tables 8.2 through 8.4, where it is evident that they closely match observed mean numbers of interest organizations, as reported in column one of the tables. The core of our analysis will consist of systematically

**TABLE 8.3.   Actual and Predicted Mean Number of Interest Organizations, by Interest Organization Type, for Three Scenarios of Interest Certainty**

| Type of Organization | Actual Mean No. of Orgs. | Pred. Scen.2-1[a] (Avg. Certainty) No. | Pred. Scen.2-2[b] (High Certainty) No.   % Increase | | Pred. Scen.2-3[c] (Low Certainty) No.   % Increase | |
|---|---|---|---|---|---|---|
| | | Profit Sector Organizations | | | | |
| Construction | 19.47 | 21.72 | 24.85 | 14.41 | 18.58 | -25.23 |
| Agriculture | 13.32 | 12.55 | 14.10 | 12.35 | 11.01 | -21.91 |
| Manufacturing | 63.08 | 62.29 | 67.49 | 8.35 | 59.10 | -12.43 |
| Subtotal | 95.87 | 96.56 | 106.44 | 10.23 | 88.69 | -16.68 |
| | | Not-for-Profit Organizations | | | | |
| Local gov't | 67.91 | 65.12 | 73.68 | 13.14 | 56.56 | -23.24 |
| Welfare | 17.87 | 21.63 | 26.52 | 22.61 | 16.73 | -36.92 |
| Environment | 10.76 | 13.19 | 14.49 | 9.86 | 11.90 | -17.87 |
| Subtotal | 96.54 | 99.94 | 114.69 | 14.76 | 85.19 | -25.72 |
| TOTAL | 192.41 | 196.50 | 221.13 | 12.53 | 173.88 | -21.37 |

[a]The number of organizations predictions for each of the six types of interests in scenario 2-1 were generated using models from chapter 7 (modified by dropping Florida and the Olson and Virginia School variables), with the mean population values of the independent variables used in those models. The manufacturing model including interest certainty was used.

[b]The number of organizations predictions in scenario 2-2 were generated with the same models used to produce the scenario 2-1 predictions, while holding constituent number and constituent interest at their actual mean values and setting the value of interest certainty at one standard deviation below the actual mean observed for the 49 states. The percentage increase values reported for scenario 2-2 represent the percentage increase in number of organizations from the figures reported for scenario 2-1.

[c]The number of organizations predictions in scenario 2-3 were generated with the same models used to produce the scenario 2-1 predictions, with the exception of setting the value of interest certainty at one standard deviation above the actual mean value observed for the 49 states. The percentage increase values reported for scenario 2-3 represent the percentage increase in number of organizations from the figures reported for scenario 2-1.

varying the value of several key variables in the models and then seeing how the resulting predicted mix of interest organizations changes in comparison with predictions of the baseline models.[3]

### Findings from the Simulation Models

Table 8.2 reports our manipulations of constituent number by increasing it 208.60 percent, an amount equivalent to a state population increase over the observed mean by one standard deviation, with corresponding

**TABLE 8.4.  Actual and Predicted Mean Number of Interest Organizations, by Interest Organization Type, for Three Scenarios of Constituent Interest**

| Type of Organization | Actual Mean No. of Orgs. | Pred. Scen.3-1[a] (Avg. Interest) No. | Pred. Scen.3-2[b] (High Interest) No. | % Increase | Pred. Scen.3-3[c] (Low Interest) No. | % Increase |
|---|---|---|---|---|---|---|
| | | | Profit Sector Organizations | | | |
| Construction | 19.47 | 21.72 | 23.80 | 9.58 | 19.57 | -9.90 |
| Agriculture | 13.32 | 12.55 | 17.19 | 36.97 | 7.88 | -37.21 |
| Manufacturing | 63.08 | 62.68 | 69.93 | 11.57 | 55.42 | -11.58 |
| Subtotal | 95.87 | 96.95 | 110.92 | 14.41 | 82.87 | -14.52 |
| | | | Not-for-Profit Organizations | | | |
| Local gov't | 67.91 | 65.12 | 86.78 | 33.26 | 43.30 | -33.51 |
| Welfare | 17.87 | 21.63 | 26.35 | 21.82 | 16.82 | -22.24 |
| Environment | 10.76 | 13.19 | 14.12 | 7.05 | 12.24 | -7.20 |
| Subtotal | 96.54 | 99.94 | 127.25 | 27.33 | 72.36 | -27.60 |
| TOTAL | 192.41 | 196.89 | 238.17 | 20.97 | 155.23 | -21.16 |

[a]The number of organizations predictions for each of the six types of interests in scenario 3-1 were generated using models froms chapter 7 (modified by dropping Florida and the Olson and Virginia School variables), with the mean population values of the independent variables used in those models. The manufacturing model including constituent interest was used.

[b]The number of organizations predictions in scenario 3-2 were generated with the same models used to produce the scenario 3-1 predictions, while holding constituent number and interest certainty at their actual mean values and setting the value of constituent interest to one standard deviation higher than the actual mean observed for the 49-state population. The percentage increase values reported for scenario 3-2 represent the percentage increase in number of organizations from the figures reported for scenario 3-1.

[c]The number of organizations predictions in scenario 3-3 were generated with the same models used to produce the scenario 3-1 predictions, with the exception of setting the value of constituent interest to one standard deviation lower than that actual mean observed for the 49-state population. The percentage increase values reported for scenario 3-3 represent the percentage increase in number of organizations from the figures reported for scenario 3-1.

changes in the values of constituent number squared. We assume that our simulated state has 208.60 percent as many welfare recipients, construction firms, manufacturing firms, local governments, farms, and environmental organizations as the actual mean numbers. The resulting predictions of subpopulations of interest organizations are reported in column three. Thus, scenario 1–2 reports numbers of each type of organization that would be expected if a state's population increased roughly from that of Maryland to that of Ohio and if all else, including relative numbers of potential constituents of each type of interest organization—the sole source of variation posited by those emphasizing a mobilization-based understanding of diversity—remained the same.

The impact on interest organization populations of this increase in constituent number varies across the interest organization guilds. Three sets of interest organizations—construction, environment, and manufacturing—evidence sharp increases in numbers over the scenario 1–1 outcomes, with the number of manufacturing interests increasing fully 65.04 percent, from 68.85 to 113.63 interest organizations. Welfare, local government, and agriculture interest organizations evidence more modest population growth, increasing, respectively, 35.41, 40.85, and 36.97 percent. These differences in growth rates result directly from variation in the responsiveness of the several interest guilds to constituency number, especially in terms of their sensitivity to density-dependent effects associated with its squared value.

The results reported in the last two columns of table 8.2 mirror those just discussed but were generated by decreasing constituent number. In this case, because population is somewhat skewed and its standard deviation is actually larger than its mean, we reduced constituent number by only 0.828 percent of its observed standard deviation (with corresponding changes in its squared value), which reflects the least populous state of Wyoming. Thus, we reduced the number of constituents of each type of interest organization to only 10.04 percent of their actual means; scenario 1–3 reports numbers of organizations that would be expected if a state's population decreased from that of Maryland to that of Wyoming and if all else, including relative numbers of potential constituents of each of the six types of interest organizations, remained the same.

The relative order of the winners and losers from increasing constituent number is only partially reproduced when constituent number is reduced. Welfare organizations, for example, which increased in number only modestly when constituent number was enhanced, declined fully 64.36 percent when constituent number was reduced. This lack of parallel responsiveness arises from the separate and unique way in which density-dependent curvilinearity in the responsiveness of number of organizations to potential constituent number is expressed for each organization guild.

Our manipulations of constituent number across ranges equivalent to those observed for Maryland, Ohio, and Wyoming have a substantial impact on the total size of the interest organization populations, but far less than an increase of 208.60 percent or a decrease of nearly 90.0 percent. Thus, the value at the bottom of column three of table 8.2 indicates that we expect a total of 304.97 interest organizations in our Ohio-like state, an increase of 50.19 percent over the baseline Maryland-like state prediction of 203.06 interest organizations. Similarly, the value at the bottom of column five indicates that we expect a total of only 104.78 organizations in our Wyoming-like state, a decrease of only 65.64 percent from the baseline prediction of 203.06 interest organizations, although this simulation entailed a reduction of nearly 90.00 percent in numbers of potential constituents.

Table 8.3 reports results from manipulating the value of interest certainty, as measured by party competition (a folded Ranney index for the decade of the 1980s). The ESA model of density suggests that when parties are competitive, policies may change if the out party comes to power. Such change is a threat or an opportunity depending on whether one is advantaged by the status quo. But in either case, we should see a more active interest organization system. Columns one and two in table 8.3 again reflect the actual distribution of organizations in our sample and the numbers that would be expected if the values for all of the variables in the ESA estimating models are set at their means, respectively.

In contrast, the predictions under scenarios 2–2 (columns three and four) and 2–3 (columns five and six) were generated holding all variables except party competition at their means. The scenario 2–2 results were generated by setting the value of interest certainty at one standard deviation below its observed mean, indicating a more competitive system. The predicted numbers of interest organizations for scenario 2–3 were produced by setting interest certainty—as measured by party competition—at one standard deviation above its observed mean, indicating a less competitive political system.

Manipulating interest certainty has an impact on both interest organization numbers and their distribution. In comparison to the baseline prediction of 196.50 interest organizations, 221.13 are expected under the scenario of high party competition (column three), an increase of 12.53 percent. Under the scenario of low competition, only 173.88 interest organizations are expected (column five), a reduction from the baseline prediction of 21.37 percent. Clearly, though, the impact of moving between these two conditions of interest certainty has far less impact on total numbers of interest organizations than did our earlier manipulations of constituent number across a narrower range.

Still, the impact is not small, nor does it fall equally across the several interest guilds. Importantly, the profit-sector interest organizations appear to be less sensitive to interest certainty than do the not-for-profit guilds. Profit-sector interest organizations increase only 10.23 percent from the baseline predictions under the scenario of high competition and fall in number only 16.68 percent under the scenario of low competition. The corresponding changes for the not-for-profit sector are 14.76 and −25.72 percent, respectively. And of all types, welfare interest organizations are clearly the most responsive to interest certainty, decreasing in number from the baseline prediction of 21.63 interest organizations to 16.73 organizations (−36.92 percent) under the scenario of low party competition and increasing to 26.52 organizations (22.61 percent) under the scenario of high competition.

Table 8.4 presents the results from manipulating the value of *constituency interest*—government activity or its potential in the area of concern to the guilds as measured uniquely for each guild. Columns one and two in table 8.4 again reflect the actual value and baseline predictions of organization number. The predictions in column three were produced by setting the value of constituent interest at one standard deviation higher than its observed mean value, while those in column five were generated by setting constituent interest at one standard deviation less than its mean.

In general, the results reported in table 8.4 are similar to those reported in our manipulation of interest certainty. Increasing constituent interest by one standard deviation raises the predicted number of interest organizations in the community from 196.89 to 238.17 (column three), an increase of 20.97 percent (column 4), while decreasing its value by the same mark reduces the predicted number to 155.23 (column 5), a population reduction of 21.16 percent (column six) from the baseline prediction.

Again, profit-sector interest organizations are on average less responsive to changes in constituent interest than are not-for-profit interest organizations. The former increase in number from the baseline predictions only 14.41 percent under the scenario of high constituent interest and fall in number only 14.52 percent under the scenario of low constituent interest. The corresponding percentage changes for not-for-profit interest organizations are 27.33 percent and −27.60 percent, respectively.

This average masks, however, differences among interest organizations within the two sectors. For example, agricultural organization numbers were more responsive to changes in constituent interest than were any of the not-for-profit sets of interest organizations—increasing from our baseline prediction by 36.97 percent under scenario 3–2 and falling by 37.21 percent under scenario 3–3. In contrast, environmental organization numbers are only modestly responsive to changes in constituent interest, as measured by levels of environmental degradation. Under the condition of high constituent interest, they increased in number from the baseline prediction of 13.19 interest organizations to only 14.12 organizations, an increase of only 7.05 percent. And under the condition of low constituent interest, they declined from the baseline prediction to only 12.24 organizations, a reduction of only 7.20 percent.

**The Diversity Implications of the Results**

What do these results say more generally about interest organization diversity? Two measures of diversity discussed in chapter 4 tap the social

TABLE 8.5.    **Numbers of Organized Interests as Proportions of Interest Organization Populations under Alternative Scenarios**

| Type of Organization | Actual Prop. | Proportions Predicted under Scenarios | | | | | | | | |
| | | 1-1 | 1-2 | 1-3 | 2-1 | 2-2 | 2-3 | 3-1 | 3-2 | 3-3 |
| | | Constit. No. | | | Interest Certainty | | | Constit. Interest | | |
| | | Avg. | High | Low | Avg. | High | Low | Avg. | High | Low |
| Profit Sector Organizations | | | | | | | | | | |
| Construction | 10.12 | 10.70 | 10.96 | 8.76 | 11.05 | 11.24 | 10.69 | 11.03 | 9.99 | 12.61 |
| Agriculture | 6.92 | 6.18 | 5.64 | 9.78 | 6.39 | 6.38 | 6.33 | 6.38 | 7.22 | 5.08 |
| Manufacturing | 32.78 | 33.91 | 37.26 | 23.61 | 31.70 | 30.52 | 33.99 | 31.83 | 29.36 | 35.70 |
| Subtotal | 49.83 | 50.78 | 53.85 | 42.15 | 49.14 | 48.13 | 51.01 | 49.24 | 46.57 | 53.39 |
| Not-for-Profit Organizations | | | | | | | | | | |
| Local gov't | 35.29 | 32.07 | 30.07 | 41.12 | 33.14 | 33.32 | 32.53 | 33.08 | 36.44 | 27.89 |
| Welfare | 9.29 | 10.65 | 9.61 | 9.96 | 11.01 | 11.99 | 9.62 | 10.99 | 11.06 | 10.84 |
| Environment | 5.59 | 6.50 | 6.47 | 6.76 | 6.71 | 6.55 | 6.84 | 6.70 | 5.93 | 7.89 |
| Subtotal | 50.17 | 49.22 | 46.15 | 57.85 | 50.86 | 51.87 | 48.99 | 50.76 | 53.43 | 46.61 |

*Note:* The proportions reported in this table, which sum to 100.00 for each column are based on the numbers of interest organizations reported in tables 8.2 through 8.4.

and economic variations in representation that are the focus of most discussions of representational diversity: the relative proportions of interests in the profit and not-for-profit sectors and Herfindahl indices of more fine-grained breakdowns of interest organization subpopulations. Both can be used to evaluate the predictions generated by our several scenarios. The raw information needed for both measures is provided in table 8.5, which presents the predicted organization numbers for the several scenarios reported in tables 8.2 through 8.4 *as proportions* of our interest organization community.

The impact that manipulating the environmental forces of constituent number, constituent interest, and interest certainty has on the relative mix of interest organization guilds is especially evident in the relative proportions of profit and not-for-profit interest organizations across scenarios 1–2 and 1–3, 2–2 and 2–3, and 3–2 and 3–3. These predicted proportions are presented in the fourth and eighth rows of table 8.5 for each of the two sectors and highlight the impact of our manipulations on the profit and not-for-profit balance in our stylized interest organization communities. Under conditions of increased constituent number (1–2), minimal interest certainty (2–3), and low constituent interest (3–3), profit-sector interest organizations comprise majorities—53.85, 51.01, and 53.39 percent, respectively. But under the opposite of these three conditions (scenarios 1–3, 2–2, and 3–2), the not-for-profit interest organizations assume majorities by similar margins—57.85, 51.87, and 53.43 percent, respectively. Indeed, the differences between the two sets of proportions as a proportion of the actual standard deviation in the proportions of the interests observed in the profit and not-for-profit sectors in the six states (9.41)—and rising from all sources of variation in diversity—are large, fully 124 percent for the manipulations of constituent number, 31 percent for interest certainty, and 72 percent for constituent interest, although all of our simulations assume a fixed set of latent interests.

Table 8.5 highlights as well the relative responsiveness of the different types of interest organizations to our three environmental variables. For example, the relative size of the government lobbying community appears to change hardly at all under our manipulations of interest certainty—as measured by party competition—in scenarios 2–1, 2–2, and 2–3, increasing from the proportion of 32.53 percent in the scenario of low party competition (scenario 2–3) to only 33.32 percent under the scenario of high party competition (scenario 2–2). But the proportion of government interest organizations in our community changes greatly under our manipulations of constituent interest (in this case, the proportion of state funding on intergovernmental aid), from 36.44 percent when aid levels are high (scenario 3–2) to 27.89 percent when aid is limited (scenario 3–3). And the relative size of the local government lobbying community is even more sensitive to changes in constituent number, as seen in the proportions reported for scenarios 1–1, 1–2, and 1–3.

In contrast, the relative size of the welfare organization component of our community is especially sensitive to manipulations of interest certainty, changing in proportion from 11.99 percent to 9.62 percent of our community between the condition of low interest certainty (scenario 2–2) and that of high interest certainty (scenario 2–3). But welfare interest organizations, unlike their local government colleagues, were largely unresponsive to manipulation of constituent interest (as measured in this case by average AFDC payments), increasing from 10.84 to 11.06 percent of our community under the two extreme conditions of scenario 3.

Comparisons of the separate guilds highlight the inadequacies of any single measure of diversity. The relative balance of interest organizations in the profit and not-for-profit sectors is produced by a simple summation of the separate guild proportions within each sector. This surely tells us something about overall diversity. But *intrasector* variation in environmental responsiveness is substantial and would be lost if we focused solely on this one measure of diversity.

A more general measure of diversity is provided via Herfindahl indices of organization diversity, a measure that is particularly useful in assessing imbalances across multiple subcategories of a population. As noted in chapter 5, Herfindahl indices are constructed by summing the squared proportions of each of the six guilds of interest organizations. Herfindahl index values are reported for our community in table 8.6. For six interest organizations guilds, the index can take a maximum value of 1.000 when all observations fall into a single organization guild and a minimum value of 0.166 when observations are distributed equitably across all six categories of interest organization. The actual average for the six sets of interest organizations, based on data from 49 states (excluding Florida, given its highly unusual population growth), is 0.268 (with a standard deviation of 0.040), indicating a fairly high degree of diversity.

Table 8.6 also reports Herfindahl index values based on the proportions generated from our several simulations, as reported in table 8.5. The interpretation of these results can be most easily illustrated by considering those presented in the second row. The Herfindahl index value of scenario 1–2, where constituent number was increased over its observed mean, is 0.258. This is 0.009 higher than the Herfindahl index

**TABLE 8.6.   Actual and Predicted Herfindahl Index Values for Scenarios Presented in Tables 8.2, 8.3, and 8.4**

| Scenarios | Herfindahl Index Value[a] | Difference in Index Value from Scenario 1[b] | Differences as % of Population St. Dev. (.040)[c] |
|---|---|---|---|
| | Constituency Number Scenarios | | |
| Scenario 1-1 (Avg.) | 0.249 | -- | -- |
| Scenario 1-2 (High) | 0.258 | 0.009 | 22.98 |
| Scenario 1-3 (Low) | 0.257 | 0.008 | 19.71 |
| | Interest Certainty Scenarios | | |
| Scenario 2-1 (Avg.) | 0.243 | -- | -- |
| Scenario 2-2 (High) | 0.240 | -0.003 | -7.50 |
| Scenario 2-3 (Low) | 0.251 | 0.008 | 20.00 |
| | Constituent Interest Scenarios | | |
| Scenario 3-1 (Avg.) | 0.244 | -- | -- |
| Scenario 3-2 (High) | 0.250 | 0.006 | 15.96 |
| Scenario 3-3 (Low) | 0.242 | -0.002 | -4.64 |

[a]The Herfindahl index is calculated by summing the squared proportions of subsets of total population one is interested in. In the case of six subsets, the minimum value of the index is 0.166, indicating complete equitability across the six categories, and the maximum value is 1.00, indicating that all of the items were in one subcategory. The Herfindahl index scores for scenarios 1, 2, and 3 reported in column one are for the predicted values of the number of interest organizations in scenarios one, two, and three of tables 8.2, 8.3, and 8.4, respectively.

[b]The differences reported in column two are from the Herfindahl index values of the predicted number of interest organizations in scenario 1 of tables 8.2, 8.3, and 8.4, respectively.

[c]The values reported in column three express the differences in column two as a percentage of the actual Herfindahl index standard deviation of 0.040 for the six subsets of interest organizations.

value for our baseline scenario (1–1), indicating that increasing constituent number reduces overall diversity. How much is diversity reduced? The last item in row two indicates that the 0.009 reduction in value represents a shift of 22.98 percent of the actual observed 49-state standard deviation of the Herfindahl index for our six interest organization guilds. Similarly, the results in row three indicate that the scenario of constituent number population decline produced an index score of 0.257, which was 0.008 higher than that observed for the baseline scenario and which constituted a standard deviation decline in diversity of 22.98 percent. Surprisingly, then, both increasing and decreasing constituent number from the values actually observed in the states reduces overall diversity as measured by the Herfindahl index.

Turning to the other two environmental constraints, increasing the level of party competition (scenario 2–2) and reducing the value of constituent interest by one standard deviation (scenario 3–3) increases diversity by 7.50 and 4.64 percent of a standard deviation, respectively. And reducing party competition (scenario 2–3) and increasing constituent interest (scenario 3–2) have the opposite impact; they reduce diversity by 20.00 and 15.96 percent of a standard deviation, respectively. Thus, while the Herfindahl index measure of overall diversity presents a somewhat different perspective on the diversity consequences of our manipulations of the ESA variables from that observed from our analysis of the relative balance of profit and not-for-profit interests, it is clear that the overall mix of communities of organized interests can change in surprising ways in response to even, across-the-board changes in the values of the ESA variables.

## Implications for Understanding Diversity

While suggestive, the results presented here are not intended to serve as a definitive analysis of interest organization system diversity in the American states. Simulations based on results for only one-third of the 1990 interest organization population in the states are an insufficient base for firm inference. Moreover, the simulations were constructed using point estimates from the results presented in chapter 7, although the coefficients are more appropriately viewed as only the most probable estimates from a series of sampling distributions. While these estimates were quite sharp, alternative combinations of estimates along their respective distributions might be selected to either enhance or diminish the diversity impacts we have presented. However, given our conceptualization of diversity as an additive outcome of the separate processes governing the densities of multiple interest guilds, simulations provide the most appropriate way to examine the diversity of populations of organized interests. A standard regression model of the type used here to test Truman's complexity hypothesis (1951) is clearly inappropriate given the many and indirect causal steps between the independent variables measuring economic complexity and the dependent variable of community diversity.

Still, our results are more appropriately viewed as exploring the implications of an ecological view of community diversity. And perhaps the key implication is that we cannot assume that any observed mix of interest organizations reflects in any automatic way the distribution of interests in society. The diversity of state interest organization populations is highly conditioned by how responsive different types of interest organizations are to the environmental constraints governing their densities. Even when the underlying distribution of interests is held constant, manipulation of those constraints produces quite different interest organization communities. Therefore, interest organization system diversity should be conceptualized as an artifact of the processes separately governing the densities of different interest organization guilds, processes that may be only partially and imperfectly reflective of actual distributions of interests in society.

Actual distributions of interests in society are not, of course, irrelevant to structuring interest organization systems: North Dakota's economy and society, for example, will produce a different mix of organized interests from that found in Michigan. But the relationship is not nearly as strong as Truman might lead us to expect. The actual mix of represented interests in the states is an outcome of processes governing the density of each interest organization guild in the community.

While we have urged caution in substantively interpreting our results, we cannot help but speculate a bit about our findings. We found profit-sector interest organizations to be more responsive to changes in constituent number than not-for-profit interest organizations. One explanation might lie in differences in the membership bases of the two sets of interest organizations. Profit-sector interest organizations are more likely to represent individual firms, while not-for-profit interest organizations, especially welfare and environmental interest organizations, are more likely to rely on individuals as members. Increasing constituent number, then, is more likely to lead to a one-for-one increase in interest organization lobbying registration for the former than for the latter.

The results reported for local government interest organizations in table 8.3 provide some indirect evidence on this hypothesis. Such interest organizations often represent a single local government in a manner comparable to the firm basis of organization of profit-sector interest organizations. Consistent with this interpretation, the responsiveness of local government interest organizations to changes in constituent interest are far more similar to that of profit-sector interest organizations than to that of their not-for-profit cousins.

The opposite pattern was found for the other two environmental constraints. A possible interpretation of the interest certainty finding, as measured by party competition, is that both parties now share a common orientation toward business interests. Many scholars have observed that the sharpest differences between parties today are drawn over social, welfare, and environmental issues. This implies that the issue uncertainty associated with party competition represents both more of a threat and more of an opportunity for interest organizations concerned about these issues. Of course, party agreement about economic policy or conflict over social policy are hardly historic constants. In other times, different patterns of responsiveness to issue certainty might be observed.

Similarly, the higher average level of responsiveness to manipulations of constituent interest on the part of the not-for-profit types of interest organizations may result from the importance of policy variation to the overall concerns of the different types of interest organizations. Changes in government spending on construction or in labor laws that influence manufacturing tap into only a small part of the broader activities of firms in these two sectors of the economy. In contrast, local governments in many states depend very heavily on state aid, as do welfare constituents. Thus, a change of one standard deviation in levels of government activity may simply mean more to interest organizations in the not-for-profit sector than to those in the profit sector.

Finally, our results may bear on the controversy between the findings of Schlozman (1984) and Schlozman and Tierney (1983), on the one hand, and those of Walker (1983), on the other, concerning the dominance of traditional economic interests. Our results suggest that both findings might have merit. Rates of interest group mobilization, and perhaps organizational survival, may have increased for nontraditional interest organizations as they gained access to more financial resources over the last two decades. But the results from our constituent number simulations indicate that higher levels of responsiveness to increasing population size on the part of profit-sector interest organizations may have led to even more rapid increases in their numbers as constituent numbers have increased for all types of interest organizations. As a result, the balance of numbers may have remained the same as the energy- or resource-induced expansion of the subpopulation in the not-for-profit sector was canceled by the relative advantage of profit-sector interest organizations in their responsiveness to changes in the growth of latent constituent numbers.

# CHAPTER 9

# The Structure of Interest Communities

Interest organization communities, no matter how dense or diverse, may be structured so that policy conflict is endemic or so that it is avoided through the balkanization of interests into isolated domains. The implications of these two alternatives for democratic deliberation may be as significant as they are obvious.[1] Not surprisingly, then, one of the most contentious issues in the interest organization literature concerns the level of policy conflict within interest systems. From Truman (1951), through Schattschneider (1960), to Walker (1983), our assessment of the degree of interest balkanization has undergone dramatic swings over the course of the postwar period. For the most part, however, this literature has been descriptive, with scholars contending over whether balkanization provides an accurate description of interest organization communities. Given the importance accorded to how we answer this question, it is surprising that much less attention has been devoted to explaining why and under what conditions balkanization can be sustained.

The best explanation we have is niche theory. J. Q. Wilson (1973, 263), although not employing the niche label, speculated that interest organizations seek to develop autonomy over resources critical to their survival. He further hypothesized (1973, 265) that in pursuing autonomy, newer organizations must adopt a strategy of *resource conflict* with more established organizations. But we have seen that Browne (1990; 1995, 216–18) developed the niche theory of interest organization more completely, arguing that the policy agenda is the most critical resource for interest organizations and that establishing policy agenda autonomy is the most important strategy used to ensure the survival of interest organizations. Such balkanization is expected to aid survival by providing interest organizations more exclusive impact on policies of concern to them. An Arkansas contract lobbyist (phone interview, 11 May 1994) put it this way: "As the legislative committees specialize more by policy interest, the lobbyist concentrates his effort there. That increases his influence." He argued that as the policy focus narrows, the lobbyist's influence over that narrow area increases: "If you get the right person [as lobbyist], they can carry a lot of water for you."

The Wilson-Browne theory provides a solid starting point from which to consider the structure of interest communities. In chapter 4, we extended their analysis by exploring the implications of population ecology's interpretation of the niche concept, especially the role of the competitive exclusion principle and the nature of niche partitioning. We explore these ideas in this chapter while examining the balkanization hypothesis.

### Assessing the Implications of Niche Theory

We use the perceptions of interest organization leaders about the nature of interest organization interactions to assess on which dimensions (or dimension) organizational identities are established, or how realized niches are defined within interest communities. Specifically, we examine their perceptions of conflict, cooperation, and partitioning within their interest communities over four of the resource dimensions identified in chapter 4: access to organization members and financial resources, control of selective incentives, and control of policy access in the form of a balkanized interest system.

One difficulty that we must confront in evaluating these perceptions is the absence of objective criteria by which to determine when values for conflict, cooperation, and partitioning are high or low. While our judgments are necessarily subjective, they are informed in three ways. First, the work of Browne (1990) and, especially, that of Heinz and his colleagues (Heinz et al. 1993, 1990; Salisbury et al. 1987) share a number of similarities with ours. Simply put, we can ask if our findings are more consistent with the balkanized system described by Browne or the somewhat more conflictual neopluralist system described in *The Hollow Core* (Heinz et al. 1993). Second, because we compare perceptions of conflict, cooperation, and partitioning across four resource dimensions, we can assess the relative levels of the variables across the comparisons. And third, we can use prior knowledge about interest organizations to inform our judgments. All other things being equal, we expect the concerns of institutions, and thus opportunities for conflict and cooperation, to be narrower than those of associations or membership groups, with membership groups—because they include numerous externality groups—having the greatest policy breadth and likelihood of interaction (Browne 1990, 488–89; Heinz et al. 1993, 259).

Another problem inherent in the use of survey data to test the implications of niche theory deserves note. Given that a likely outcome of competition is niche partitioning, participants may be unaware of the contest we assume they are in. Certainly, many of the contract lobbyists we interviewed saw their world as a highly competitive one. One South Dakotan lobbyist (phone interview, 29 April 1994), for example, noted that, "There is more competition among lobbyists; it is the last unregulated market in capitalism." Still, partitioning should minimize perceptions of competition. But as Hannan and Carroll (1992, 27) note, "Whether two or more actors dependent on the same limiting resources come to recognize their relation as competitors poses an interesting and possibly important question. But the absence of such recognition surely does not cause competitive constraints to dissipate." Thus, given this inherent difficulty of testing niche and competition theory with survey data on the perceptions of interest organization leaders, we must interpret our findings with care.

Still, we have ample evidence that competition, driven by resource scarcity, characterizes the organizations we study. In population research, the defining sign of competition is evidence of density dependence (Hutchinson 1959, 149; Lack 1954; Hannan and Carroll 1992, 29). Because of increasing competition for limiting resources, population growth rates slow as density increases. Therefore, presence of the latter is taken as evidence of the former. And clear evidence of density dependence for state interest organization populations as a whole and for several subpopulations of interests in the states was reported in chapter 7. Also consistent with our expectation of intense competition is our report in chapter 6 that interest organization mortality increases with density. Thus, whether recognized by the participants or not, intense resource competition characterizes interest communities.

## The Interest Organization Survey

Since financial resources did not allow us to survey interest organizations in every state, we selected six states for analysis: Arkansas, South Dakota, Pennsylvania, North Carolina, Michigan, and Minnesota—the same six states used in our analysis of entry and exit rates in chapter 6. Again, they constitute a broad cross section in terms of size, economic complexity, and region. More importantly, while in aggregate they nearly mirror the national distribution of institutions, associations, and membership groups, the six states are distributed across the full range of states in terms of the densities of their interest organization populations.[2] At the same time, they include one of the fastest-growing state populations of interest organizations (Michigan) and one of the slowest-growing (Arkansas). Thus, these six states should both constitute a plausibly representative sample of all states and provide needed variation on variables critical to our interpretation of populations of interest organizations. While individual state results are presented where theoretically appropriate, on most questions there were few systematic differences in the responses of the interest organization leaders across the states.[3] Therefore, most of our analyses merge the responses for all six states.

Our samples were drawn from lists of interest organizations registered to lobby the six state legislatures in 1990–91. Since we are interested in a broad range of interests, the lobbying organizations in each state were classified into three categories: institutions, associations, and membership groups. For each of the three categories of organizations, separate random samples of 55 organizations (or the entire population in the few cases where there were slightly fewer than 55 organizations) were drawn for each state, producing a maximum of 165 organizations for each state. Because only three of the states provided the addresses of the organizations in their lobbying registration lists, relevant directories were used to find addresses for each organization. Questionnaires were then directed to each interest organization's executive director or government relations officer, as appropriate.

A number of surveys from our initial mailing in December 1993 and January 1994 were returned because organizations had disbanded or moved. This necessitated another address search. In several cases, we obtained new registration lists from the state, visited the state capitol, and phoned lobbyists, as well as employing other search procedures. Some organizations were never located and are presumed to have disbanded. Based on our revised lists, a second mailing to organizations that had not responded to the initial wave was conducted approximately six weeks after the first. A reminder postcard followed a month later.

The response rates, relative to our initial sample of approximately 165 organizations for each state, are as follows: Minnesota 42.94 percent, North Carolina 45.45 percent, South Dakota 46.97 percent, Arkansas 35.86 percent, Michigan 35.37 percent, and Pennsylvania 34.38 percent. If we exclude from the initial sample those organizations for which no current address could be found after extensive search, and which are presumed to have disbanded, the effective response rate improves somewhat: Minnesota 44.30 percent, North Carolina 46.05 percent, South Dakota 49.04 percent, Arkansas 39.10 percent, Michigan 41.13 percent, and Pennsylvania 37.67 percent.

How do these rates compare with previous surveys of interest organizations? Most previous surveys have been of membership groups, with relatively few surveying institutions and associations; and most have been conducted at the national, rather than the state, level. Perhaps most directly comparable are the mail surveys of lobbyists conducted in connection with the Hrebenar and Thomas studies of state interest organizations (1992, 1993a, 1993b). The response rates reported there for our states were 35.0 percent for Michigan (Browne and Ringquist 1993, 144), 33.0 percent in North Carolina (Fleer 1992, 361), 44.0 percent in Minnesota (Grau 1993, 153), 25.0 percent in Arkansas (English and Carroll 1992, 369); 33.0 percent in South Dakota (Burns and Cheever 1993, 296), and 5.0 percent in Pennsylvania (P. M. Crotty 1994). However, the unit of analysis in these studies was not the organization but the individual lobbyist, for whom addresses from state registration lists are probably more reliable. On balance, though, we believe that our response rates compare favorably with those reported in previously published work on state interest organizations.[4]

**Findings of the Survey**

Figures 9.1A through 9.1D present results based on interest organization leaders' perceptions about the nature of the policy system. The first two sets of results provide some support for the balkanization thesis. Figure 9.1A presents responses to the statement "In this policy area, there are only a few key legislators who make decisions that really matter." Fewer than a quarter of our respondents in each set of organizations indicated that this statement is *rarely true*.[5] A strong majority of more than 75.0 percent answered that the statement was *always* or *sometimes true*. As expected given their narrower policy focus, institutional interest respondents were somewhat more likely (28.09 percent) to answer *always true* than were association (21.48 percent) or membership group (16.67) respondents. In general, however, these results indicate that our respondents believe that they interface with a relatively small number of influential legislators when pursuing their policy objectives.

This pattern is mirrored by figure 9.1B, which presents responses to the statement "Legislative jurisdiction over issues in this policy area is restricted to only one or a few committees." Fewer than 10.0 percent of the respondents in any of the sets of interest organizations indicated that this statement was *rarely true,* and more than 45.0 percent answered that the statement was *always true.* Surprisingly (given their naturally narrower policy focus), institutional respondents were somewhat less likely (52.87 percent) to answer *always true* than were association leaders (61.36 percent). Still, it is quite clear that interest organization representatives view their policy arena as highly structured in terms of both jurisdictional locus and involvement by key legislators, results that seem consistent with the balkanization thesis.

This consistency disappears, however, when we examine what happens within that structured setting. As seen in figure 9.1C, a majority of

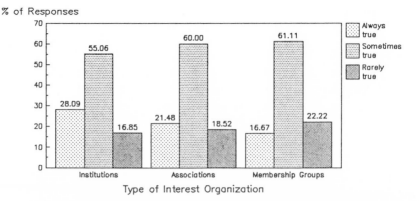

Fig. 9.1. *A,* **Agreement with statement that policy area is dominated by a few key legislators. Total institutions = 89; total associations = 135; total memberships = 144.**

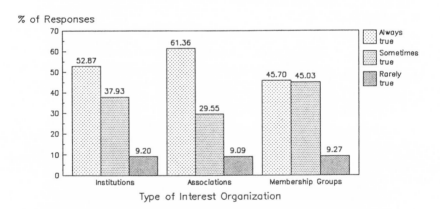

Fig. 9.1. *B,* **Agreement with statement that jurisdiction is restricted to one or a few committees. Total institutions = 87; total associations = 132; total memberships = 151.**

our association and membership group respondents indicated that the statement "This policy area is marked by intense conflict and disagreement over fundamental policy goals" is *sometimes true.* When these responses are combined with the *always true* responses, it is clear that most of our respondents in all three sets (two-thirds or more) view their policy arena as at least occasionally providing a setting for serious policy disagreements. Indeed, it is especially surprising that our institutional interest respondents, given their inherently narrower policy focus, an-

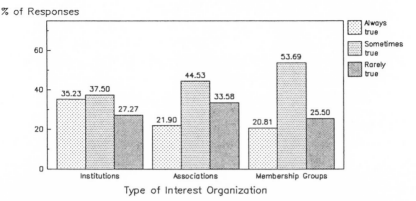

**Fig. 9.1. *C,* Agreement with statement that policy area is marked by intense conflict. Total institutions = 88; total associations = 137; total memberships = 149.**

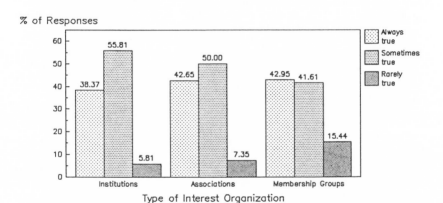

**Fig. 9.1. *D,* Agreement with statement that leaders surveyed often face same opponents in policy area. Total institutions = 86; total associations = 136; total memberships = 149.**

swered *always true* more often (35.23 percent) than did our association (21.90 percent) or membership group (20.81 percent) respondents. This is a level of policy conflict that seems inconsistent with strict balkanization.

And this conflict is not haphazard. As seen in figure 9.1D, a very strong majority of our respondents indicated that the statement "In making our case in this policy area, we repeatedly face the same opponents on each issue that comes up" is *sometimes* or *always true.*

Indeed, a plurality of membership group leaders and more than a third of the leaders of the other two sets of interest organizations indicated that the statement was *always true*. Although highly structured, the policy system does not seem especially successful in segregating policy opponents to avoid policy confrontation.

In sum, while our respondents believe that the arena in which they pursue their interests is highly structured—that is, comprised of one or a few committees and a small set of legislative actors—it is not an arena that protects them from confrontation over core policy values with long-standing policy opponents. Given the importance of the former to pluralist theorists, these results, on balance, fail to support the balkanization hypothesis. In the case of many of the organizations in our sample, either they have failed to establish a strong policy identity of the type described by Browne (1990; 1995, 216–18), or their niche identities must be rooted somewhere other than in control of a narrow policy issue agenda.

To begin to determine where such identities are rooted, we turn to our second set of analyses in figures 9.2A through 9.2C, which assess perceptions of frequencies of interaction with potential competitors and allies. We have argued that low levels of policy interaction, as a result of partitioning along the policy access/control dimension, should be expected given Browne's policy niche model. Figures 9.2A and 9.2B provide this expectation little support.

The responses in figure 9.2A were generated by the question "In lobbying the state legislature, how often do you find yourself in direct competition with other organizations opposed to your position?" Taken together, fewer than a quarter of our respondents answered *rarely* or *never,* although as expected, leaders of institutional interests were somewhat more inclined to do so. If the respondents indicated that policy opposition occurred *always, often,* or *sometimes,* they were then asked to identify up to five organizations that opposed them within the last three years. Even when the *rare* and *never* response cases were assigned a value of zero, the mean number of opponents identified by each of the full set of respondents was 2.35 for membership groups, 2.18 for associations, and 1.97 for institutions. In sum, consistent with the results presented in figures 9.1C and 9.1D, there appears to be at least a modest level of interaction among policy opponents.

Similar to the findings of Heinz, Laumann, Nelson, and Salisbury in *The Hollow Core* (1993), an even stronger level of interaction was found among policy allies, as seen in figure 9.2B. A majority or near majority of respondents in each of the three sets of organizations answered *often* to the question "In conducting your lobbying activity with the state legislature, how often do you consult, communicate, or cooperate with

Type of Interest Organization

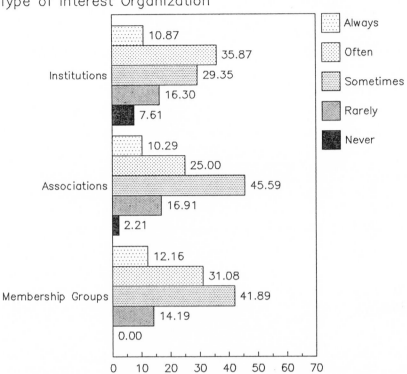

Fig. 9.2. *A*, Perception of frequency of competition with interest organizations opposed to own organization's position. Total institutions = 92; total associations = 136; total memberships = 148.

other organizations sharing your goals and also engaged in lobbying the state legislature?" When the *often* responses are combined with the *always* responses, it is clear that interaction among policy allies is frequent. Again, if the respondents indicated that consultation, communication, or cooperation occurred *always, often,* or *sometimes,* they were then asked to identify up to five organizations with whom they had so interacted within the last three years. Even when the *rare* and *never* response cases were assigned a value of zero, the mean number of allies so identified by each full set of respondents was 3.53 for membership groups, 3.43 for associations, and 3.09 for institutions. These results are quite consistent with those reported in *The Hollow Core* and inconsistent with the balkanization model. Given these high levels of interaction

# Type of Interest Organization

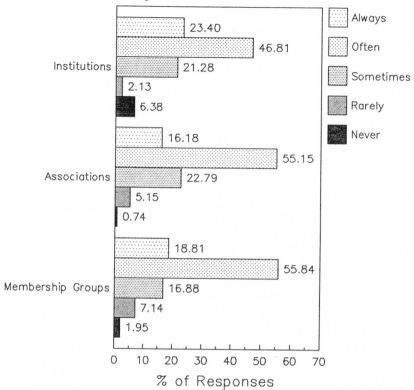

**Fig. 9.2. _B_, Perception of frequency of consulting, communicating, and cooperating with interest organizations with similar goals. Total institutions = 94; total associations = 136; total memberships = 154.**

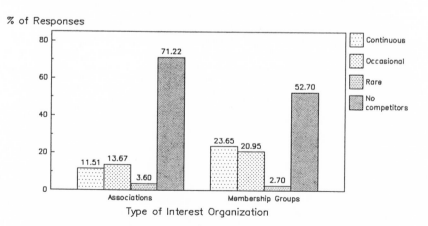

**Fig. 9.2. _C_, Perception of frequency of competition with organizations with similar goals for new members, funds, contracts, and other resources. Total associations = 139; total memberships = 148.**

among adversaries and allies, it seems unlikely that the limiting similarity threshold is being defined along the policy access/control dimension of interest organization niches.

So, where is it being defined? The answer can be found in figure 9.2C, which combines responses to two questions. First, respondents were asked, "Are there associations in your state with broadly similar purposes with whom your organization competes for new members, funds, contracts, or other resources?" (Only leaders of associations and membership groups were asked this question, as well as those used to construct figures 9.3A through 9.3D, given that these resources are generated internally for institutional interest organizations.) If they responded *yes,* they were then asked, "How frequent would you say this competition is for members, funds, contracts, or other resources?" Fully 71.22 percent (99 of 139) of the association respondents and 52.70 percent (78 of 148) of the membership group respondents indicated that they had *no* competitors for these vital resources. The minority of respondents who answered *yes* were asked to name up to five organizations with whom their association competed for new members, funds, contracts, or other resources over the previous three years. When the *no* responses were assigned a score of zero, the mean number of competitors named was 1.19 for membership groups and only 0.61 for associations.

These are shocking results given that we know from extensive evidence on density dependence and interest organization mortality that competition for such resources must be intense, so intense that many organizations cannot sustain viable realized niches. We might expect such intense competition to be more obvious to the competitors. But these results are also highly consistent with niche and competition theories. It is on these internal resource dimensions that the limiting similarity threshold is being defined. Interest organizations are responding to competition for internal resources by so partitioning them that they can each have a secure—if necessarily shrunken and perhaps nonviable— resource base. Once so partitioned, competition in any direct or overt form is unnecessary.

We can test this hypothesis even more directly by looking at the strategies competitors adopt toward one another. Respondents were presented with a set of paired statements and asked, "Which best characterizes your organization's strategy when faced with real or potential competition for influence in a policy area with other organizations with similar goals?" Similar questions were asked about competition for new members, about providing services to members (including publications, conferences, in-service training, and tours), and about financial resources (including dues, contract, grants, gifts, and sales revenue). The paired statements for each of the respective questions, presented along with a *neither* response, were as follows:

—*We work very hard to make sure that we are a major player on all issues relevant to our policy concerns; or We cooperate with our competitors by letting them take the lead on some issues, while we take the lead on others.*

—*We work very hard to make sure that we secure the membership and that our competitor does not; or We cooperate with our competitors, either directly or indirectly, to minimize competition over members. We each have our own turf.*

—*We try to provide all or most of the services provided by our competitors, with the goal of delivering better-quality services; or We try to make sure that the package of services offered our members is different from that of our competitors.*

—*We work very hard to make sure that we secure the financial resources and that our competitor does not; or We cooperate with our competitors, either directly or indirectly, to minimize competition over financial resources. We respect their turf.*

In short, the responses were designed to elicit whether an organization employs a strategy of direct conflict with competitors on the four niche dimensions or whether they respond to competition by partitioning.

We encountered some initial difficulty in analyzing these responses, because for all but the policy control resource, anywhere from half to two-thirds of the respondents answered *neither*. Given our findings in figure 9.2C, this is problematic because it might indicate either that an organization has no strategy or that it believes that it has no competitors. The magnitude of this problem became evident when we cross-tabulated responses on the strategy questions with responses on the question used to construct figure 9.2C; on all four strategy questions for both sets of interests, those indicating that their organization has no competitors were much more likely (in most cases, by a more than a two to one margin) to answer that they employed neither strategy.

Given this problem, the *neither* response was divided into two categories. Those indicating that their interest organization had no competitors were identified as having a *passive partitioning* response to competition. The resource had been so partitioned that competition was no longer recognized. Respondents who recognized that their organization has competitors but who responded *neither* to the strategy questions were identified as having no strategy. As reinterpreted, then, the first of the paired statements indicates reliance on a resource conflict strategy, while the second represents a strategy of *active partitioning*—one in which the competitor is recognized while partitioning is taking place. The minority of respondents who indicated that their organization has no competitors in answer to the question used in figure 9.2C and who still answered the strategy questions by selecting one of the paired statements were not recoded as *passive partitioners*. These are a small number of cases, but they inflate modestly the reported percentages for the active partitioning and resource conflict responses.

Distributions on these measures are presented in figures 9.3A through 9.3D. As seen in figure 9.3A, high levels of both resource conflict (42.52 percent for associations and 45.33 percent for membership groups) and active partitioning (38.58 percent for associations and 45.33 percent for membership groups) are evident in competition over policy control. When the *active* and *passive partitioning* responses are combined, they exceed the *resource conflict* response, but not by a great margin. Thus, this niche dimension exhibits both high levels of partitioning and high levels of overt conflict.

This stands in marked contrast to, and is placed into perspective by, the results presented in figures 9.3B and 9.3C for competition over members and financial resources, respectively. On both, we see very little use of the resource conflict strategy—no more than 14.0 percent in all four cases. Instead, active and passive partitioning—which account for roughly two-thirds of the responses on both questions, are the strategies of choice of both associations and membership groups. Given that niche theory leads us to expect that partitioning will be especially evident on the shared niche dimensions that define limiting similarity thresholds, these results provide strong evidence that for those organizations having members, interest organization identities—their realized niches—are established on these resource dimensions.

Our least clear findings are presented in figure 9.3D. They are less clear because the pattern of strategic response to competition for control of services to members falls somewhere between that observed for the policy control dimension, on the one hand, and the members and financial resources dimensions, on the other. For both sets of organizations, respondents were nearly equally split between the *passive partitioning* and *resource conflict* responses. While this dimension is probably less important in defining the realized niche of interest organizations than are those representing membership and financial resources, it also seems to be more important than controlling a narrow issue domain.

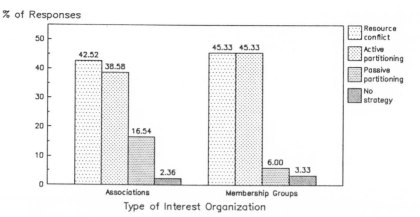

Fig. 9.3. *A*, Dominant strategy on competition for agenda control by interest organization. Total associations = 127; total memberships = 150.

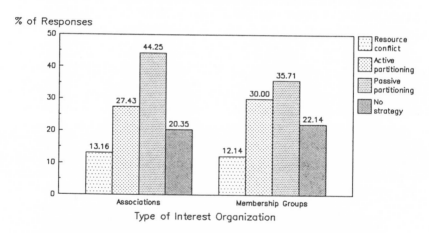

Fig. 9.3. *B*, Dominant strategy on competition for members of interest organization. Total associations = 114; total memberships = 156.

What accounts for the degree of reliance on the partitioning strategy? One hypothesis is provided by J. Q. Wilson (1973, 265) in his assertion that newer organizations must forgo the safety of partitioning to engage in resource conflict in order to establish autonomy. In contrast, population ecology's interpretation of niche theory suggests that partitioning is the first and dominant strategy in response to potential competition and that its use will be ubiquitous, irrespective of time in an organization's life cycle.

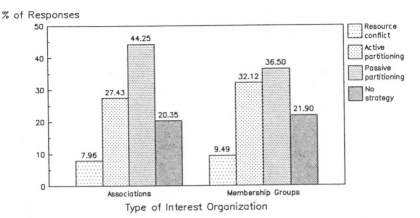

**Fig. 9.3. *C*, Dominant strategy on competition for financial resources of interest organization. Total associations = 113; total memberships = 137.**

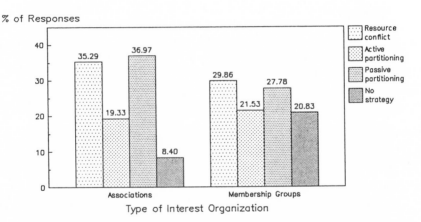

**Fig. 9.3. *D*, Dominant strategy on competition for services to members of interest organization. Total associations = 119; total memberships = 144.**

We test the first of these accounts by examining differences in the mean ages of the organizations in our sample across the competitive strategies for all four resources. These comparisons are presented in table 9.1 and provide little support for Wilson's expectations. The mean age of organizations adopting the resource conflict strategy is actually greater on all four resource dimensions for associations and on all but the policy control dimension for membership groups than the

**TABLE 9.1. Average Age of Interest Organizations by Responses to Competition for Policy Control, Members, Financial Resources, and Membership Services**

| Object of Competition | Response to Competition | Average Age in Years | |
|---|---|---|---|
| | | Associations | Membership Groups |
| Competition for Agenda Control | | | |
| | Resource Conflict | 44.65 (34.27) [n = 52] | 47.75 (30.93) [n = 56] |
| | Active Partitioning | 42.64 (29.45) [n = 48] | 44.01 (38.76) [n = 67] |
| | Passive Partitioning | 41.59 (40.30) [n = 21] | 59.79 (50.69) [n = 9] |
| | No Strategy | 48.00 (54.80) [n = 3] | 55.40 (69.30) [n = 5] |
| Competition for Members | | | |
| | Resource Conflict | 56.07 (33.40) [n = 15] | 53.24 (43.73) [n = 11] |
| | Active Partitioning | 31.05 (21.39) [n = 26] | 50.54 (35.38) [n = 41] |
| | Passive Partitioning | 40.17 (32.06) [n = 48] | 48.90 (33.03) [n = 47] |
| | No Strategy | 53.50 (31.97) [n = 18] | 34.67 (38.88) [n = 31] |
| Competition for Financial Resources | | | |
| | Resource Conflict | 48.22 (38.06) [n = 9] | 57.83 (47.04) [n = 12] |
| | Active Partitioning | 38.29 (27.44) [n = 31] | 48.73 (31.04) [n = 44] |
| | Passive Partitioning | 36.90 (29.09) [n = 49] | 48.33 (31.67) [n = 47] |
| | No Strategy | 46.89 (32.83) [n = 23] | 36.38 (43.13) [n = 30] |

**TABLE 9.1.   Continued**

Competition
  for Membership Services

| | | |
|---|---|---|
| Resource | 52.93 | 56.21 |
| Conflict | (37.32) | (38.95) |
| | [n = 41] | [n = 42] |
| Active | 35.83 | 47.10 |
| Partitioning | (23.50) | (35.26) |
| | [n = 23] | [n = 29] |
| Passive | 37.41 | 50.68 |
| Partitioning | (27.16) | (33.88) |
| | [n = 44] | [n = 38] |
| No | 45.90 | 32.83 |
| Strategy | (26.87) | (38.31) |
| | [n = 10] | [n = 30] |

*Note:* Figures in parentheses are standard deviations. Number of observations reported here differ slightly from those reported in the figures because of missing data on interest organization age. Age was calculated by subtracting the date of founding of the organization from 1994.

mean age of organizations adopting either partitioning strategy, the opposite of Wilson's expectations. This does not mean, however, that partitioning is a strategy of the young. The differences between the mean ages are not great, and only that between the resource conflict and partitioning strategies on the membership resource dimension for associations is statistically discernible. Therefore, the most appropriate interpretation is that partitioning is the strategy of choice on resource dimensions perceived to be critical to interest organization survival, and that use of this strategy is not related to life cycle, especially not in the manner suggested by Wilson.

Alternatively, we might expect reliance on the several strategies to vary with levels of interest organization population density. We saw in chapter 6 that mortality rates among membership groups and associations are associated with population density in relation to economic size as measured by GSP-BASE. Dense systems, it seems, extract a steep price for not adopting the most optimal survival strategy. This finding would lead us to expect that avoidance of resource conflict in favor of partitioning would be especially important in states with dense interest organization populations.

Evidence on this hypothesis is presented in table 9.2, which reports for both associations and membership groups the proportion of respondents opting for the resource conflict strategy on each of the four resource dimensions. Further, the states are arrayed from the most to the least dense as inversely measured by 1990 GSP-BASE. Our hypothesis

**TABLE 9.2.  Proportion, by Resource and State, of Associations and Membership Groups Opting for Resource Conflict Strategy, with States Arrayed by GSP-BASE**

| State | 1990 Density GSP-BASE | Finances | Resource Members | Policy | Services |
|-------|------------------------|----------|------------------|--------|----------|
| Associations | | | | | |
| SD | 34.26 | 0.00 | 5.26 | 57.14 | 31.58 |
| MN | 98.06 | 4.67 | 0.00 | 34.78 | 28.57 |
| MI | 156.75 | 5.88 | 5.56 | 31.58 | 31.58 |
| AR | 160.82 | 21.05 | 23.81 | 48.00 | 38.10 |
| PA | 193.13 | 13.04 | 26.09 | 48.00 | 50.00 |
| NC | 271.58 | 0.00 | 14.92 | 28.57 | 26.67 |
| Membership Groups | | | | | |
| SD | 34.26 | 4.17 | 7.69 | 42.86 | 23.08 |
| MN | 98.06 | 3.70 | 3.70 | 32.14 | 28.57 |
| MI | 156.75 | 14.29 | 19.05 | 66.67 | 43.48 |
| AR | 160.82 | 14.29 | 14.29 | 42.86 | 33.33 |
| PA | 193.13 | 16.67 | 26.32 | 52.38 | 33.33 |
| NC | 271.58 | 7.69 | 7.69 | 39.29 | 20.00 |

would lead us to expect that the proportions relying on a strategy of resource conflict should decline as we move down the columns, especially for the critical dimensions of financial resources and access to an exclusive membership pool.

Unfortunately, the evidence is tantalizingly mixed. As expected, the South Dakota and Minnesota proportions for associations and membership groups on the finance and membership resources are lower—markedly so in most cases—than those reported for Michigan, Arkansas, and Pennsylvania. North Carolina, however, does not follow the pattern. The minimal reliance of its interest organization leaders on strategies of resource conflict mirrors that of the states with the most dense interest organization populations, although its population is among the least dense of all of the states. And with data on only six states, we simply cannot know if North Carolina is an outlier or if it represents a counterfactual situation of sufficient generalizability to undermine our hypothesis. Clearly, data on many more states will be needed before we can more confidently test this hypothesis.

## Implications of Niche Analysis

Our primary goal in this chapter has been to examine the issue of interest community balkanization using population ecology's niche concept and its understanding of competition. This approach, we believe, has great promise for enabling us to address simultaneously the internal organizational maintenance and external political requirements of interest organizations in such a way that a more integrative understanding of interest representation might be developed. We have also argued that such an integrative interpretation will be required if we are to stop begging a fundamental theoretical issue—explaining why interest communities are structured as they are.

Our empirical analysis was designed to illustrate at least some of this potential by examining partitioning behavior across a set of resource dimensions bearing on both internal and external behaviors of interests. Our findings indicate that, for state interest communities as a whole, partitioning of the shared resource dimensions of members, financial resources, and, to a lesser extent, member services may be more important in defining limiting similarities than is exclusive control of a policy agenda. This suggests that interest group niches—and thus the structure of interest group communities—are more strongly determined by the internal needs of organized interests than by their patterns of interface with government. Lest this be thought a trivial conclusion, it is worth noting that it contrasts sharply with prevailing public choice models. These models often assume that officials design the jurisdictions of legislative committees so as to extract rents, and that this relationship then determines the structure of interest communities (Mueller and Murrell 1986; Coughlin, Mueller, and Murrell 1990; Mitchell and Munger 1991).

Our findings also challenge the generalizability of Browne's conclusions (1990) about the importance of strict partitioning of the policy access dimension in both defining the nature of interest group niches and accounting for policy balkanization. Indeed, the relatively high levels of policy cooperation, communication, and overt conflict we find among allies and enemies leads us to question whether policy balkanization provides an apt description of state interest communities. In this regard, our findings are far more consistent with those reported in *The Hollow Core* by Heinz and his colleagues than with those reported by Browne.

This incongruence does not mean that Browne's findings are invalid. We examined a sample of the organized interest universe in the American states, while Browne (1990) studied Washington interest groups in a well-defined policy arena. Interest group niches in the states may differ from their counterparts in Washington. Or, more likely, the agricultural domain may be unusual in its high level of balkanization (Heinz et al. 1993, 247–61). The incongruence between our and Browne's studies thus suggests that niches may vary in fundamental ways across jurisdictions, policy areas, and, perhaps, time as well, with limiting similarities being established on distinct resource sets under different conditions. If so, then explaining this variation should be a high-priority topic in any research program attentive to the niches of interest organizations.

Another, and perhaps related, form of variation meriting research concerns *niche width*—the level of specialization entailed in a niche. Encompassing interests have broad niche widths, while the niche widths of more specialized interests are narrow. Accounting for the relative abundance of these two forms of organized interests over time and across policy arenas and jurisdictions deserves attention. And an obvious starting point for such inquiries is niche research in organizational ecology (Hannan and Freeman 1989, 91–116; Hannan and Carroll 1992, 159–169; Aldrich et al. 1990), which accounts for such variation by reference to patterns of environmental stability, with more stable resource environments favoring generalist organizations.

Accounting for these two sources of variation in niche structure has important implications for the nature of interest representation. Indeed, it is possible to imagine a scenario where the variables associated with a population ecology approach enhance policy balkanization. As economies expand and populations grow, more interest organizations with relatively narrow concerns will pass the threshold requirement for organization. Presumably, many of these potential interest organizations will already comprise elements of more encompassing umbrella interest organizations. Therefore, simply passing the threshold need not generate interest fragmentation.

But if there are policy disagreements among members of more encompassing organizations, fragmentation will be more likely. Such breakups are not unknown. A North Carolina lobbyist (phone interview, 20 April 1994), for example, rapidly noted "the insurance industry breaking-up over health care, a trade association no longer able to function as an umbrella organization, [and the] example of generalist doctors and specialists no longer agreeing on [a] health care bill." A Minnesota lobbyist (phone interview, 22 September 1994) noted that breakups are especially likely when states face fiscal crises: "The fragmentation is caused by the general economy. It is easy to have an umbrella organization when there is a lot of money to go around. When dollars are tight, it is hard to generate consensus to hold the group together." Over time, then, it is not implausible to expect umbrella organizations to fragment.

Given the competitive exclusion principle, these narrower interest organizations will partition their multidimensional niche space with existing, more general interest organizations where fundamental niches overlap. With the advantages of greater specificity of representation (Heinz et al. 1993, 376) and more targeted selective incentives, this partitioning may favor the newer, narrower interest organizations. As a result, the influence of more encompassing interest organizations will at least be diluted or even depleted, creating the necessary condition for balkanization. In this scenario, balkanization is the result not of the search for viable niches per se but of conducting that search in the context of a rapidly expanding interest community under conditions governed by the competitive exclusion principle.

Absent specific conditions of uncertainty that might shift the advantage to generalist organizations in the partitioning of shared niche space (Hannan and Freeman 1989, 105–16), and absent government action to institutionalize encompassing organizations in some form of corporatist arrangement, the long-term implications of our speculative account are quite grim. As interest communities expand in size from the very tiny to the very dense, it seems quite plausible that the remorseless operation of the competitive exclusion principle might transform the system from something that Truman (1951) would recognize into something much more like that described in *The Hollow Core*. As even more time passes, and as the system becomes even more dense, the more extreme level of balkanization described by Browne (1990) for the Washington agriculture domain may even become commonplace.

An even more basic type of research must address resource dimensions. Our enumeration of the resources potentially important to niche design was drawn from prior research, none of which was intended to provide a comprehensive list of the things interest organizations need to survive and prosper. In short, our list has a necessarily ad hoc flavor. Additional research informed more explicitly by the niche concept, along with careful review of the extensive case literature on interest organizations, should generate a list of resource dimensions about which we can be more confident.

More research is needed on the questions examined in this chapter. While suggestive, our analysis was conducted at a very high level of aggregation. In ecological research, such questions are more often addressed by examining the niche structures of two, or at most a few, closely related species. Researchers tease out how the species partition overlapping fundamental niches so that either only one survives or both survive in more tightly defined realized niches. Some of this research has been experimental. Park's classic study (1948) of niche partitioning, for example, entailed observing patterns of survival over time of two species of flour beetles after placing them in glass jars filled with flour. Given the stringent oversight of modern human subject committees, it seems unlikely that we will be able to place lobbyists representing similar business interests in glass jars filled with flour, although this procedure has its attractions. Instead, such research will have to mirror MacArthur's classic field study (1958) of niche partitioning among six species of warblers, which entailed painstaking monitoring of minute differences in resource utilization.[6] Comparative case studies of related interest organizations, therefore, may be the most appropriate method for studying at least some of the theoretical issues raised by niche theory.

CHAPTER 10

# Interest Communities and Legislative Activity

Every civics textbook presents a complex figure outlining the torturous path that a bill must travel to become law. While such figures have the status of cliché, the ability to successfully process bills into law is one of the essential requirements of democratic governance. And it is not one that is to be taken for granted. When governments must be financed by continuing resolution because appropriation bills cannot be passed, we mark the event as a failure of governance. When deficits grow because legislators and executives cannot agree on strategies of remediation, we speak of gridlock. And when comprehensive and decisive action is taken, as with the Tax Reform Act of 1986, we celebrate the event as exceptional (Birnbaum and Murray 1988).

What accounts for variation in the ability of governments to introduce and enact legislation? Or, to state the issue in negative terms, what accounts for gridlock? Recently, a great deal of attention, with very mixed results, has been directed toward divided government as the cause of gridlock (Mayhew 1991; Fiorina 1992). In this chapter, we focus on another explanation. We examine how interest organization populations, especially their properties of density and diversity, influence legislative activity. While blaming interest organizations for either too much legislation or too little is not new, empirical analyses of their role are extremely rare. We address this opportunity by examining the relationship between interest organization density and diversity, on the one hand, and, on the other, legislative activity—bill introductions, enactments, and their ratio—in the American states. First, we consider a number of speculations about interest organizations and legislative activity. We then test these hypotheses with data on state legislative activity during 1990 and 1991. Along the way, we test the divided government hypothesis as well.

## Too Little or Too Much Legislation?

While there is little in the way of direct hypotheses about the impact of interest organization density and diversity on legislative activity, we have seen that the literature offers a number of implicit speculations. Some of the more pessimistic evaluations of density have been offered by economists. To Stigler (1971) and Peltzman (1976), of course, interest organizations approach government to secure regulations serving their needs, not the public interest. This implies that where there are more interest organizations, we will find more regulatory activity. Virginia School scholars have generalized this hypothesis to nearly all policy areas. To Virginians (Mueller and Murrell 1986; Coughlin, Mueller, and Murrell 1990; Shugart and Tollison 1986), the malign axis of organized interests and vote-maximizing politicians leads to almost inevitable deadweight losses to society in the form of more protectionist policies and subsidies. Nearly as pessimistic, Olson's *Rise and Decline of Nations* (1982) argues that the steady accumulation of organized interests leads to greater complexity of regulations, especially regulations that comfort the inefficient, thereby slowing economic growth. All three perspectives lead us to expect that more interest organizations will lead to more legislative activity.

Some neopluralists (Walker 1983; Heclo 1978; Heinz et al. 1993) have found—as we did in chapter 9—unexpectedly extensive conflict among interest organizations. These findings are important because they suggest that conflict occurs. If conflict occurs, then securing desired legislation may not be as easy as some scholars assume. Logrolling may still provide a detour around legislative roadblocks, but the transaction costs associated with logrolling and coalition building increase markedly as numbers of interest organizations increase (Heinz et al. 1993). As a Michigan contract lobbyist (phone interview, 26 April 1994) observed, "[Increased] competition creates a perception at least of gridlock. Almost every group has something to say on every issue. The legislature has little wiggleroom. Some group squeals about every thing they do." In such uncertain and conflict-ridden systems, more activity on the part of interest organizations may actually act to "cancel out" interest influence, which, of course, would not surprise Truman (1951).

What do these varying perspectives yield in terms of testable hypotheses? While the perspectives cover a broad array of analytic foci, and while some of their ideas about interest organizations and legislative activity are only implicit, we think that the following hypotheses are reasonable: models of interest organizations that stress their power and influence would lead us to expect that density of interest organizations is associated with greater numbers of bill introductions and enactments and a higher ratio of enactments to introductions as legislatures serve the narrow and protectionist preferences of special interests; in contrast, neopluralists would lead us to expect that greater density will reduce the number of enactments and the ratio of introductions to enactments as coalitions become unwieldy and as opponents raise barriers to bill passage.

Hypotheses about diversity are often simple extensions of analyses of density. Economists, we have seen, assuming either that policy making is balkanized or that logrolling is costless, subsume issues of diversity under considerations of density. They would expect that greater diversity of interests would increase the flow of legislation—which is always assumed to serve the needs of organized interests—only if it was associated with an increase in numbers of interest organizations. While different types of policies may be produced in more diverse interest systems, diversity, per se, would not be expected to be associated with level of activity.

Political scientists might reach quite different conclusions. Though they are silent on this issue, most political science analysts of diversity probably would assume that no fewer proposals supportive of traditional interests would be forthcoming as the interest system becomes more diverse. Traditional interests seeking benefits will still do so even in the presence of other interests. But as diversity increases, the potential for conflict over those proposals should increase. To neopluralists (Salisbury 1992, 345–46), more diversity means more conflict and, therefore, a greater potential for legislative roadblocks. As a result, fewer proposals of traditional interests should be enacted in diverse systems.

At the state level, Thomas and Hrebenar's analysis of experts' ratings of the influence of interest organizations on politics seems to support this view. In an explanation that echoes well the findings of Heinz and his colleagues (Heinz et al. 1993), Thomas and Hrebenar (1990, 138) argue that economic and social development has made interest systems more diverse, which has undermined the power of traditionally dominant business interests. This implies that we should find that the ratio of enactments to bill introductions will decline as representational diversity increases.

Would diversity also impact proposals supportive of the interests of those formerly poorly represented before legislatures? It seems reasonable to assume that such interests will be concerned about more than constructing roadblocks to the proposals of traditional economic interests. And here the issue is whether or not the proposals of the newly represented were previously on the policy agenda. If already on the agenda in all systems, then we would not expect to find more bill introductions in systems with greater diversity than in those with lesser diversity. We would, however, expect to find more of the proposals of nontraditional interests being enacted in diverse systems as the newly organized bring their influence to bear on legislative decisions. Alternatively, if mobilization of bias is sufficiently great in nondiverse systems to preclude the introduction of proposals supportive of nontraditional interests, then we should find that greater diversity is associated with increased bill introductions.

In the remainder of this chapter, we consider evidence bearing on these competing hypotheses. But before examining the data, it is worth keeping in mind Salisbury's caution (1992, 99) that politics and policy involve more than simply counting heads in a committee room or checking off names on a PAC contribution list. Thus, the null hypothesis that the population-level properties of interest communities have little impact on legislative activity is a viable alternative to the competing hypotheses we have considered until now.

### Testing the Legislative Activity Hypotheses

Data and Operationalizations

In examining the governance consequences of different configurations of interest organization populations, we focus on three measures of legislative activity: the number of bills introduced for consideration by the legislature, the number of those bills enacted, and the ratio of enacted to introduced bills. High levels of legislative activity would be indicated by high numbers for both of the first two variables. And a high ratio of enacted to introduced bills would be indicative of a high level of governance capacity in the sense of ability to process proposed legislation into law.

Measures of each of these variables are reported in *The Book of the States* for the regular sessions of state legislatures in 1990 and 1991. Our measures, therefore, exclude two types of legislative activity. First, we count only bills, not resolutions. There is substantial variation in use of resolutions by state legislatures, and they are often honorific rather than substantive in nature. Therefore, we examine bills as the core of legislative activity.[1] Second, we do not consider actions during special sessions. States vary widely in their use of special sessions and in the degree to which they restrict the focus of introductions and enactments. For the most part, however, the number of bills enacted in special sessions during 1990 and 1991 were small. The major exceptions were Texas and West Virginia, which in special sessions over these two years enacted 80 and 51 bills, respectively. Still, these numbers are small compared to the number of bills they enacted in regular session over 1990 and 1991— 4,684 and 2,941, respectively.

We focus on 1990 and 1991 to include in our sample all seven states with biennial sessions and, more importantly, to validly compare annual and biennial legislatures. Because biennial legislatures must adopt legislation in anticipation of needs that will develop in the following year, it is possible that, all other things being equal, they both introduce and enact more legislation per annual session than do annual legislatures. Still, looking at two years of legislative activity has its own potential threats to valid inference. Over two years, a biennial state may accomplish a particular purpose, such as an appropriation, with one bill, whereas annual legislatures will use two. To assess this possibility, we tested the models presented here separately with 1990 and 1991 data. The results were substantively the same as those from models using the combined 1990 and 1991 data, although modestly weaker. Still, we include a biennial-legislature dummy variable in our models to account for this effect.

Turning to the independent variables, we are interested in the impact of different configurations of interest organization populations on the pace of legislative activity. The density of interest organization populations is measured by the number of interest organizations registered to lobby state legislatures in 1990. We do not use the GSP-BASE measure of density here, because we include population in our impact models. GSP and population are so strongly correlated that it would be impossible to interpret what the GSP-BASE coefficients mean. We use two measures of diversity: the Herfindahl index of interest organization diversity across ten categories of activity, and the proportion of interests representing government and social interests. All three measures were discussed in chapter 5.

To validly assess the relationship between legislative activity and interest density and diversity, we must control for a number of other influences on the pace of legislation. In accordance with previous research (Rosenthal and Forth 1978a, 1978b), we control for differences across the states in *preferences* for legislation, *capacities* for processing bills, *opportunities* to introduce and enact legislation, and *need* for legislation.

In regard to preferences, we include several control variables. The first concerns the preferences of citizens for government activity. While legislation is in and of itself inherently neither conservative nor liberal, conservatives often sleep more easily when government does little or nothing. Liberals, favoring active government, will tend to support greater levels of legislation. If state legislatures mirror the *ideological* preferences of citizens, as Erikson, Wright, and McIver (1993) suggest they do, then we should find that states with more liberal electorates will have more active legislatures. To tap the concept of ideology, we employ Erikson, Wright, and McIver's measure (1993, 16) of state public opinion liberalism from 1976 to 1988.

We expect ideologically based preference for legislation among legislators to reflect well preferences among the public. But there is an additional dimension of preference that applies only to legislators. This, of course, is V. O. Key's hypothesis (1949) that legislatures in competitive party systems are more attentive to the have-nots of society as the out party tries to become the in party by appealing to those yet to be fully integrated into the political system. This *electorally*-based preference for legislation suggests that states with competitive parties will have more active legislatures. We measure party competition with a folded Ranney index of party competition for the period from 1981 to 1988, where high values indicate little competition.

While the Ranney index will capture the long-term implications of party competition for levels of legislative activity, contemporaneous patterns of party control might also be expected to influence introductions and enactments. We expect legislatures controlled by Republicans to consider and pass fewer bills, and we expect states with GOP governors to have less-active legislatures. Three variables, scored one for a GOP governor and GOP majorities in the upper and lower legislative chambers, were calculated for 1990 and 1991. For annual legislatures, the GOP governor, Senate, and House variables in the models are the average of their respective scores for the two years. Thus, a state with a Republican governor in both years was scored one, a state with a Democratic governor in both years was scored zero, and a state that switched from one to the other was assigned a value of 0.50.[2] For biennial legislatures, only the pattern of party control in the year in which the session was held was counted in scoring the party control variables.

States also vary in their capacities to develop and process legislation. The institutions of state government vary in terms of their "potential for effective, efficient, and responsive actions" (Bowman and Kearney 1988, 343). The most comprehensive analysis of state government capability is Bowman and Kearney's factor analysis (1988) of 32 state institutional variables from the early 1980s, which identified four dimensions of capability. We include three in our models. The first, labeled *staffing and spending,* includes measures of legislative compensation, staffing, expenditures, and session length as well as indicators of gubernatorial budget and staffing levels. The second factor addresses legislative *accountability and information management* and includes measures of legislative committee staffing patterns and use of data processing technology. Factor three, labeled *executive centralization,* includes such variables as the number of elected agency heads and the responsibilities of the lieutenant governor. We expect that all three factors will be associated with greater legislative activity.

The fourth Bowman and Kearney factor addresses representation as reflected in indicators of both the absolute size of legislatures and their size relative to the population being represented. The latter concept is measured by population in our models. And while we might think that larger legislatures might do more work, this factor produced discernible coefficients in none of our preliminary analyses. Therefore, it was excluded from the final model to preserve degrees of freedom.

We also need to control for opportunities to legislate. We have already noted that a biennial-legislature dummy variable is included in the models. Additionally, some elements of opportunity have already been tapped through the Bowman and Kearney staffing and spending measure, which includes a session length variable. But this refers only to the potential length of sessions. We should also control for the actual 1990 and 1991 session lengths used to generate counts of introductions and enactments. Therefore, we include session length as measured by number of days legislatures were in session. Since some states report only the calendar days legislatures were in session, estimates of legislative days were developed under the assumption that legislatures are typically in session only three days per week. Thus, calendar days were multiplied by 0.429 to yield estimated legislative days.[3]

Opportunities may also be influenced by a number of rules governing the pace of legislation. These include provisions for prefiling bills, rules governing the carryover of bills from a prior session and companion bills, and various deadlines for the introduction of bills. Of these, the carryover provision strikes us as potentially the most important; if bills do not have to be reintroduced, opportunities for carryover would reduce the number of new introductions in the second session of a legislature. To test the influence of these rules, we developed a dummy variable indicating whether states allowed carryover as well as a larger index counting the number of rules a legislature has that facilitate easier bill introduction. When included separately and together in the models presented in this chapter, both produced very tiny coefficients and *t*-values, while nothing else of substance changed in the estimates. As a result, neither measure is included in the models in this chapter.

In models examining bill enactment and the ratio of enactments to introductions, we also include the number of bill introductions as a control. Number of bill introductions defines opportunities for enactments.

While we believe that inclusion of this variable is appropriate to define the context in which enactments take place, excluding it from the models has no other impact than slightly decreasing the coefficient of determination. In a similar manner, we include in the introductions model a dummy variable scored one for New York and Massachusetts. Both states allow citizen introduction of bills. It is not surprising, then, that the legislatures of these two states had significantly more introductions than had any other state.

The last element of opportunity concerns the unusual case of Nebraska and its nonpartisan, unicameral legislature. Since we are by nature optimistic and charitable individuals, we scored the Nebraska legislature as held by Democrats in both years. However, coding Nebraska as held by the GOP had no substantive impact on the results. Also, a unicameral legislature may influence the pace of activity in a number of contradictory ways, which makes interpretation of the Nebraska case highly uncertain. However, since exclusion of Nebraska from the analyses presented in this chapter altered nothing in our findings, we continue to include it in our sample.

The final control variable concerns the need for legislation. Clearly, there is no objective measure of need for legislation. Still, it is plausible that, all other things being equal, bigger and more complex states will need more legislation than will smaller and simpler states. Therefore, 1990 state population is included in all three models of legislative activity.

The final variable in the model—the influence of divided government—is not a control but is designed to test a rival account for gridlock. For both 1990 and 1991, states with less than uniform party control of the governor's office and the upper and lower chambers of the legislature were assigned a value of one for split party control. The final variable for split party control is the average of the 1990 and 1991 scores for states with annual legislatures. Thus, a state fully controlled by one party in both years was assigned a value of zero, a state with divided government for both years was scored one, and a state experiencing both conditions over the two years was assigned a value of 0.50. For biennial legislatures, either the 1990 or 1991 value for split party control was used with the year matched to the legislative session year.

When each of the independent variables was regressed on the remaining independent variables, relatively high collinearity was found for three of our measures: density as measured by number of interest organizations (R-square = 0.855), population (0.873), and the staffing and spending dimension of legislative capacity (0.891).[4] Dropping either population or the Bowman and Kearney measure did not alter our results in a substantive manner. Still, we were able to generate statistically discernible estimates for the interest organization density and diversity variables even when all of the measures were included in the models. Thus, collinearity does not seem to greatly influence our results, despite the many variables in the models.

Finally, four states are excluded from our analysis. First, including Florida would severely bias the interest organization number estimates, given that state's unusual number of interests in 1990. Also, Wright, Erikson, and McIver do not report measures of opinion liberalism for Alaska, Hawaii, and Nevada, necessitating their exclusion.[5]

## Findings for Legislative Activity Models

OLS regression results for the models examining bill introductions, enactments, and ratio of enactments to introductions are presented in table 10.1. Only three of the control variables have a discernible impact ($p < 0.10$) on the number of bills introduced in state legislatures: the Bowman and Kearney staffing and spending variable, party competition, and the dummy variable for citizen introduction of bills. Further, the signs of these estimates are plausible. Bill introductions increase in states with professionalized state governments, greater party competition, and citizen introduction.

What were the effects of the interest organization variables? Neither of the diversity measures—the proportion of not-for-profit organizations and the Herfindahl index—generated discernible coefficients. Diversity does not appear to greatly influence bill introductions. Density, however, does matter. The coefficient of $-6.419$ is, we will see later in this discussion, quite large in substantive terms and is statistically significant at nearly the 0.05 level. And its negative sign indicates that, all other things being equal, states with denser interest organization populations consider less legislation.

The enactments results are presented in the second column of table 10.1. A number of the control variables influence bill enactments. As expected, enactments increase with executive centralization, party competition (which is inversely scored), and population; and they decline when Republicans control the upper chamber of legislatures. With t-values falling just below the 0.10 criterion level, the coefficient for number of legislative days indicates that longer sessions *may* increase number of enactments, while the coefficient for divided government indicates that nonuniform party control *may* depress bill passage; but the evidence that they do so is not very strong. And contrary to the fears of conservatives, states with more ideologically liberal electorates actually produce fewer enactments.

**TABLE 10.1.  Tests of Interest Organization Impact on Legislative Process**

| Independent Variable | Dependent Variable No. of Bill Introductions | No. of Bills Enacted | % of Bills Enacted |
|---|---|---|---|
| No. of interest organizations, 1990 | -6.419* (3.277) [-1.959] | -1.091** (0.443) [-2.466] | -0.043*** (0.015) [-2.815] |
| % of Not-for-profit organizations | 77.415 (120.527) [0.642] | 48.303*** (15.469) [3.123] | 1.621*** (0.530) [3.060] |
| Herfindahl index: interest diversity | -67.016 (73.745) [-0.909] | -9.767 (9.325) [-1.047] | -0.164 (0.319) [-0.512] |
| BK-staffing and spending | 1917.089* (1129.954) [1.697] | 181.146 (152.537) [1.188] | 8.036 (5.222) [1.539] |
| BK-accountability and management | 333.441 (709.978) [0.470] | 73.674 (91.752) [0.803] | 2.145 (3.141) [0.683] |
| BK-executive centralization | -124.842 (553.987) [-0.225] | 133.962* (71.347) [1.878] | 3.941 (2.443) (1.613) |
| Biennial legislature | -2384.714 (1435.220) [-1.662] | -63.287 (182.574) [-0.347] | 16.064** (6.251) [2.570] |
| EWM-opinion liberalism | 37.362 (86.905) [0.430] | -19.117* (11.221) [-1.704] | -0.846** (0.384) [-2.202] |
| Party competition | -11289.880* (5803.348) [-1.947] | 1297.950* (748.912) [1.733] | 13.252 (25.640) [0.517] |
| No. of legislative days | -18.650 (1.639) [-1.639] | 2.283 (1.442) [1.583] | 0.032 (0.049) [0.652] |
| Population 1990 | 0.307 (0.215) [1.431] | 0.074*** (0.027) [2.792] | 0.001 (0.001) [1.184] |
| Republican governor | -1066.739 (1221.380) [-0.873] | -154.271 (158.453) [-0.974] | -0.682 (5.425) [-0.126] |
| Republican Senate | 325.534 (1223.250) [0.266] | -477.983*** (157.673) [-3.031] | 1.467 (5.398) [0.272] |
| Republican House | -2201.052 (1342.093) [-1.640] | 95.650 (173.100) [0.553] | 7.700 (5.926) [1.299] |

**TABLE 10.1.  Continued**

| | | | |
|---|---|---|---|
| Split party control | -474.275<br>(1296.364)<br>[-0.366] | -262.444<br>(167.269)<br>[-1.569] | -4.744<br>(5.727)<br>[-0.828] |
| Citizen bill introduction | 18741.074***<br>(2607.422)<br>[7.188] | -- | -- |
| No. of bills introduced | -- | 0.153<br>(0.014)<br>[1.069] | -0.001**<br>(0.000)<br>[-2.239] |
| Constant | 23596.708 | -155.168 | 0.602 |
| $R^2$ | 0.847 | 0.730 | 0.687 |

*Notes:* Figures in parentheses are standard errors; figures in brackets are *t*-values.
\* = $p < .10$; \*\* = $p < .05$; \*\*\* = $p < .01$, two-tailed tests

Two of the three interest organization variables—all but the Herfindahl index—produced statistically discernible coefficients. The negative estimate (−1.091) for number of interest organizations indicates that density reduces enactments. In contrast, the positive estimate (48.303) for the proportion of organizations representing not-for-profit interests indicates that having relatively more organizations in the not-for-profit sector is associated with more enactments. Given our earlier results, having a greater proportion of not-for-profit organizations is associated not with *consideration* of more legislation but with more *passed* legislation.

The last set of results in table 10.1 employs the ratio of enactments to introductions as the dependent variable. Only two of the control variables—public opinion liberalism and the biennial-legislature dummy—are statistically significant. The negative estimate of the former again indicates that states that are more ideologically liberal have lower success rates in translating introductions into enactments, while the positive coefficient for the latter indicates that biennial legislatures have somewhat enhanced passage ratios.

And as in our previous results, both the interest organization density variable (−0.043) and the proportion of not-for-profit interest organizations' measure of diversity (1.621) produce significant estimates. The signs of the estimates are consistent with those of the enactment model. Greater interest organization density is associated with a lower batting average on legislation, while having a greater proportion of interests in the not-for-profit sector is associated with higher passage ratios.

**Interpreting the Findings**

Our results provide only the weakest support for the notion that divided government is to blame for gridlock. While the variable for split party control produced the expected negative coefficients in all three models, none of the reported *t*-values exceed the standard criteria for statistical significance. The *t*-values for the divided government coefficients in the introductions and ratio models, especially, were quite small.

Our findings indicate, in contrast, that interest organization populations influence the pace of legislative activity. But what are the magnitudes of these effects? A number of predictions based on the results in table 10.1 were used to answer this question. The value of all of the variables in the three models were set at their actual population means and were multiplied by the estimates reported in table 10.1. When summed and added to their respective constants, the resulting values constitute predictions of bill introductions, enactments, and their ratio for the average state. These predictions are presented in the second row of table 10.2. The actual mean values of the three dependent variables for the 46 states are presented in the first row.

TABLE 10.2.    **Responsiveness of Legislative Processes to Changes in Interest Organization Density and Diversity**

| Prediction Manipulations | No. of Bill Introductions | No. of Bills Enacted | % of Bills Enacted |
|---|---|---|---|
| Actual mean value for 46 states | 4193.587 | 876.022 | 30.235 |
| Predicted value for avg. state from table 10.1 eqs. | 4193.587 | 876.022 | 30.235 |
| Predicted value for avg. state with +1 std. dev. in org. no. | 2266.251 | 548.366 | 17.429 |
| Predicted value for Avg. state with -1 std. dev. in org. no. | 6120.922 | 1203.677 | 43.042 |
| Predicted value for avg. state with +1 std. dev. in % not-for-profit org. | 4613.658 | 1138.127 | 39.028 |
| Predicted value for avg. state with -1 std. dev. in % not-for-profit org. | 3773.515 | 613.916 | 21.442 |

While leaving all else the same, we then manipulated the values of number of interest organizations and the proportion of not-for-profit interests to generate additional predictions for states that were otherwise quite "average" but that had more or fewer interests or a greater or lesser proportion of not-for-profit interest organizations than the typical state. Thus, the values in the third row of table 10.2 are the predicted number of introductions and enactments and the ratio of enactments to introductions for an otherwise average state with greater-than-average density in interest organizations.

Before examining the results from our simulations, we should first ask if our manipulations are plausible? There certainly are states with similarly-sized populations but quite different sizes of interest organization populations. Georgia and Virginia, for example, are the tenth and eleventh most populous states in our sample. Yet, Georgia had 904 interest organizations in 1990, while Virginia had only 496, a difference constituting a spread of 1.359 standard deviations around the mean number of interest organizations. Minnesota and Alabama, twentieth and twenty-first in population, even exceed this difference between the sizes of their interest organization populations—by 2.215 standard deviations. There are also a number of states with similar interest organization numbers but very different proportions of not-for-profit interests. Arizona and Colorado, for example, rank fifteenth and sixteenth in number of interest organizations. But only 25.97 percent of Arizona's registered organizations represented government or social interests, while Colorado's comparable proportion was 44.27 percent, a difference representing a spread of 3.362 standard deviations around the mean proportion of not-for-profit interests, or substantially more than the manipulated spread in table 10.2. Nearly as large is the difference for Tennessee and Wyoming, with the twenty-eighth and twenty-ninth largest interest populations; the difference in this pair's proportions of not-for-profit interests represents a spread of 3.223 standard deviations around the mean proportion of not-for-profit interests. In short, the real-world differences we observe in interest organization population size and diversity among otherwise similar states are equivalent in magnitude to those underlying our simulations.

Do these differences matter? Clearly having more interest organizations matters. Instead of 4,193 introductions, only 2,266 would be expected in a state with an interest organization population larger by one standard deviation than the mean. Instead of 876 enactments, only 548 would be expected. And instead of introduced bills being passed at a rate of 30.23 percent, only 17.43 percent of bills would be

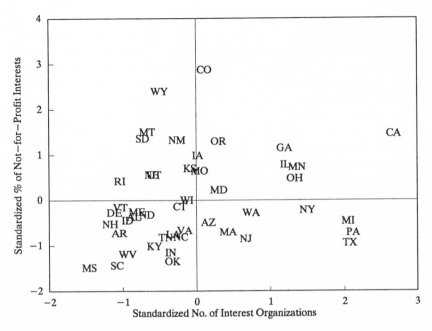

**Fig. 10.1.   State interest communities**

expected to be enacted. As seen in row 4, an otherwise average state with an interest population one standard deviation smaller than the mean should have 6,120 introductions, 1,203 enactments, and a passage rate of 43.04 percent. Predictions for similar manipulations of the proportion of not-for-profit interests are presented in the last two rows of the table, and their impact on the measures of legislative activity, with the major exception of introductions, is nearly as great as that of density. In short, legislative activity is extremely responsive cross-sectionally to the density and diversity of interest organization systems.[6]

Interest organization population density and diversity matter. Thus, we can characterize the capacity for governance among the states—insofar as it is influenced by interest organizations—by examining how states are distributed across the two interest organization population properties. Figure 10.1 reports the distribution of states by standardized scores of interest organization number and the proportion of not-for-profit interests. The capacity to legislate is greatest for those states in the upper left of the distribution. They have relatively few interest organizations—which enhances introductions, enactments, and their ratio—and a relatively large number of not-for-profit interests—which is associated with more enactments and a higher ratio of enactments to introductions. With the exception of Rhode Island, the states in this group are smaller mountain and plains states. While we are not controlling here for all of the other influences on legislative activity, these states, as expected, have the highest average ratio of enactments to introductions of any of the four groups of states considered (36.74 percent, s.d. = 15.00).

In the lower right of the figure are those states facing relative gridlock. They have both relatively more interest organizations and a lower proportion of not-for-profit interests, factors that make legislative action more difficult. With the exceptions of Arizona and Washington, these states—Massachusetts, New York, New Jersey, Michigan, Pennsylvania, and Texas—are all large industrial states. As expected, these states have the lowest average ratio of enactments to introductions (13.27 percent, s.d. = 9.035).

The remaining two quadrants face different combinations of competing forces influencing the pace of legislative activity. In the lower left of the figure are a number of New England, southern, and border states. Legislative activity is promoted in these states by their smaller-than-average interest organization populations, but it is inhibited by their lower-than-average proportion of not-for-profit interests. The opposite pattern obtains for the upper right quadrant, which contains our most heterogeneous mix of states, although all range from midsized to large in population and have diverse economies. The average enactment ratios in these two quadrants fall between those of the first two (34.51 percent, s.d. = 16.22, and 30.06 percent, s.d. = 14.56, respectively), although they are both closer to our first group than to the states we have characterized as facing relative gridlock in their legislative processes.

The cross-sectional responsiveness of legislative activity to interest organization density and diversity is impressive. But lest we get too carried away with the size of these effects, it is also worth remembering that these relationships represent only a snapshot in time. Numbers of interest organizations have been increasing markedly over the last two decades, with the average number of registered organizations increasing from 195.57 in 1975 to 587.04 in 1990 for all states, excluding the unusual case of Florida. Thus, all of the states have been moving over time to the right side of figure 10.1. At the same time, however, we saw in chapter 5 that there has been no counterbalancing trend in the proportion of not-for-profit interests represented in the states. Such organizations accounted for 28.20 percent of registrations in 1975. And while some gains were made by 1980, with the proportion increasing to 29.35 percent, they were lost over the course of the 1980s. By 1990, the 49-state average proportion was nearly back to the level of 1975—28.94 percent. With increasing density and no change in average diversity, legislating should have become progressively more difficult.

Has this development resulted in less legislation? Surprisingly, it has not. The number of enactments by the 46 legislatures and the ratio of enactments to introductions in 1975 and 1976 (863.46 and 30.22, respectively) were nearly the same as those observed for 1990 and 1991 (876.02 and 30.23, respectively). This stability suggests that the state legislatures have been adjusting across the board to the presence of greater numbers of interest organizations.

Interviews with long-term contract lobbyists in six states hint at what this adjustment entails. Nearly all of the veterans report a marked change in legislative workloads, a change that has made legislating more difficult. As one Michigan lobbyist (phone interview, 29 April 1994) put it, "There is now much more intense competition over every issue. It complicates the hell out of public policy. It is healthy for democracy, having more points of view, but it makes life difficult for the policymaker. It now takes months and years to do things instead of weeks." A North Carolina lobbyist agreed (phone interview, 20 April 1994): "legislators are getting more work to do every year. Even with more staff it is hard for them to keep up."

To produce the same amount of legislation, both legislators and interest advocates must endure more conflict, negotiation, bargaining, and gaming, and they are by all reports having to work many more hours in the legislative day. As another Michigan lobbyist (phone interview, 21 April 1994) noted, "Civility has disappeared. The legislators can't distinguish the professional from the personal. . . . They don't get along with one another any more; they don't have any fun. This spills over into the lobbyists, so that most have no enthusiasm for their jobs." While the lobbyists may view their environment as less congenial, such changes probably account for why we observe no marked change in the level of bill production.

Does this mean that the cross-sectional impact of interest organization density and diversity on legislative activity has no long-term implications? We suspect that the answer is no. There is good reason to believe that this secular accommodation of greater numbers of interest organizations is incomplete. First, we should view the stability of enactments as surprising in and of itself. Nearly all observers of state politics and policy have noted a dramatic increase in policy responsibilities and controversies during the 1980s, including battles over hazardous waste disposal, prison construction, Medicaid, abortion, and industrial policy, and all of this within the context of rapidly shifting fiscal conditions (Roeder 1994). A Minnesota lobbyist (phone interview, 23 September 1994) adds that "The intensity of activity has increased due to the legislature getting involved in so many damn issues." That number of enactments has not changed in the face of this expanding policy agenda suggests either that decisions are not being made or that their locus is being shifted to other arenas—to governors and to administrative agencies, perhaps.

There is also reason to think that the accommodation of expanding interest organization populations is only partially successful given variations across the states in changes in levels of legislative activity over time. For all 46 states, there was an average *increase* of 1.46 percent in number of enactments from 1975–76 to 1990–91. But the eight states in the upper left of figure 10.1, where density and diversity least depress legislative activity, experienced an average *increase* of 5.37 percent in enactments over the same period, from 622 to 655 enacted bills. In contrast, the eight relatively gridlocked states in the lower right of figure 10.1 experienced an average *decrease* of 12.33 percent in enactments from 1975–76 to 1990–91, from 863 to 757. These results suggest that recent expansion of interest organization populations may have diminished the ability of some state legislatures to keep pace with their expanding policy agendas.

And of course, 20 states are undergoing a radical change in their operation with the introduction of term limits. It is interesting to speculate about the impact of limited terms on the productivity of legislatures. Will legislators introduce more bills to accomplish their objectives in a shorter period of time? Will legislators, being on average less experienced, pass a smaller proportion of introduced bills? And will organized interests become the chief purveyors of ideas to amateur legislators? While none of these directions is certain, we think it quite plausible to expect legislative productivity to change in these states.

## Interest Communities and Governance

On balance, then, the density findings provide strong support for the expectations of neopluralists. Having more interest organizations makes it more difficult to enact legislation. States with dense interest organization populations have fewer enactments and a lower ratio of enactments to bill introductions. Neopluralists would account for these findings by reference to either or both the difficulty in dense systems of constructing coalitions when many players are involved and the greater number of players who can work to block legislation. Perhaps more surprising is that such states even have fewer bill introductions. It may be relatively costless for legislators to introduce legislation at the behest of an interest organization in nondense interest systems. But when there are many interest organizations, the potential for such introductions to offend someone increases. As a result, introductions may be considered more carefully in dense systems.

We have also found evidence that interest organizations are powerful consumers of legislation. A greater proportion of not-for-profit interests is associated with more enactments and higher passage rates, although not with more introductions per se. And while we cannot know for sure without evaluating the kinds of legislation that are passed in the different types of systems, it seems plausible that having greater representation by organizations in the not-for-profit sector increases the likelihood of passing legislation supportive of particular interests. Schattschneider (1960), Schlozman and Tierney (1986), and Walker (1991) were correct to worry about "bias" in interest organization populations. The balance of interests in a population matters, at least in terms of the amount of legislation that is produced by legislatures, and plausibly in terms of its content as well.

It is also clear that the impacts of these two properties of interest communities are quite independent of each other. As a result, changing patterns of density and diversity may interact to either reinforce or counteract each other. The impact on legislative activity of an increasingly dense state interest community, for example, may be minimal if most of that increasing density is comprised of interest organizations in the not-for-profit sector. Alternatively, increasing gridlock would be expected if that enhanced density resulted from a rapid expansion of the profit-sector interest community. As reported in chapter 5, however, little change has been observed in the average proportion of not-for-profit interests within state interest communities since 1975, while average density has increased markedly.

Still, we must be very cautious in characterizing our results. Our findings address only the amount of legislation processed by legislatures, not its content. We do not know if more or fewer laws mean *different* legislation, not only in substance but in significance as well. But the fact that there are very real differences in the amount of legislation processed by states with different configurations of interests suggests that studying the content of enactments should move to the front of our agenda. One strategy is to follow Mayhew (1991) by focusing on important legislation, rather than all legislation. In our case, this would entail identifying controversial policy issues of concern to all or many of the states. The ease, for example, with which states were able to make tough budget decisions during the fiscal crises of the early 1990s is a possible focus for further analysis. Two other strategies, which we pursue in the next chapter, are to examine specific policies of importance to interests and to search for more general consequences of policy on the economy and the size of government.

Finally, we return to the question of governance. Except for the extreme case of being unable to respond to a widely perceived crisis, the normative meaning of diminished legislative activity is very much in the eye of the beholder. For conservatives, gridlock may be only a libelous term used by liberals to describe prudent and efficient government. Indeed, to Stigler (1971), Peltzman (1976), Coughlin, Mueller, and Murrell (1990), Shugart and Tollison (1986), and Olson (1982), our findings on interest organization density should represent good news. They suggest that *economic* institutional sclerosis—in the form of ever-accumulating protectionist enactments and subsidies—might be checked by *political* institutional sclerosis, as more and more interest organizations strangle their collective ability to influence legislators.

Many other observers, however, will share our concern about the increasing difficulty of passing legislation in high-density, low-diversity states. If we review the recent history of the states to identify which governments "work" in the sense of making effective policy in a timely, deliberative, and responsive manner, not many would rank highly the states in the lower right quadrant of figure 10.1. While having many virtues, Massachusetts, New York, Michigan, Pennsylvania, and New Jersey share a recent reputation for conflictual policy making and a nasty style of politics. Our results suggest that part of the explanation for why this is so, though surely not the only reason, lies in their configurations of interest organizations, which act to make the journey from bill to law especially arduous.

# CHAPTER 11

## Impacts on the Economy, Policy, and Politics

Running throughout our analysis of interest organization populations have been a number of speculations by economists and political scientists about the impacts of density and diversity on economics and politics. Our finding in chapter 10 that the pace of legislative activity varies with the density and diversity of interest organization populations brings these issues to the fore. Given that legislatures confronting different configurations of interest organizations legislate at different rates, we must be concerned about whether this in turn generates different types of legislation with attendant economic and political consequences. Evidence about such differences inevitably will weigh heavily on our final assessment of the role of organized interests in society.

Given the breadth of this topic, our review cannot be comprehensive. Rather, we examine what seem to us to be the four most widely discussed claims about interest organization impact, all of which have been reviewed in the course of our analysis. The first is Olson's claim (1982) that the presence of a large number of organized interests slows economic growth. The second is the Virginia School (Mueller and Murrell 1986; Coughlin, Mueller, and Murrell 1990) and public choice (Bush and Denzau 1977) hypothesis that expanding interest communities underpin or are underpinned by an expanding public sector. The third is the hypothesis of Stigler (1971), Peltzman (1976), and Bush and Denzau (1977) that larger interest populations lead inevitably to the adoption of ever more policies designed to either shield those interests from competition and/or provide them subsidies. And finally, we examine the Morehouse (1981) and Thomas and Hrebenar (1990, 1995) typologies of interest organization power to determine if more, and more diverse, interest organizations are associated with greater or lesser political power.

Before beginning, however, we must note that the specifications we present in this chapter are driven not by population ecology but by the impact theories we are testing. Indeed, a number of the specifications do not make a great deal of sense given our tests of the ESA model in chapter 7. Still, we try to assess the impact hypotheses on their own terms. After considering what they have to tell us, we reconsider their specifications from a population ecology framework. Switching to a population ecology perspective, we will see, will help clarify a number of puzzling findings.

### Interest Organizations and Economic Growth

While we credit the economic growth hypothesis to Olson (1982), the ideas that underlie it run throughout economic analyses of interest organizations. Stigler (1971) and Peltzman (1976) were concerned about narrow protectionist regulations because they inhibit market competition, thereby diminishing economic growth. Similarly, the Virginians and other public choice scholars are so exercised about government growth because they view it as detracting from the share of economic resources devoted to the private sector, which they assume to be the engine of economic growth. Thus, Olson's hypothesis is common to economists' thinking about the impact of interest organizations.

### The Economic Growth Models

Unlike legislation, which starts from a number of zero when a new legislature convenes, the size of the economy does not start from a new base each year. Therefore, we need to examine change over some period. We examine change in the size of the economy as percentage change in GSP from 1977 to 1989 and from 1982 to 1989. The latter period, we will see, more closely matches the time periods for our independent variables. However, 1982 was a year of severe recession. And since we are using GSP measures, focusing exclusively on the 1982 to 1990 period may bias our results by setting 1982 values at artificially low levels for states that suffered the most in the Reagan recession.

Change in total GSP over the two periods constitutes the primary dependent measure in our tests of the economic growth hypothesis because it matches closely Olson's focus (1982) on the total size of the economy. However, we also examine a slightly different version of the GSP indicator as well. Change in total GSP could be influenced by changes in the state and local government component of GSP. This could be a serious problem if such changes are large, given that the underlying, if implicit, premise of the Olson hypothesis is that government actions depress growth in the private sector. Therefore, we also examine changes in GSP *excluding state and local government GSP* for the 1977–89 and 1982–89 periods to control for this potential threat to inference.

Turning to the independent variables, we are most interested in the influence of the interest organization population properties of density and diversity. Unlike in our analyses in chapter 10, we are able to employ two measures of density here, because population is not included in the models. Thus, both number of interest organizations and GSP-BASE are used, both of which were described in chapter 5. As in chapter 10, both the Herfindahl index and the proportion of not-for-profit interest organization measures of diversity are employed as well. But since we are examining change over an extended period, 1990 measures are not used. Rather, we look at the average of 1980 and 1990 values of all four interest organization variables, which should better reflect the actual levels of the interest organization population properties over the decade.

We also include in the model a number of the control variables included in our analyses of legislative activity. Again, because population is not in the model, we are able to include all four of the Bowman and Kearney (1988) measures of government capability, as well as the Erikson, Wright, and McIver (1993) measure of opinion liberalism and the Ranney index of party competition. All are expected to be associated with more active government, which critics of the public sector suggest should be associated with diminished economic growth.

Finally, we include measures of per capita GSP and of the share of GSP devoted to state and local government for either 1977 or 1982, whichever year is appropriate given the dependent variable. The per capita GSP measure is included to control for initial levels of economic development given Brace's observation (1993) that much of the variation in economic growth rates in the last two decades has been a function of less-developed economies catching up with more developed economies. State and local share of GSP is included to control for the initial size of the government sector and to capture the argument of public choice scholars that public spending is a drag on economic growth.

Because the interest organization variables were generated using both 1980 and 1990 data, and because we again employ Erikson, Wright, and McIver's opinion liberalism measure, a number of states are not included in these tests: Florida, Nevada, Alaska, Rhode Island, Hawaii, Alabama, and West Virginia. When regressed on each other, only one of the variables produced an exceptionally high R-square value—the Bowman and Kearney staffing and spending indicator (0.846). However, we were still able to generate discernible estimates for this variable. Therefore, it seems unlikely that collinearity is influencing our findings.[1]

**TABLE 11.1.  Tests of Interest Organization Impact on Economic Growth**

| Independent Variable | Dependent Variable | | | |
|---|---|---|---|---|
| | % Change in GSP | | % Change in Non-S&L GSP | |
| | 1977-89 | 1982-89 | 1977-89 | 1982-89 |
| No. of interest organizations | 0.144*** (0.453) [3.401] | 0.062** (0.024) [2.561] | 0.147*** (0.044) [3.377] | 0.063** (0.025) [2.544] |
| GSP-BASE measure of density | 0.141 (0.087) [1.616] | 0.083 (0.050) [1.672] | 0.142 (0.089) [1.592] | 0.082 (0.051) [1.601] |
| % of Not-for-profit organizations | -2.190 (1.435) [-1.527] | -0.791 (0.770) [-1.027] | -2.228 (1.466) [-1.520] | -0.829 (0.791) [-1.048] |
| Herfindahl index: interest diversity | 0.139 (0.828) [0.168] | 0.147 (0.481) [0.306] | 0.139 (0.846) [0.165] | 0.131 (0.494) [0.265] |
| BK-staffing and spending | -37.150*** (11.103) [-3.346] | -15.516** (6.423) [-2.416] | -37.503*** (11.344) [-3.306] | -15.534** (6.597) [-2.355] |
| BK-accountability and management | -28.076*** (8.402) [-3.342] | -13.022*** (4.659) [-2.962] | -28.718*** (8.584) [-3.345] | -13.884*** (4.786) [-2.901] |
| BK-executive centralization | 15.672*** (5.780) [2.711] | 8.218** (3.287) [2.500] | 16.442*** (5.906) [3.287] | 8.647** (3.376) [2.561] |
| BK-representation | 17.283*** (4.879) [3.542] | 6.934** (3.001) [2.304] | 18.346*** (4.985) [3.010] | 7.027** (3.092) [2.273] |
| EWM-opinion liberalism | 1.711 (1.072) [1.596] | 1.633*** (0.604) [2.704] | 1.879* (1.095) [1.716] | 1.689*** (0.620) [2.723] |
| Party competition | 88.700 (59.553) [1.489] | 19.618 (33.683) [0.582] | 91.858 (60.848) [1.510] | 20.636 (34.598) [0.596] |
| % of S&L gov't GSP, 1977 | 15.775*** (5.771) [2.734] | -- | 16.165*** (5.896) [3.187] | -- |
| Per capita GSP, 1977 | -4.541 (4.689) (-0.968) | -- | -5.203 (4.791) [1.108] | -- |
| % of S&L gov't GSP, 1982 | -- | 5.114 (3.187) (1.605) | -- | 5.445 (3.273) [1.664] |

**TABLE 11.1. Continued**

| | | | | |
|---|---|---|---|---|
| Per capita<br>GSP, 1982 | -- | -4.673***<br>(1.108)<br>[-4.217] | -- | -4.865***<br>(1.138)<br>[-4.275] |
| Constant | -0.466 | 58.322 | 2.959 | 61.378 |
| $R^2$ | 0.689 | 0.760 | 0.701 | 0.763 |

*Notes:* Figures in parentheses are standard errors; figures in brackets are *t*-values.
* = $p < .10$; ** = $p < .05$; *** = $p < .01$, two-tailed tests

### Findings for Economic Growth

Results for the economic growth models are presented in table 11.1, with the total GSP models for the 1977–89 and 1982–89 periods presented in the first two columns. Starting with the controls, we have a number of surprising findings. Contrary to the expectations of public choice scholars, the size of state and local governments in 1977 and 1982 has a positive effect on economic growth over the periods spanned by the respective models. The estimate in the 1977 model is significant at the 0.01 level, while the 1982 model coefficient falls just below the 0.10 criterion level. Similarly, the opinion liberalism coefficients, the t-values of which also fall just below the 0.10 criterion level in one model while being highly significant in the other, are positive, indicating that liberal electorates are associated with faster economic growth. And all of the Bowman and Kearney capability estimates are significant in both models, although their signs are mixed. Greater professionalism in the legislature and the governor's office are associated with less growth, while a more centralized executive branch and a more representative legislature are associated with more robust growth. Finally, the negative per capita GSP coefficients support Brace's catch-up hypotheses, although only the estimate in the 1982–89 model is discernibly different from zero.

Our primary interest, however, lies in the interest organization variables. Neither of the diversity measures produced significant coefficients, although their signs are consistent. The negative signs of the proportion of not-for-profit interest estimates indicate that relatively more not-for-profit interests depress growth, while the positive signs for the inversely coded Herfindahl index suggest that greater diversity across economic sectors has a similar effect. Still, neither impact is strong. In contrast, density—as measured by number of interest organizations—produced significant coefficients that contradict Olson's hypothesis (1982). Having more interest organizations is associated with more rapid economic growth. This is somewhat balanced by the GSP-BASE coefficients, however, the *t*-values of which fall just below the 0.10 criterion level. Given the inverse coding of GSP-BASE, they indicate that, all other things being equal, greater density of interest organizations relative to the size of the economy may depress economic growth.

Given these conflicting signs, we need to assess the net impact of interest organization density on economic growth. We do so by comparing the relative responsiveness of GSP growth to manipulations of the two variables. We set the variables at their observed means and multiplied through by the estimates in the second column of table 11.1 to produce a predicted economic growth rate for the 1982–89 period for the average state. This prediction was the same as the observed average for the states—61.86 percent. We then manipulated the value of number of interest organizations, either by itself or in the GSP-BASE measure of which it is a component (while leaving the GSP numerator of GSP-BASE at the observed average) by plus and minus one standard deviation of the actual mean. The difference between the simulations employing plus one and minus one standard deviation manipulations of interest organization number was 27.58 percentage points, a large difference in expected growth rates. But a large portion of this predicted expansion of the economy is canceled by the impact of GSP-BASE. When the number component of GSP-BASE was manipulated plus and minus one standard deviation, the difference between the simulations was 21.58 percentage points. Thus, the predicted net difference in economic growth rates of two states that were otherwise typical but, respectively, had larger-than-average and smaller-than-average interest organization populations is only 5.72 percentage points over seven years.

Alternatively, we reestimated the model by dropping GSP-BASE to see if its exclusion altered the estimate for number of interest organizations. Results virtually identical to those presented in the second column of table 11.1 were produced. The coefficient of interest organization number was nearly the same (0.061 instead of 0.062) and had a significant t-value of 2.468, while the R-square value (0.736) declined only slightly. This suggests that the positive impact of interest organization number on growth of the economy is indeed substantial and largely independent of the GSP-BASE effect.

How are we to choose between these two assessments? Staying within the theoretical orientation implicit in this specification, we think that the most appropriate interpretation is that density as number of organized interests has a large positive impact on economic growth. That the estimate for number of interest organizations changed hardly at all when GSP-BASE was dropped from the model suggests strongly that

GSP-BASE is tapping something other than the density of interest organizations. Otherwise, the coefficient for number of organized interests should have changed to reflect the exclusion of GSP-BASE. What might GSP-BASE have been tapping if not interest organization density? We saw in chapter 5 that GSP-BASE is closely related to GSP, with GSP-BASE increasing as economies decrease in size. If, therefore, there were differences in the economic growth rates of small and large states, then the GSP-BASE coefficients in table 11.1 could be reflecting these differences. And smaller states did experience slower growth over the 1982–89 period. The GSP of the 15 smallest states—many of them mountain and plains states—expanded an average of 52.74 percent over the period, while the economies of the 15 largest states grew an average of 74.03 percent. Therefore, as long as we remain within the theoretical framework used to justify this specification, a case can be made that economic growth is strongly influenced in a positive manner by interest organization density as reflected in the interest organization number estimate.

This finding is not a function of looking at total GSP, which includes GSP associated with state and local government. The results in the third and fourth columns of table 11.1 were generated by the same models used to produce the estimates in the first two columns of the table, except that total GSP *excluding state and local government GSP* is now employed as our dependent variable. A simple comparison across the columns indicates that the results are virtually identical. Indeed, the coefficients of determination and the magnitudes of the number of interest organization coefficients are slightly larger, which indicates that the results for total economic growth were not being masked by changes occurring solely within the public sector. Having a greater number of interest organizations is associated with economic growth in the *private sector,* a result that again contradicts Olson's hypothesis.

This does not mean that Olson (1982) was entirely wrong. His core argument was that government actions that protect the inefficient can slow economic growth. He also assumed, however, that interest organization density would be associated with such actions, that protectionist policies would accumulate as organized interests accumulate. And it is this second part of Olson's argument that may have been mistaken. As we saw in our earlier analysis of bill introductions and enactments, larger populations of interest organizations are actually associated with lower rates of legislative activity, an outcome neopluralists would interpret as a function of interests checking interests. Accordingly, greater interest density might inhibit adoptions of the kinds of policies that Olson argues act to restrain economic growth. Thus, with this rather major switch in assumptions, and pending our finding evidence that less legislation means less *protectionist* legislation, our economic growth results could still be consistent with at least the central part of Olson's argument.

But there is another explanation for our findings that may be even more plausible. The specification underlying these results makes little sense from a population ecology perspective. Our specification assumes that the direction of causality runs from number of interest organizations to economic growth. The ESA models presented in chapter 5, in contrast, used GSP as a surrogate indicator of the space needed for interest organizations to survive. It suggests, then, that the causal arrow runs from size of economy to number of interests. When economies expand, the ESA model would lead us to expect that interest populations will too.

**Interest Organizations and Government Growth**

Our second hypothesis about the impact of different configurations of interest organizations—the Virginia School and public choice hypothesis that interest organization density is related to the size of the public sector—also has an established pedigree within economics. Actually, we have seen that strong versions of the Virginia School model (Mueller and Murrell 1986; Coughlin, Mueller, and Murrell 1990) suggest that the direction of causality actually runs from government size to interest organizations, the form of the hypothesis we considered in chapter 7. But other public choice scholars have suggested the opposite (Bush and Denzau 1977), and many conservative critics of big government seem to have little difficulty switch-hitting in causal direction as the needs of the immediate argument require.

The Government Growth Models

The government growth hypothesis, like the economic growth hypothesis, is about rates of change. Therefore, similar to our analysis of economic growth, we measure change in the size of government as percentage change in state and local government GSP from 1977 to 1989 and from 1982 to 1989. We examine state and local GSP to control for differing levels of fiscal centralization and because local governments are highly constrained by decisions made by state governments. Public choice scholars are concerned about growing government spending, but they are especially attentive to expansion of the public sector's *share* of the economic pie (Berry and Lowery 1987). Therefore, we examine two additional measures as well: change in the state and local government *proportion* of GSP for both the 1977–89 and 1982–89 periods.

The independent variables in the models are the same as those used in the economic growth models, including both measures of interest organization density and both measures of diversity. The control variables, for the most part, have similar interpretations. The government and political variables are again expected to be associated with levels of government activity, which might be related to the size of government. Two of the control variables, however, have somewhat different interpretations in the government growth models. State and local share of GSP for either 1977 or 1982, whichever year is appropriate, are included in the models to control for initial differences in the sizes of government. Smaller governments may have more room for expansion within the domain of programs and policies generally viewed as appropriate for state and local governments than do governments that are already engaged in a wide range of activities. And the per capita GSP measures for either 1977 or 1982 are included in the government growth models to account for the traditional observation that government is a luxury good, the demand for which expands as societies become more wealthy (Berry and Lowery 1987).[2]

### Findings for Growth of Government

Tests of the government growth models with percentage change in state and local GSP are presented in the first two columns of table 11.2. The results are easily summarized in that they are very similar to those presented in table 11.1. With the exception of the per capita GSP measure in the 1977–89 results in column one, all of the coefficients in the first two columns of table 11.2 mirror those reported in table 11.1. The one exception was not discernibly different from zero. This means that the variables influencing growth of the private economy similarly influence the public sector.

This common pattern of impact is especially evident for the estimates of the interest organization variables. Again, none of the diversity estimates are significant, and their signs indicate that the two dimensions of diversity have contradictory effects on growth of the public sector. Density, however, does matter. And again, the interest organization number estimate is significant in both models. In this case, GSP-BASE (number relative to the size of the economy) produced a significant coefficient in only the 1982–89 equation.

Perhaps the most striking thing to note about the results is that the

**TABLE 11.2. Tests of Interest Organization Impact on Size of Government**

| Independent Variable | % Change in S&L GSP 1977-89 | % Change in S&L GSP 1982-89 | % Change in S&L Gov't GSP Share 1977-89 | % Change in S&L Gov't GSP Share 1982-89 |
|---|---|---|---|---|
| No. of interest organizations | 0.125*** (0.041) [3.030] | 0.054** (0.021) [2.563] | -0.007 (0.010) [-0.708] | -0.001 (0.009) [-0.552] |
| GSP-BASE measure of density | 0.134 (0.084) [1.590] | 0.095** (0.043) [2.196] | 0.004 (0.021) [0.197] | 0.005 (0.019) [0.255] |
| % of Not-for-profit organizations | -1.826 (1.390) [-1.314] | -0.551 (0.669) [-0.824] | 0.141 (0.353) [0.401] | 0.044 (0.290) [0.153] |
| Herfindahl index: interest diversity | 0.073 (0.802) [0.091] | 0.271 (0.418) [0.647] | 0.030 (0.203) [0.147] | 147.854 (180.910) [0.817] |
| BK-staffing and spending | -34.613*** (10.754) [-3.219] | -16.223*** (5.580) [-2.907] | -0.124 (2.733) [-0.045] | -0.890 (2.415) [-0.368] |
| BK-accountability and management | -21.184** (8.138) [-2.603] | -12.898*** (4.048) [-3.186] | 2.307 (2.068) [1.115] | -0.030 (1.752) [-0.017] |
| BK-executive centralization | 7.480 (5.598) [1.336] | 3.687 (2.856) [1.291] | -2.333 (1.423) [-1.639] | -2.223* (1.236) [-1.799] |
| BK-representation | 6.445 (4.726) [1.364] | 5.900** (2.615) [2.256] | -2.572** (1.201) [-2.141] | -0.232 (1.132) [-0.205] |
| EWM-opinion liberalism | -0.086 (1.038) [-0.082] | 0.975* (0.525) [1.858] | -0.720*** (0.264) [2.729] | -0.548** (0.227) [-2.411] |
| Party competition | 60.421 (57.684) [1.047] | 13.025 (29.265) [0.445] | -6.801 (14.660) [-0.464] | 1.109 (12.665) [0.088] |
| % of S&L gov't GSP, 1977 | 10.516* (5.590) [1.881] | -- | -2.002 (1.421) [-1.410] | -- |
| Per capita GSP, 1977 | 3.968 (4.542) (-0.968) | -- | 3.791*** (1.154) [3.284] | -- |
| % of S&L gov't GSP, 1982 | -- | 1.908 (2.769) (0.689) | -- | -1.571 (1.198) [-1.311] |

**TABLE 11.2  Continued**

| | | | | |
|---|---|---|---|---|
| Per capita GSP, 1989 | -- | -1.685* (0.963) [-1.750] | -- | 3.228*** (0.417) [7.748] |
| Constant | -34.924 | 16.863 | -28.184 | -56.837 |
| $R^2$ | 0.433 | 0.573 | 0.687 | 0.834 |

*Notes:* Figures in parentheses are standard errors; figures in brackets are *t*-values.
* = $p < .10$; ** = $p < .05$; *** = $p < .01$, two-tailed tests

estimates of the density variables are very similar in magnitude to those reported for the total GSP and private-sector GSP models. The number of organized interests estimate in the second column of table 11.2 is slightly smaller than its counterpart in column two of table 11.1. Conversely, the GSP-BASE coefficient in the second column of table 11.2 is slightly larger than its counterpart in table 11.1. Given that their signs (remembering that high values of GSP-BASE indicate low density) suggest that the two dimensions of density have contradictory impacts on the growth of government, we again need to assess the relative magnitudes of their impacts on government growth.

As we did for the economic growth models, we first set the variables at their means and multiplied through by the estimates in the second column of table 11.2 to produce a predicted public-sector growth rate for the 1982 to 1989 period for an average state. We then manipulated the value of number of interest organizations, both by itself and in the GSP-BASE measure of which it is component—while leaving the GSP numerator at the observed average—by plus and minus one standard deviation of the actual mean. The difference between the simulations employing plus one and minus one standard deviation manipulations of interest organization number was 24.05 percentage points, a large difference in expected growth rates. But this was more than canceled by the GSP-BASE effect. The difference between the simulations employing plus one and minus one standard deviation manipulations of organization number component of GSP-BASE was 24.95 percentage points. Thus, the net difference in growth rates between two states that were otherwise typical but, respectively, had larger-than-average and smaller-than-average interest organization populations is 0.90 percentage points over seven years, with the state with the larger interest organization population having the smaller, albeit very similar, growth rate.

Alternatively, we reestimated the model by excluding GSP-BASE to see if its exclusion altered the estimate for number of interest organizations. Results virtually identical to those presented in the second column of table 11.2 were produced. The coefficient of interest organization number was nearly the same (0.053 instead of 0.054) and it produced a significant t-value of 2.389, while the R-square value (0.502) declined only slightly. This suggests that the positive impact of interest organization number on growth of the public sector was indeed substantial. And there is again reason to believe that this latter interpretation is to be preferred given the possibility that GSP-BASE is again picking up differences in the rates of government growth between large and small states. Over the 1982–89 period, the 15 largest states experienced an average expansion of public-sector spending of 68.57 percent, while public-sector spending in the 15 smallest states increased only 56.15 percent.

Again, though, we might reject the entire logic of specification underlying this model, opting instead for the ESA interpretation of causality as running from government GSP to numbers of organized interests. Expanding government GSP, just like expanding private-sector GSP, is a broad surrogate both for the space term of the ESA model for interests oriented toward the public sector and for the constituent interest term of the model for many private- and public-sector interests. When government expands, then, we might expect numbers of interests to increase. Indeed, we believe that this should be the preferred interpretation.[3]

The last two columns in table 11.2 address government's share of GSP. And given that numbers of organized interests influence the growth of public and private sectors in the same manner, their impact on the share of GSP devoted to the state and local sector should be predictable. But first, we should consider the results for the control variables in the GSP share models. Our clearest finding is that greater wealth, as measured by per capita GSP, is associated with a growing government share of GSP. Contrary to expectations, states with liberal electorates actually experienced a decline in their state and local public sectors relative to the size of their economies. While one of the Bowman and Kearney variables generated a significant estimate in one or the other of the two GSP share models, none of the other controls produced consistent findings of any substance.

More importantly, none of the interest organization coefficients generated t-values greater than one. The coefficients of the two density measures indicate that greater interest representation enhances the growth of government relative to the economy as a whole, while the signs of the two diversity measures indicate that the two dimensions of diversity have contradictory associations with change in the size of the public sector. But the estimates are so weak that it is difficult to place any weight on interpretation of their signs.

As noted earlier, greater density does lead to an expansion of the public sector in absolute terms. Those opposed to any expansion of the public sector will not be comforted by this finding. But because number of interests is positively associated with an expansion of the economic pie, growth in the absolute size of government is not associated with an expansion of the public sector's share of economic activity. Thus, our results should assuage the fears of public choice critics of organized interests to the extent that they are concerned about the *relative size* of government.

The null results for the diversity measures in all of the government growth models also deserve special note. We saw in chapter 10 that having a greater proportion of government and social interest organizations is associated with higher rates of legislative enactments and higher bill passage ratios. We might expect that this would entail passage of a greater number of bills supportive of the interests of government and social groups, bills that might entail an expansion of the public sector. That we do not find such expansion associated with variation in proportions of interests representing not-for-profit organizations suggests that greater legislative activity does not necessarily mean a different kind of activity.

### Interest Organizations and Public Policy

While we have spent a considerable amount of time considering the impact of interest organization density and diversity on economic growth and expansion of the public sector, the former variables do not act directly on the latter. Instead, many economists assume that density and diversity are associated with adoption of protectionist policies and subsidies, the effects of which are reflected in patterns of economic growth and government size. It is important, then, that we consider these more direct consequences of the properties of interest organization populations.

It is also important that we do so given our alternative explanation for the results presented in tables 11.1 and 11.2. This is the population ecology perspective, which suggests that the specifications of the models presented in tables 11.1 and 11.2 are flawed in reversing the actual causal path running between numbers of organized interests and the sizes of the public and private sectors. A failure to find evidence that having more interest organizations leads to different kinds of policies, especially policies that inhibit economic growth, will indirectly support our alternative account.

## The Policy Models

We consider four types of government protectionist policies and subsidies. The first is occupational regulation. Following Stigler (1971) and Peltzman (1976), we should find that greater density, and perhaps greater diversity of interests, is associated with greater reliance on regulations designed to shelter interests from the pressures of competitive markets. This argument has been made forcefully by critics of state occupational regulations (Rottenberg 1980; Friedman 1962), who view such regulations as constraints on market competition that are adopted at the behest of the regulated (Meier and Garman 1995, 61–63). We measure the level of occupational regulation by the number of 61 occupations that were regulated by the states in 1990 as reported by the *Book of the States*. This variable ranges from Missouri's regulation of only 13 occupations to Oregon's regulation of 39. Unlike our previous analyses, we do not measure change in occupational regulations given the lack of common categories of occupations in tallies of regulatory activity from one year to the next. However, we include in the model the number of 64 occupations regulated by states in 1980 as a control, given the incremental nature of change in occupational regulation. Although the two lists are not sufficiently similar to construct a valid change score, we expect states with a proclivity to regulate will rank high on both lists.

The second protectionist policy is use of earmarked taxes. While some public choice scholars have recently tried to rehabilitate the reputation of earmarked taxes by relabeling them user fees, they are traditionally viewed as a mechanism by which preferenced programs are excused from the uncertainties of budgetary competition. As Fisher (1987) has noted, "If earmarking makes it more difficult, either procedurally or politically, to reduce expenditures in an area, then there is more certainty for providers and recipients in that area." Because tax policies are strongly incremental (Hansen 1983; Lowery 1987), we employ percentage change in the proportion of taxes that are earmarked from 1979 to 1988 as our dependent variable. We also include the 1979 proportion of earmarked taxes as a control, expecting that states making less use of earmarking than do their neighbors have more opportunity to expand its use.

The remaining policy areas are spending subsidies provided to two specific interests: AFDC benefits for the poor and state and local government contracts for construction. These, of course, are two of the six interest guilds that we examined in chapter 7. Indeed, our models here are simply more complex specifications of the reverse causality tests reported for these two interest guilds in that chapter. Our hypothesis is that interest density in the respective guilds is associated with level of subsidy. For welfare recipients, the dependent variable is the percentage of change in the average AFDC benefit level from 1980 to 1989. We include in the model the 1980 AFDC benefit level, given that states with lower benefits levels have more opportunity politically to expand welfare spending. For construction interests, the dependent variable is change in the proportion of state and local government spending on construction from 1977 to 1989. We focus on change in the proportion rather than change in spending per se to assess how construction interests fare relative to other interests in the competitive budgetary process. We also include the 1977 proportion as a control, for the same reason used to justify inclusion of the 1980 AFDC benefit level in the welfare subsidy model.

The four interest organization variables employed in the economic and public-sector growth models are included in the occupational regulation and earmarked tax models since the two policy mechanisms are attractive to a broad number of interests. In the welfare and construction spending models, however, we measure density only with numbers of welfare and construction interest organizations, respectively. Thus, the interest organization number measures are the average of 1975 and 1990 numbers of welfare and construction interest organizations, respectively. And the GSP-BASE measures of organized interest density relative to the size of the economy are the average of 1977 and 1989 GSP figures divided by the average number of welfare or construction interest organizations. The general population diversity measures are still included in the welfare and construction models. We expect greater diversity—especially as measured by the proportion of not-for-profit interests—to be associated with more rapid expansion of AFDC benefits and less growth in construction spending.

The remaining independent variables are the opinion liberalism, party competition, and government capability measures used in our earlier tests. Higher levels of party competition and liberalism should be associated with greater attention to consumer interests, hence with more extensive occupational regulation (Meier and Garman 1995, 63). Following V. O. Key's hypothesis (1949) about the role of competitive parties, we expect competitive states to have faster rates of AFDC benefit growth. More liberal electorates should also be associated with more rapid expansion of benefit levels. Since levels of earmarking and construction spending are often credited to the power of special interests, we expect that they will be negatively associated with liberalism and party competition. Our weakest expectations are for the capability

**TABLE 11.3. Tests of Interest Organization Impact on Policies**

| Independent Variable | % of Regulated Occupations | % Change in Earmarked Taxes 1979-88 | % Change in AFDC Benefit 1980-89 | % Change in S&L Construc. Expend. 1977-89 |
|---|---|---|---|---|
| No. of interest organizations | 0.014<br>(0.664)<br>[0.021] | -0.007<br>(0.014)<br>[-0.481] | 0.097[a]<br>(0.296)<br>[0.328] | 0.157[b]<br>(0.257)<br>[0.611] |
| GSP-BASE measure of density | -0.898<br>(1.232)<br>[-0.729] | -0.004<br>(0.025)<br>[-0.150] | 0.002**<br>(0.001)<br>[2.096] | 0.005*<br>(0.003)<br>[1.868] |
| % of Not-for-profit organizations | -0.227<br>(0.196)<br>[-1.158] | -0.001<br>(0.004)<br>[-0.265] | -0.102<br>(0.722)<br>[-0.014] | 0.815<br>(0.927)<br>[0.879] |
| Herfindahl index: interest diversity | -153.977<br>(127.105)<br>[-1.211] | 0.199<br>(2.679)<br>[0.074] | 0.035<br>(0.442)<br>[0.080] | 0.480<br>(0.593)<br>[0.810] |
| BK-staffing and spending | 1.000<br>(1.644)<br>[0.608] | -0.004<br>(0.034)<br>[-0.122] | 1.670<br>(3.390)<br>[0.493] | -11.890**<br>(5.993)<br>[-1.980] |
| BK-accountability and management | 0.661<br>(1.281)<br>[0.516] | -0.022<br>(0.024)<br>[-0.902] | 1.106<br>(3.953)<br>[0.280] | -8.807<br>(5.247)<br>[-1.678] |
| BK-executive centralization | 0.196<br>(0.901)<br>[0.218] | -0.009<br>(0.019)<br>[-0.483] | 0.396<br>(3.207)<br>[0.123] | -4.844<br>(4.434)<br>[-1.093] |
| BK-representation | 0.222<br>(0.770)<br>[0.288] | -0.016<br>(0.015)<br>[-1.054] | 7.374**<br>(2.798)<br>[2.636] | -2.821<br>(3.420)<br>[-0.825] |
| EWM-opinion liberalism | 0.214<br>(0.156)<br>[1.373] | 0.007*<br>(0.004)<br>[1.932] | 1.474**<br>(0.570)<br>[2.585] | 0.410<br>(0.772)<br>[0.531] |
| Party competition | 3.259<br>(9.214)<br>[0.354] | -0.194<br>(0.205)<br>[-0.947] | 47.620<br>(33.609)<br>[1.417] | 25.221<br>(41.355)<br>[0.610] |
| No. of regulated occupations, 1980 | 0.706***<br>(0.223)<br>[3.165] | -- | -- | -- |
| % of earmarked taxes, 1979 | -- | -0.189<br>(0.115)<br>[-1.644] | -- | -- |
| Per capita GSP, 1977 | -- | -- | -3.546<br>(2.441)<br>[-1.453] | 0.359<br>(3.357)<br>[0.107] |

**TABLE 11.3.  Continued**

| | | | | |
|---|---|---|---|---|
| Avg. AFDC<br>benefit, 1980 | -- | -- | -0.029**<br>(0.002)<br>[-2.418] | -- |
| % of S&L expend.<br>for construc, 1977 | -- | -- | -- | -2.675**<br>(1.278)<br>[-2.093] |
| Constant | 25.935 | 0.305 | 78.056 | -98.626 |
| $R^2$ | 0.449 | 0.407 | 0.512 | 0.371 |
| n | 42 | 38 | 42 | 42 |

*Notes:* Figures in parentheses are standard errors; figures in brackets are *t*-values.

[a]In the welfare model, the number of interest organizations is the average of 1980 and 1990 welfare interest organizations, not the total number of interest organizations. GSP-BASE in the welfare model is the average of 1982 and 1989 GSP divided by number of welfare interest organizations.

[b]In the construction model, the number of interest organizations is the average of 1980 and 1990 construction interest organizations, not the total number of interest organizations. GSP-BASE in the construction model is the average of 1977 and 1989 GSP divided by number of construction interest organizations.

$* = p < .10; ** = p < .05; *** = p < .01$, two-tailed tests

variables. In general, however, we expect that more capable governments are better able to resist special interests. Therefore, lower levels of all four dependent measures should be expected when the four capability variables take on high values.[4]

### Findings for the Policy Models

The protectionist and subsidy policy results are presented in table 11.3 and are easily summarized since few of the variables generated coefficients of any magnitude. Few of the control variables have much influence on occupational regulation. The only variable with a significant estimate is number of occupations regulated in 1980. Similarly, only the opinion liberalism measure is discernibly greater than zero in the earmarked taxes model,[5] and its estimate suggests that earmarking grew at a slower rate over the 1980s in states with more liberal electorates. AFDC benefit levels increased at a faster rate in states with more representative legislative bodies, more liberal electorates, and lower initial benefit levels. Finally, growth in the proportion of state spending devoted to construction was lower in states with better funded and better staffed executive and legislative branches and higher relative levels of construction spending in 1977. While many of our expectations for the controls were not supported, all of the detected relationships are in the expected direction.

What was the impact of the interest organization measures? With but two exceptions, none of these measures produced coefficients that approached the standard criteria for statistical significance. The exceptions are the GSP-BASE measures of density relative to economic size in the welfare and construction spending models. And given the inverse coding of these measures, the estimates indicate that lower density is associated with greater spending, the opposite of what we would expect given traditional interpretations of the power of special interests. In general, then, these results provide little support for the notion that having more, or more diverse, interests is associated with levels of protectionist public policies.

These findings bear greatly on our interpretation of the legislative activity results presented in chapter 10, as well as on how we understand the economic and government share results presented earlier. Interest density is negatively associated with legislative activity, while the proportion of not-for-profit interests is positively associated with bill passage rates. The findings presented in table 11.3 suggest, however, that these results are not associated in any aggregate way with the kinds of legislation enacted by the states. And without evidence that specific policies change as interest organization populations change, it is difficult to place great weight on our earlier findings that greater density is associated with rapid growth of both the public and private economies. Accordingly, we interpret these findings as providing at least indirect support for our alternative interpretation that the specifications underlying the models of economic and government growth are fundamentally flawed by misunderstanding the direction of causal association between interest organization density and the size of the public and private sectors.

## Interest Organizations and Power

Whereas economists have an enduring fascination with the sources of economic growth, political scientists are attentive to power. Despite the difficulty of measuring the concept, scholars since Belle Zeller (1954) have attempted to gauge the power of organized interests in the political process. But it is not clear what power means in terms of the population properties we are examining. On the one hand, the "power" of interest organizations may be unrelated to such system-level concepts as population diversity and density. Only one, two, or a few organizations may be extremely influential across a broad array of issues. Thus, while certain interest organizations might be very powerful in a state, that political influence may be unrelated to the state's overall distribution of interests (Thomas and Hrebenar 1994, 5–6). On the other hand, power may reflect influence derived from such system-level characteristics as the density and diversity of interest organizations. In their interpretations of their typologies of interest organization power, this seems to be the position of Morehouse (1981) and Thomas and Hrebenar (1990, 1995).

Even more importantly, economists and political scientists offer markedly different perspectives on the relationship between power and the population properties of density and diversity. As we have seen in our tests of the economic impact hypotheses, economists tend to assume that density, and perhaps diversity of interests as well, is positively associated with political influence. In contrast, political scientists, especially pluralists (Truman 1951) and neopluralists (Heinz et al. 1993), observe that interests—at least under some circumstances—compete with each other, and that this competition can serve as a check on interest influence. Given these competing expectations, we need to examine the relationship between power and the population properties of density and diversity.

### Data and Operationalizations

The dependent variables in the analyses to follow are the rankings of state interest organization power developed by Morehouse (1981) and by Thomas and Hrebenar (1990) for the late 1970s and late 1980s, respectively. Morehouse's measure identifies three types of interest systems that vary, in her interpretation, on the basis of "interest organization strength," including strong, moderate, and weak categories. Although this implicitly rests on the broader definition of power in terms relative to that of other political actors, Thomas and Hrebenar have criticized Morehouse's measure as positing the existence of absolute levels of influence (1990, 147). In contrast, they employ labels making specific reference to the relative power of interest organizations (Thomas and Hrebenar 1990, 141). And this is not the only difference. Their typology includes five sets of interest organization systems, including four that are observable and another type (e.g., subordinate) that is missing empirically, although still theoretically viable. The four observable types range from dominant, through dominant/complementary and complementary, to complementary/subordinate.

Although separated by a decade and employing somewhat different ranking schemes, the two typologies are quite strongly related, as seen in the cross-tabulation presented in table 11.4. For example, Morehouse's "strong" interest organization states match well with

Thomas and Hrebenar's interest organization "dominant" states. In short, and allowing for some variation over the ten-year gap separating the two measures, the two indicators are broadly consistent with each other and provide at least some implicit support for their authors' assumption that interest organization power is an enduring characteristic. Because both measures have a limited range of values, logistic regression is used in the tests that follow.

The independent variables in the analysis are our four indicators of properties of interest organization populations and the core set of controls used in the models presented earlier in this chapter, measuring

**TABLE 11.4.  Comparison of Morehouse Power Ranking with Hrebenar and Thomas Power Ranking**

| Hrebenar and Thomas Rank | Morehouse Rank | | |
|---|---|---|---|
| | Strong | Moderate | Weak |
| Dominant | Alabama<br>Alaska<br>Florida<br>Louisiana<br>Mississippi<br>New Mexico<br>South Carolina<br>Tennessee<br>West Virginia | | |
| Dominant/<br>  complementary | Arkansas<br>Hawaii<br>Georgia<br>Kentucky<br>Montana<br>Nebraska<br>Oklahoma<br>Oregon<br>Texas<br>Washington | Arizona<br>California<br>Idaho<br>Nevada<br>Ohio<br>Utah<br>Virginia<br>Wyoming | |
| Complementary | Iowa<br>New Hampshire<br>North Carolina | Illinois<br>Indiana<br>Kansas<br>Maine<br>Maryland<br>Missouri<br>Pennsylvania<br>South Dakota | Colorado<br>Massachusetts<br>Michigan<br>New Jersey<br>New York<br>North Dakota<br>Wisconsin |
| Complementary/<br>  subordinate | | Delaware<br>Vermont | Connecticut<br>Minnesota<br>Rhode Island |
| Subordinate | | | |

government capability, party competition, and opinion liberalism. Their interpretation here is straightforward. The measures of interest organization power purport to tap relative power. Therefore, more capable executive and legislative branches should weaken the influence of organized interests. Competitive parties are thought to be stronger—better organized and more disciplined. Therefore, competitive parties should be associated with weaker interest organizations. Liberal electorates should be more open to democratic influences on policy, which should also weaken the power of organized interests.[6]

### Findings for Interest Organization Power

Given that the power variables are scored so that high values indicate more powerful interest systems, the estimates for the control variables presented in table 11.5 provide some indication that power is indeed relative. In the Morehouse results, states with better staffed and better funded legislatures and executives, more competitive parties, and better managed legislatures tend to have less powerful interest systems. Relative interest organization power, as measured by the Hrebenar and Thomas index, is lower in states with more representative legislatures, more competitive parties, and more liberal electorates. In contrast, the interest organization properties of density and diversity do not seem to matter much. With conflicting signs across the two models and very tiny t-values, the interest organization estimates suggest that interest organization power is a function of something other than the population-level properties of interest communities.

### The Impact of Interest Communities

Several null conclusions are justified. We found little support for the hypotheses of economists about the deleterious effects of growing interest organization populations. We found no evidence that the density and diversity of interest communities are associated with adoptions of several specific subsidies and protectionist policies. And worse from the perspective of economists, density was found to be positively associated with economic growth. Only for change in total state and local spending were the expectations of the economists met, although we found no evidence that spending growth is associated with an expansion of government's share of economic activity. The most plausible explanation for this odd set of findings is that many of our traditional hypotheses about the impact of interest organization populations are founded on a fundamental misunderstanding of causal relationships.

**TABLE 11.5. Tests of Interest Organization Impact on Power**

| Independent Variable | Dependent Variable Morehouse Index | Hrebenar and Thomas Index |
|---|---|---|
| No. of interest organizations | 0.005* (0.003) [1.750] | -0.000 (0.002) [-0.045] |
| GSP-BASE measure of density | 0.005 (0.006) [0.824] | 0.003 (0.005) [0.627] |
| % of Not-for-profit organizations | -0.013 (0.078) [-0.171] | 0.051 (0.073) [0.700] |
| Herfindahl index: interest diversity | -0.027 (0.050) [-0.535] | -0.006 (0.047) [-0.136] |
| BK-staffing and spending | -1.586* (0.832) [-1.906] | 0.393 (0.665) [0.590] |
| BK-accountability and management | -1.684*** (0.609) [-2.764] | -0.646 (0.490) [-1.317] |
| BK-executive centralization | -0.198 (0.370) [-0.533] | 0.144 (0.345) [0.416] |
| BK-representation | 0.048 (0.321) [0.150] | -0.563* (0.331) [-1.701] |
| EWM-opinion liberalism | -0.068 (0.058) [-1.183] | -0.142** (0.059) [-2.427] |
| Party competition | 6.891* (3.878) [1.778] | 6.893* (3.893) [1.865] |
| Intercept 2 | -3.062 | -8.459 |
| Intercept 3 | - - | -5.547 |
| Constant | -5.578 | -11.070 |

*Notes:* Figures in parentheses are standard errors; figures in brackets are *t*-values.
* = $p < .10$; ** = $p < .05$; *** = $p < .01$, two-tailed tests

We also found little support for the notion that interest organization power is associated with the interest community properties of density and diversity.

This leaves us with two important questions. First, does this mean that interest organizations have little influence on public policy? The answer is almost certainly that they do matter. We have not examined all aggregate measures of policy impact. But while we may be missing the real locus of population-level influence on aggregate policy outcomes, we are not optimistic that impacts of the traditional sort reflected in the hypotheses we have tested will be found. Even more importantly, specific interests clearly can have an important influence on legislative and executive actions in certain circumstances (Heinz et al. 1993). Our results indicate not that organized interests are unimportant but that the population-level characteristics of density and diversity do not bear in an obvious manner on policy outcomes. If we are to look for the real influence of special interests, we need to examine specific interests at specific times in specific places; we should not simply infer aggregate-level policy outcomes from the population-level properties of interest organization communities.

Second, does this mean that the population properties of density and diversity do not matter? Despite the limited evidence of impact reported here, we think that they do matter. But they may matter more to how government decision making is conducted than to the policies it produces. As we saw in chapter 10, having more interests and fewer not-for-profit interests makes legislating more difficult, an impact that is of considerable importance to those interested in how governments function. As a Pennsylvania contract lobbyist (phone interview, 28 April 1994) put it, "It started in Washington with people hiding behind front groups. The sides have hardened on issues, [making it] difficult to find a compromise point." Having more interest organizations means that coalition formation will be more difficult and the resulting coalitions more fragile (Browne 1995; Heinz et al. 1993). As well, greater density means that there will be more potential roadblocks to bill passage.

The enhancement of passage rates when non-for-profit interests are relatively better represented is more difficult to understand given that we have found little evidence that having more such interests is associated with specific policy outcomes. But here, our common understanding of such interests may be flawed. Government and social interests are typically assumed to be more liberal than are traditional economic interests. But examination of lists of social interests, in particular, indicates that they include many religious groups (i.e., fundamentalist churches), hobby interests (i.e., gun control opponents), and cause groups (i.e., taxpayer coalitions) that are far from liberal. When such interests, as well as government interests, add their weight to efforts to pass legislation, it has a greater likelihood of passage, all other things being equal. But given the diversity of interests involved, their net impact on the global direction of policy seems to be minimal.

CHAPTER 12

# Findings and Future Work

The population ecology theory of interest organizations explored in the preceding chapters offers, we believe, a number of new insights into the nature of interest representation. After summarizing our empirical findings, we examine some of the broader implications of these insights for both what social scientists should be studying about interest communities and how their studies should be conducted, as well as for how we interpret the role of interest communities in democratic political systems.

## Findings and Substantive Contributions

While many more quite specific substantive findings were noted in the individual chapters testing hypotheses derived from the population ecology theory of interest representation, the following—numbered by chapter and the order in which they were presented—constitute our principal findings.

6.1: Contrary to prior work on national interest communities, state interest organizations frequently withdraw from lobbying.

6.2: Contrary to Salisbury's hypothesis (1984), institutions withdraw at higher rates than do associations or membership organizations.

6.3: Withdrawal from lobbying is far more likely to indicate organizational death for associations and membership organizations than for institutions.

6.4: Patterns of exit greatly influence the diversity and density of organized interest systems, although not to as great a degree as does entry.

6.5: Density dependence in interest communities is expressed primarily through increased mortality, not through reduced entry of new organizations.

7.1: No support was found for the Olson and Virginia School explanations of interest community density.

7.2: Interest organization number is positively associated with potential constituents number, but at a declining rate; that is, interest organization number has a density-dependent relationship with number of potential constituents.

7.3: Interest organization number is positively associated with governmental actions of specific concern to potential constituents.

7.4: Interest organization number is positively associated with party competition.

8.1: Little or no support was found for Truman's complexity explanation (1951) of interest community diversity.

8.2: The diversity of state interest organization populations is highly conditioned by how responsive different types of interest organizations are to the environmental constraints governing their densities.

9.1: Competition within interest organization guilds is expressed through partitioning of membership and financial resources.

9.2: The intensity of partitioning is not related to the life cycle of interest organizations.

9.3: The intensity of this partitioning may be related to the density of interest communities, with greater reliance on partitioning in highly dense systems.

9.4: Interest group niches—and thus the structure of interest group communities—are more strongly determined by the internal needs of organized interests than by their patterns of interface with government.

10.1: Legislatures in states with dense interest populations have fewer bill introductions, fewer enactments, and a lower ratio of enactments to bill introductions than do legislatures in states with less dense interest communities.

10.2: Legislatures in states with high proportions of not-for-profit interests have more enactments and a higher ratio of enactments to bill introductions than do legislatures in states with low proportions.

11.1: Interest organization density, but not diversity, is positively associated with the rate of economic growth, and there is good reason to expect that causality runs from the latter to the former.

11.2: Interest organization density, but not diversity, is positively associated with the rate of state and local government growth, and there is good reason to expect that causality runs from the latter to the former.

11.3: Neither density nor diversity of interest communities is associated with changes in government's share of economic activity.

11.4: Neither density nor diversity of interest communities is associated with state adoptions of several specific subsidies and protectionist policies.

11.5: Neither density nor diversity of interest communities is associated with the Morehouse (1981) and Thomas and Hrebenar (1990) measures of interest system power.

These findings contribute most directly to at least two distinct literatures in political science. The first is the literature on state politics. It should be understood, though, that we do not view our analysis of interest organization populations as work with exclusive meaning for the literature on state politics. It just so happens that the best available opportunity to study interest organization populations entails attention to the American states.

Still, through this choice of analytic locus, our research makes a number of contributions to the state politics literature. Indeed, this work offers a rigorous, systematic examination of state interest communities that is comparable to the work at the national level by Schlozman and Tierney (1986), Walker (1983, 1991), and Aldrich and his colleagues (Aldrich and Staber 1988; Aldrich et al. 1990, 1994). The work on state interest organizations has heretofore been too descriptive, and as a result the interest representation subfield has lagged behind other areas of state politics scholarship. We hope our study will encourage others to adopt a more theoretical orientation toward the study of state interest organizations and to take better advantage of the power of comparative analysis that the states provide us.

While our analysis is quite different from that typical of the early days of comparative state politics, we think that our themes are relevant to the old "economics versus politics" debate. Obviously, we judge the influence of state economies on politics to be quite significant; a number of our density and diversity measures are constructed with reference to the size and diversity of state economies. But our density and impact models also include variables attentive to political factors, including measures of policy need, government policy activity, party control of state legislatures and governorships, party competition, public opinion, and the number of claimants seeking government action. Thus, our models are hardly founded on economic determinism. Rather, they suggest that politics matters.

While our central measures of density and diversity were not found to be related to interest organization power—the central and defining concept of prior research on state interest organization politics—we nonetheless believe that our analysis contributes to the power literature.

Our analysis suggests that interest organization power is not founded on the aggregate composition of interest organization communities per se but on some other factor. The most plausible alternative explanation is that measures of interest community power are tapping the influence of a few select interests within specific states. This does not mean that the properties of interest organization populations do not matter for how states are governed, as is amply demonstrated in the summary of our findings on legislative gridlock.

While our analysis contributes to the state politics literature first, its second and major contribution is to the broader literature on interest representation. Our measures of organized interest populations cast a wider net than most studies, by including institutions among the objects of study. As others have speculated, we found a growing dominance of institutions among interest organization populations. But interestingly, their dominance appears to be due to their flexibility—their ability both to enter and to exit the lobbying scene at will. It is not, as others had thought, simply their innate capacity to mobilize more easily that matters. We do not know what institutions do while they are politically moribund; perhaps they drop out of politics altogether, or perhaps they operate a PAC instead of lobbying. Those questions await another study. We simply know that interest organization communities are very fluid beneath the appearance of stability.

Also, the population ecology models performed well, especially in contrast to the Virginia School and Olson perspectives. As we saw time and again, the Virginia School interpretation is not founded on a plausible model of politics, nor does it predict well either interest organization population density or interest organization impact. The Olson incentive theory of mobilization, which works so well at the micro level, simply is not a useful guide to generating valid inferences about the societal-level properties of interest organization communities, largely because it ignores context, the environment in which interest representation takes place.

Finally, our analysis contributes to the debate over the governance and policy consequences of interest representation. We discuss these contributions more fully when we consider the implications of our findings for democratic government. For now, though, it is sufficient to note that in the debate between neopluralist political scientists and Virginia School and public choice economists over the impact of interest organizations, our findings place us firmly in the camp of our disciplinary colleagues. While variations in the density and diversity of interest organization populations were found to exercise considerable impact on the pace of legislative activity, they had little impact on highly aggregated measures of public policy. While examination of more narrowly gauged measures of public policy and legislative activity is still needed, both of these findings match well the expectations of neopluralist scholars.

## Analytic Contributions

By far, the most important contribution of this analysis is the development—based on population biology and the study of organization ecology in sociology—of a population ecology theory of interest organizations. From that theory, a model of interest organization density was developed, as well as a radical new interpretation of the nature of interest organization diversity. Despite the frequency with which prior scholarship has used the concepts of density and diversity, no prior analysis has offered a compelling theoretical account of the former or a nuanced interpretation of the latter. While far from complete, this approach offers a broad theoretical base from which to understand how interest communities are constructed.

How does the population ecology approach relate to more traditional research programs on mobilization and impact? This is an important question. After all, our attention to population-level phenomena was motivated at least in part by a suspicion that mobilization and impact cannot be explained without attention to population-level issues. Our empirical analysis of interest organization entry and exit suggests that the connections between mobilization and population-level phenomena is weak. Interest organization population density does not appear to feed back so as to alter mobilization rates. While not a necessary outcome of our population-level theory, this empirical finding is very good news because it indicates that mobilization studies need not be attentive to population-level issues in explaining why interest organizations originate or how members join them. Still, our finding that interest organization density influences the mortality rates of interest organizations suggests strongly that we cannot draw inferences about the composition of interest organization communities directly from mobilization studies.

The study of populations of interest organizations appears to have a more complex relationship with the literatures on interest community interactions with government. Although the evidence was more suggestive than definitive, our findings on niche partitioning indicate that rigor of partitioning varies with the density of interest communities. Further, interest organization identities seem to rest very heavily on many of the same variables governing the density of interest communities. If further research replicates and strengthens these findings, then we may have to consider population issues when examining interactions among interests as they seek to influence government. Such variables may not matter if we study single populations at one point in time. But they may matter a great deal across time and across interest communities.

By focusing on population-level characteristics of interest organization systems, we were compelled to develop several new measures of the properties of interest communities. Several of these measures of density and diversity are useful for describing interest organization populations. But for purposes of explanation, raw numbers of interest organizations must be the focus of further work. It is interest organizations themselves—not their relationships to GSP or to other interest organizations—that form, lobby government, and then perish at a surprisingly high rate.

The measures we developed have no counterpart in prior research on interest organizations. The literature on mobilization focuses almost exclusively on individual interest organizations. The concepts of density and diversity, quite simply, have no meaning in terms of individual interest organizations. Individual interest organizations and their political and organizational behavior are clearly important objects of study. Indeed, we have pointed to a number of areas of inquiry where attention to one or a few organizations offers the most appropriate research strategy. But it is also important to study populations *as populations*. We hope that other scholars will use these measures, as well as explore the validity and reliability of indicators of other population-level properties of interest communities.

Our inquiry also experimented with several modes of analysis that we believe have merit for the further study of organized interests. First, instead of the usual single-minded focus on Washington, D.C., we analyzed interests in the 50 states, something necessitated by our need to ensure variance in the population-level properties of interest systems. Interest communities vary across the states, from the handful of full-time lobbyists in Little Rock, Arkansas, to perhaps a thousand full-timers in Lansing, Michigan. Each state's political community thinks that it is unique, and in some sense each is. But the purpose of comparative research is to illuminate what is common among states as well as highlighting their differences. Indeed, our ability to account for differences among the states in the densities of their interest organization populations suggests strongly that they share much in common as interest organization systems. The processes governing the composition of their interest populations are the same, irrespective of the diversity of communities thereby generated.

Second, instead of a single cross section, we used data from three time periods: 1975, 1980, and 1990. By doing so, we found that the rate of increase in organized interests, while alarming in the 1975–80 period, has since slowed considerably. Moreover, we were able to analyze accurately the mortality of interest organizations using detailed population records from 1980 and 1990. With these findings in mind, we hope future researchers will not make rash statements derived from studies of a single population at a single point in time.

Third, our design included institutions registered to lobby as well as the oft-studied membership groups and associations. Few other scholars have included institutions within their samples of lobbying organizations. Yet, at the state level, they constituted nearly half (49.02 percent) of all registered organizations in 1990. Further, their numbers are increasing far faster than those of any other type of interest organization. More to the point, we found that institutions behave differently than associations and membership groups; they enter and exit lobbying communities more frequently. This suggests rather strongly that future investigators need to study the full lobbying community, not just membership groups and associations.

Fourth, our design included data from a range of sources: aggregate data taken from the registration lists of all 50 states, simulation analyses based on the aggregate data findings, survey data collected from registered organizations in 6 states, and interview data gathered from lobbyists in the same 6 states. In addition, one of the authors just finished a four-year stint as a volunteer lobbyist in the Minnesota legislature, while the other had an earlier career as a legislative staffer being lobbied in the Michigan legislature. Thus, we brought to our interpretation of the data experience as participants in the representation of interests.

## A Population Ecology Research Agenda

Examining interest organization populations offers any number of possible routes for further theoretical and empirical analysis. As noted earlier, some of our empirical findings, especially those generated from analyses of only a limited number of states, need to be replicated. We have also suggested that the analysis of interest organization impact must shift away from attention to excessively broad measures of policy impact toward much more detailed assessment of the specific content of legislation produced by political systems with varying configurations of interest organization populations. Further work on these questions is obviously required given our findings, and the direction of such work is sufficiently clear so as to need little further elaboration.

The most important opportunities for further analysis, however, may entail examining some less obvious implications of our population-level findings for the survival and influence strategies and life histories of *individual* interest organizations. While our focus has been on populations as populations, the forces that shape populations operate by influencing the behaviors of specific interest organizations. Fully developing a population ecology theory of interest representation will require that we better understand how the structure of interest organization populations influences the members of those populations. Several such questions arise from our findings and merit further research, questions that will require both further elaboration of the population ecology theory of interest organizations and research designs and data different from those employed here.

First, we need to consider in much greater detail the nature of selection processes as they are experienced by individual interest organizations. Some of our key findings are that interest organizations frequently exit lobbying communities, that they do so at an increasing rate as interest communities become more dense, and that many of these organizations—especially membership groups and associations—cease to exist once they leave registration rolls. How can we account for why some organizations survive and continue to lobby while others perish? In accounting for interest organization density, the ESA model developed in chapter 4 and tested in chapter 7 points to the variables of government activity—or the perceived need for activity—and the constituency-base of interest organizations. Our analysis also emphasizes the primacy of constituents and finances in the niche strategies of interest organizations. But how are changes in the values of these quite general variables experienced by specific lobbying organizations, especially in terms of how they influence an organization's decision to disband or to become politically inactive?

It is vital that we answer this question if we are to fully understand how population-level phenomena influence the composition of interest organization communities. And it cannot be studied with the kind of data employed here. An approach that would be far more successful would entail identifying a set of new interest organizations and tracking their development over a number of years. Given the high exit rate of interest organizations, we should be able to observe sufficient mortality over a five- or ten-year period to be able to determine how government activity or potential activity, membership and financial factors, and other variables implicit in our analysis of populations influence the survival chances of these interest organizations. This research strategy would have the added advantage of linking the study of interest organization populations to the literature on interest organization strategy and leadership.

Second, how do selection processes influence the composition of interests represented before government? Here, we are concerned with the breadth of interests that are represented, with the potential variation in the composition of interest communities ranging from those comprised largely of encompassing interests to those composed of a large number of organized interests attentive to only very narrow policy concerns. The implications of such differences in interest communities for the play of democratic politics has concerned many scholars. But little research attention has been devoted to explaining why one interest organization system has more encompassing interest organizations than another.

The population ecology theory we have explored in this book suggests that we look to the operation of the competitive exclusion principle and environmental uncertainty in accounting for such differences. Environmental uncertainty may encourage the fragmentation of interests as components of existing umbrella organizations pass the threshold size required for independent organization. As interest communities thereby become more dense, the newer interest organizations with more narrow issue agendas and more focused constituencies may slowly deprive older and more encompassing interest organizations of the means of survival. Their realized niches may be reduced below the size needed for organizational viability. Over time, then, the composition of interest organization systems could evolve so that narrow interests replace encompassing interests.

While population ecology theory clearly supports this hypothesis, and while several of the contract lobbyists we interviewed agreed with it, the data employed here are not sufficient to put it to a clear empirical test. A valid test will likely entail merging long-term tracking of an interest organization population—like that we have proposed for the study of selection processes—with focused analysis of an issue domain— like that conducted by Heinz and his colleagues in *The Hollow Core* (Heinz et al. 1993). Such a long-term study will be a major undertaking, but one fully justified by the implications such evolutionary developments in the composition of interest communities have for the viability of democratic politics.

Third, our findings provide strong evidence of niche partitioning among interest organizations, partitioning that occurs primarily on the critical internal resource dimensions of membership and financial resources. How does such partitioning take place? How do interest organizations with initially similar potential memberships signal to each other primacy in some portion of their shared potential constituency? Is such signaling active in the form of some explicit or implicit negotiation and bargaining or simply a passive recognition of where their greatest opportunities for growth are? And how does such partitioning constrain the evolution of specific interest organizations and the issues they represent? Given limited attention to policy conflict among interest organizations in the traditional literature, such questions have rarely been asked, much less examined empirically. But one important implication of population ecology theory is that partitioning, rather than overt conflict, is likely to be the dominant mode of strategic interaction among interest organizations sharing overlapping fundamental niches.

This shift in analytic focus brings with it, of course, a rather severe impediment for empirical research. Conflict can be observed and its meaning easily interpreted. Lack of conflict, too, can be observed. But determining whether it is a function of prior partitioning or of a lack of fundamental niche overlap entails comparing a known outcome with some potential outcome that is unobservable. And capturing interest organizations at the precise moment they recognize a potential area of conflict and engage in partitioning is unlikely, as generations of population biologists have learned in the study of interactions among related species. Biologists, however, can retreat to experimental manipulation in the laboratory, a luxury we do not have as students of interest organizations. Thus, a more complete understanding of interest organization populations will require developing new measures and more powerful research designs, tasks we leave to future research projects.

### Interest Communities and Democratic Government

What can be said about democracy in the American states as a result of this study? A number of our findings speak to this most global of governance issues, but not always with a single voice. In many senses, they suggest that democratic government is alive and well in the states. In other ways, they suggest that the business of government has become more difficult even as it has become more open.

In the regulation of lobbying, the disclosure of representation, and the reporting of expenditures, our contract lobbyists report that new laws have made a difference in their professional lives. Lobbying is much "cleaner" now, they report. A Minnesota lobbyist (phone interview, 22 September 1994), for example, reported that "There is more emphasis on technical information, less on socializing." A North Carolina lobbyist (phone interview, 26 April 1994), agreed, noting that "The good ole boy system is gone. Wining and dining is gone. Legislators are more sophisticated, [and] they want to know the issues." A Pennsylvania lobbyist (phone interview, 3 May 1994) added that "[Legislators] are less interested in whether you golfed with them than with the quality of your information." So, the business of lobbying has changed over the last decade as regulation has increased.

Such regulation, however, does not seem to have greatly influenced which interests are represented or how many organizations decide to engage in lobbying. Nor has it seemed to reduce their influence. Most of the interviewed lobbyists rated their collective influence as remaining about the same over the same period. And at least one Arkansas lobbyist (phone interview, 25 April 1994) suggested that increased professionalism among legislators over the same time period has actually made the lobbying task even less difficult: "They are more professional, have more staff. Agendas are prepared ahead of time. It makes our job easier; everything is more open."

Attention to lobbying regulation and the professionalization of the lobbying function, however, sidestep the more fundamental issue of lobbyists' influence on governance and public policy.[1] Our findings speak directly to only one part of this question. We found little evidence that interest organization populations *as populations* influence several global measures of policy outcomes or political power. Our results say little or nothing about the specific influence of specific interest organizations on specific issues, although, more generally, dense communities seem to make legislative decision making more difficult.

Though lobbyists' influence goes beyond the issues examined in this work, the contract lobbyists we spoke to reported that their influence was very limited under certain circumstances. While not surprisingly confident about their abilities to represent their clients' interests, many observed that professional lobbying is influential only until the public gets involved. Then, they argued, lobbyists take a backseat. As one Arkansas lobbyist (phone interview, 21 April 1994) put it, "The tobacco lobby is one of the strongest lobbies; yet in the 1991 session the nursing home people got a cigarette tax slapped on. So the grassroots organization won over an embedded lobbying organization. All those little old ladies on their walkers was [sic] appealing." This assessment was echoed by a South Dakota lobbyist (phone interview, 29 April 1994), who noted that "the people still have power. Hobby lobbyists can stop bills if they get riled up." And a Michigan lobbyist (phone interview, 26 April 1994) added, "If the people are united on something, they get it. We have to get out of the way." Thus, these senior lobbyists almost uniformly believed that their influence is at least potentially checked by public opinion.

More generally, our findings do not indicate that interest organizations are arrayed vis-à-vis the legislative process in a manner that precludes competition over issues of policy. Rather, and consistent with the findings reported in *The Hollow Core,* we found evidence of both co-operation among policy allies and routine conflict among policy opponents. More importantly, perhaps, we found that policy balkanization is neither a necessary outcome of increasing interest organization density nor required to establish viable interest organization niches. This may provide at least the opportunity for some of the kind of interaction among interests of the type lauded by pluralists and neopluralists.

At the same time, we found little evidence that interest organization communities are becoming more diverse. Contrary to the expectations of those who thought that the observed increase in the number of public interest organizations during the 1970s would transform interest communities, traditional economic interests continue to dominate lobbying communities in the states. Indeed, numbers of institutional interest organizations increased markedly relative to membership groups and associations over the decade of the 1980s. Perhaps our most optimistic finding in this regard is that the high mortality rate of interest organizations suggests that state interest organization communities are, at least potentially, highly fluid in their composition.

Interest community density does lead to lower rates of legislative activity, which raises the potential of governmental gridlock. However, the presence of more not-for-profit organizations leads to higher passage rates, perhaps implying that the broader public interest can be served. And we found little evidence that interest communities are expanding exponentially as many fear. Indeed, perhaps the central implication of the ESA density model is that there are very real limits on the size of interest organization communities. Environmental constraints operate to moderate the pace of growth; indeed, they set the carrying capacities of political systems for interest organizations.

On balance, then, our findings should make us more sanguine about democracy's prospects in the American states. They do not insure, however, that hyper interest group politics and gridlock will not be a part of our future. If potential constituencies increase in number, if government engages or fails to engage in actions of concern to these constituencies, and if uncertainties over policy outcomes increase, interest communities will grow, perhaps significantly so. But the resulting changes in the nature of politics will be less a function of organized interests and more a reflection of the changing nature of politics. As a Pennsylvania lobbyist (phone interview, 28 April 1994) put it, "Issues are more contentious now, solutions more difficult. This is a function of how politics has changed, not how lobbying has changed."

# APPENDIX 1

## On the Use of Lobby Registration Rolls

The 1975 registration lists were obtained from Marquis Academic Media (1978), while the 1980 data was collected by Conover and Gray (1983). Complete lists for these years were available for only 44 states, with Hawaii, Rhode Island, Utah, West Virginia, Alabama, and Nevada missing from the data set. The 1990 data were developed from lists of registered lobbyists provided by all 50 states. Lobby registration rolls provide lists of lobbyists and identify the organizations they represent. We do not count registered lobbyists as our measure of interest organization populations, as some have done (Hunter, Wilson, and Brunk 1991). Focusing on individual lobbyists confounds organizational representation with the intensity of organizational effort. While the intensity of lobbying effort may be an interesting subject in its own right, our attention is on populations of interest organizations. Therefore, organizations with multiple representatives are entered into our census only once, and lobbyists registered as individuals were not recorded. After careful consideration of the lobbying laws of the several states, traditional state agencies (e.g., the office of the governor, departments and executive agencies, etc.) were also excluded from the lists of those states where they are required to register as lobbyists.

The 1975, 1980, and 1990 registration data were coded by economic sector represented. Complete lists for 1990 and registration rolls for six states in 1980 were coded by form of organization (i.e., membership groups, associations, or institutions). Procedures were the same in both cases. Initial codings of organizations were checked by a second coder, and discrepancies were resolved through discussions between the primary and secondary coders. At this point, another coder consulted various sources—including several directories of organizations, associations, and groups—in an attempt to ascertain values for organizations that remained unidentified. After this verification process was completed, 3.80 percent of the 1990 organizations could not be coded by economic sector. Only 3.05 percent of the 1990 cases and 3.37 percent of the 1980 cases could not be coded by organizational form.

Do variations in the restrictiveness of lobby registration requirements and their enforcement influence lobby registrations? The answer
seems to be that they do not. First, it is not at all clear what the direction of
impact should be. Political scientists typically assume that more rigorous
registration laws and more rigorous enforcement stimulate registrations
of interest organizations already engaged in lobbying (Hamm, Weber,
and Anderson 1994). In contrast, economists view lobbying regulations as
*barriers to entry* into the political market (Brinig, Holcombe, and
Schwartzstein 1993). As such, they expect strict regulations and strict
enforcement to *reduce* registrations by inhibiting lobbying activity. It is
possible, of course, that both effects are small and/or that they cancel each
other out. Thus, it is not implausible to expect that regulation has little net
impact on registrations.

Second, we can test the hypotheses implicit in these expectations by
using published indices that purport to measure the rigor of a broad
range of restrictive provisions in lobbying regulations as well as the
degree to which they are enforced. Opheim (1991), for example, has
constructed a 22-item index using 1987 data that taps three dimensions
of regulatory rigor: statutory definitions of lobbying used in the laws,
their disclosure requirements, and their oversight and enforcement provisions. Alternatively, Brinig, Holcombe, and Schwartzstein (1993) offer
a multi-item index, one that emphasizes the severity of penalties associated with violation of a broad range of lobbying regulations. While the
two indices are only weakly correlated with each other ($r = 0.169$), both
are substantially more comprehensive and more valid in content than
other measures used in the literature.

Our tests entail including the two indicators of regulatory restrictiveness in a simplified model of state interest organization numbers. This is a
polynomial model with 1990 gross state product (GSP) and its squared
value as our predictors. The theoretical rationale for the model and more
extensive tests of both it and a number of more complex, but related,
models are presented in chapter 7.[1] Registrations in 1990 are used to
match as closely as possible the time periods captured by the Opheim and
Brinig, Holcombe, and Schwartzstein indices. Opheim did not report
scores for Montana, South Dakota, and Virginia, and we exclude Florida
because its registrations skyrocketed by 1990 for unexplained reasons, at
a rate of increase not evident in our 1975 and 1980 data.[2]

The results for our base model—reported in columns one and three
of table A1.1—differ from each other only in the number of observations employed so as to match those used to construct the two indices of
restrictiveness. The results in column two are those for the base model
plus the Opheim indicator, the estimate of which, while positive as

suggested by political scientists, has a *t*-value of only 1.128. The results in column four are for the base model plus the Brinig, Holcombe, and Schwartzstein index. Its coefficient is negative, suggesting that regulatory restrictiveness actually *decreases* registrations. Again, however, it produces a minuscule *t*-value of only −0.816. In short, the impact of lobbying regulation on registrations appears to be minimal and of uncertain direction.

Why do lobby registration laws have so little impact? Two reasons seem most plausible. One is that registration regulations were adopted at the behest of interest organization entrepreneurs so as to enhance monopoly status *within* their organizations, as "official" spokespersons vis-à-vis the government. While plausible, we presently have no evidence on this account. Another is that lobby laws are exercises in symbolic politics whereby, following episodes of reported corruption, legislatures can appear to do something while changing little. This account fits well the pattern of cycles in revision of lobby laws; the current generation of regulations were produced in the mid-1970s in response to Watergate-era scandals (Thomas and Hrebenar 1991, 7–10). Indeed,

**TABLE A1.1.  Tests of Lobby Regulation Impact**

| Independent Variables | Dependent Variable: 1990 Interest Organization Registrations | | | |
| | Model 1 | Model 2 | Model 3 | Model 4 |
|---|---|---|---|---|
| GSP | 0.382* (0.054) | 0.374* (0.054) | 0.369* (0.051) | 0.383* (0.054) |
| GSP$^2$ | -0.337* (0.088) | -0.333* (0.088) | -0.317* (0.085) | -0.336* (0.088) |
| Opheim index | -- | 5.790 (5.134) | -- | -- |
| Brinig et al. index | -- | -- | -- | -6.206 (7.603) |
| Intercept | 243.389 | 194.577 | 249.208 | 298.766 |
| $R^2$ | .709 | .718 | .705 | .709 |
| n | 46 | 46 | 49 | 49 |

*Notes:* Figures in parentheses are standard errors. *Measures:* "1990 interest organization registrations" is the number of organizations registered to lobby state legislatures in 1990; "GSP is 1989 gross state product, and "GSP$^2$" is its squared value. GSP is expressed in units of hundreds of millions, and GSP$^2$ is expressed in trillions for ease of presentation of the resulting coefficients. The Opheim index is provided in Opheim 1991, 409. The Brinig et al. index is provided in Brinig, Holcombe, and Schwartzstein 1993, 379.
* = $p < .01$

recent legislative scandals (e.g., in Arizona, South Carolina, and California) have set off another round of ethics reforms during the early 1990s. In any case, the lack of impact of regulatory restrictiveness and enforcement on numbers of lobby registrations suggests that registration rolls can provide valid and reliable indicators of interest organization political activity. In short, they can be used to define the boundaries of our populations.

## APPENDIX 2

## Survey of Interest Organization Leaders

Department of Political Science
University of North Carolina at Chapel Hill
Chapel Hill, North Carolina 27599

*(Please fill in the appropriate blanks with the requested information or circle the most appropriate response when several are provided.)*

[Questions Asked of All Respondents]

1. What is the official name of your organization?

   _____

2. In what year was it founded? _____
3. Which of the following best characterizes how this organization was founded?
   1. It was a brand new organization started from scratch.
   2. It was started through the merger of older organizations.
   3. It was started by splitting off from a parent organization.
   4. None of the Above
   5. Don't Know
4. Your organization was selected for this survey because it was registered to lobby your legislature in 1990. Is it still registered to lobby?
   1. Yes   2. No   3. Don't Know
5. In conducting your lobbying activity with the state legislature, how often do you consult, communicate, or cooperate with other organizations sharing your goals and also engaged in lobbying the state legislature?
   1. Always  2.  Often  3.  Sometimes  4.  Rarely  5.  Never
      6. Don't Know
6. If you answered always, often, or sometimes to question 5, please identify up to five such organizations with which you have consulted, communicated, or cooperated in the last three years.

_____

_____

_____

_____

7. In lobbying the state legislature, how often do you find yourself in direct competition with other organizations opposed to your position?
   1. Always  2.  Often  3.  Sometimes  4.  Rarely  5.  Never  6. Don't Know

8. If you answered always, often, or sometimes to question 7, please identify up to five organizations with which you have competed in the last three years.

_____

_____

_____

_____

9. Considering all of the policy areas (such as education, environment, business regulation, taxation, and so on) that government works in, what does your organization lobby for?

_____

_____

10. Do the following statements apply to the policy area in which your organization is *most directly involved* in lobbying? (Please circle the most appropriate answer after each item.)
    1. This policy area is marked by intense conflict and disagreement over fundamental policy goals.
       1. Almost Always True  2. Sometimes True  3. Rarely True  4. Don't Know

2. In this policy area, there are only a few key legislators who make the decisions that really matter.
   1. Almost Always True   2. Sometimes True   3. Rarely True   4. Don't Know
3. In making our case in this policy area, we repeatedly face the same opponents on each issue that comes up.
   1. Almost Always True   2. Sometimes True   3. Rarely True   4. Don't Know
4. Legislative jurisdiction over issues in this policy area is restricted to only one or a few committees.
   1. Almost Always True   2. Sometimes True   3. Rarely True   4. Don't Know

11. In addition to your organization's lobbying activity, does it also sponsor a political action committee, or PAC?
    1. Yes   2. No   3. Don't Know

12. In what year was the Political Action Committee (PAC) established?
    _____

13. Which of the following statements best characterizes your organization's efforts to lobby the state legislature?
    1. Lobbying the state legislature is the single most important activity engaged in by my organization.
    2. Lobbying the state legislature is one of several important activities my organization engages in.
    3. Lobbying the state legislature is a minor but nonetheless important activity among all of the activities my organization engages in.
    4. Lobbying the state legislature is only an incidental part of the activities engaged in by my organization.
    5. Don't Know

14. Do you think your organization will continue registering to lobby your state legislature for the foreseeable future?
    1. Very Likely   2. Somewhat Likely   3. Not Very Likely   4. Don't Know

15. Sometimes, the very existence of an organization is challenged, whether by internal or external factors. Within the next five years, would you estimate that your organization will face a serious challenge to its existence?
    1. Very Likely   2. Somewhat Likely   3. Not Very Likely   4. Don't Know

[Questions Asked of Only Association and Membership Group Respondents]

16. Some groups are made up of organizations (the Chamber of Commerce, for example, is usually composed of businesses who are members). Some groups are made up of individuals (the nursing association, for example). And some groups have both organizations and individuals as members. To which membership category does your association belong?
    1. Membership composed of organizations
    2. Membership made up of individuals
    3. Membership a mixture of individuals and organizations
17. If your association has organizations as members, which of the following best represents your association's position on independent lobbying activity by member organizations?
    1. We *encourage* members to lobby independently in addition to representation of their interests by our association.
    2. We *discourage* members from lobbying independently in addition to representation of their interests by of our association.
    3. We *neither encourage nor discourage* members from lobbying independently in addition to representation of their interests by our association.
    4. Don't Know
18. What is the total membership of this association? _____
19. How large was the membership five years ago?
    1. Association not in existence five years ago
    2. Larger than current size
    3. Approximately the same size as today
    4. Smaller than current size
    5. Don't Know
20. What are the principal benefits received by members of this association? (Indicate in the space provided the level of importance of the benefit: 1. = important; 2. = not important; 3. = not provided.)
    1. ____ Informative Publications
    2. ____ In-Service Training
    3. ____ Conferences and Meetings
    4. ____ Low-Cost Insurance
    5. ____ Advocacy of Important Policies
    6. ____ Contacts with Professional Colleagues
    7. ____ Organized Tours or Trips
    8. ____ Discounts on Consumer Goods
    9. ____ Representation of Members' Opinions before Government Agencies
    10. ____ Opportunity for Members to Participate in Public Affairs
    11. ____ Friendship with Other Members

12. ___ Coordination of the Activities of Other Voluntary Organizations in This Field
13. ___ Other (Please Specify) _____

21. Most associations receive financial support from many different sources. Please indicate whether the following financial sources are used by this association and circle the percentage of the association's total financial support provided by each source during the last fiscal year.
    1. Membership Dues
       1. Yes   2. No
    If yes, please circle percentage of total financial support:
       1. 1–10%   2. 11–30%   3. 31–70%   4. 71–100%
    2. Sales and Services (including publications, insurance, conference fees, and fees for other staff services)
       1. Yes   2. No
    If yes, please circle percentage of total financial support:
       1. 1–10%   2. 11–30%   3. 31–70%   4. 71–100%
    3. Government Contracts
       1. Yes   2. No
    If yes, please circle percentage of total financial support:
       1. 1–10%   2. 11–30%   3. 31–70%   4. 71–100%
    4. Funds (including gifts) from Other Associations, Foundations, and Individuals
       1. Yes   2. No
    If yes, please circle percentage of total financial support:
       1. 1–10%   2. 11–30%   3. 31–70%   4. 71–100%
    5. Interest on Loans
       1. Yes   2. No
    If yes, please circle percentage of total financial support:
       1. 1–10%   2. 11–30%   3. 31–70%   4. 71–100%
    6. Other (Please Specify) _____
    Please circle percentage of total financial support:
       1. 1–10%   2. 11–30%   3. 31–70%   4. 71–100%

22. Are there other associations in your state with broadly similar purposes or goals with whom your association competes for new members, funds, contracts, or other resources?
    1. Yes   2. No   3. Don't Know

23. If you answered yes to question 22, please specify up to five associations or organizations with whom you have competed for new members, funds, contracts, or other resources over the last three years.

---
---
---
---

24. If you answered yes to question 22, how frequent would you say this competition is for members, funds, or other resources?
    1. Is Continuous   2. Occurs Sometimes   3. Occurs Rarely   4. Don't Know
25. Which of the following statements best characterizes your organization's strategy when faced with real or potential competition over *financial resources* (including dues, contracts, grants, gifts, sales revenue) with other organizations with similar goals?
    1. We work very hard to make sure that we secure the financial resource and that our competitor does not.
    2. We cooperate with our competitors, either directly or indirectly, to minimize competition over financial resources. We respect their turf.
    3. Neither statement is accurate for our organization.
    4. Don't Know
26. Which of the following statements best characterizes your organization's strategy when faced with real or potential competition over *new members* with other organizations with similar goals?
    1. We work very hard to make sure that we secure the membership and that our competitor does not.
    2. We cooperate with our competitors, either directly or indirectly, to minimize competition over members. We each have our own turf.
    3. Neither statement is accurate for our organization.
    4. Don't Know
27. Which of the following statements best characterizes your organization's strategy when faced with real or potential competition for *influence in a policy area* with other organizations with similar goals?
    1. We work very hard to make sure that we are a major player on all issues relevant to our policy concerns.
    2. We cooperate with our competitors by letting them take the lead on some issues, while we take the lead on others.
    3. Neither statement is accurate for our organization.
    4. Don't Know

28. Which of the following statements best characterizes your organization's strategy when faced with real or potential competition in *providing services to your members* (including publications, conferences, in-service training, and tours) with other organizations with similar goals?
    1. We try to provide all or most of the services provided by our competitors, with the goal of delivering better quality of services.
    2. We try to make sure that the package of services offered our members is different from that of our competitors.
    3. Neither statement is accurate for our organization.
    4. Don't Know

[Questions Asked of Only Institution Respondents]

29. Does your organization belong to any associations of organizations (such as the Chamber of Commerce, a trade association, the Municipal League) that are also engaged in lobbying your state legislature?
    1. Yes   2. No   3. Don't Know
30. If you answered yes to question 29, please identify up to five such coalitions/associations of which your organization is a member.

————————————————————————

————————————————————————

————————————————————————

————————————————————————

————————————————————————

31. Whether or not your organization is *now* a member of these or similar associations, has your organization been a member of such associations in the *last decade*.
    1. Yes   2. No   3. Don't Know
32. What are the principal reasons that your organization has decided to represent itself directly to state legislators rather than exclusively relying on a civic, professional, or trade association? (Indicate in the space provided the level of importance of the reason to your organization's decision to lobby directly: 1. = very important; 2. = somewhat important; 3. = not important.)
    1. ____ There was no civic, professional, or trade association inter-

ested in our concerns. Therefore, we had to work with legislators on our own.

2. ____ Our concerns are very specific, while those of most associations that we might join are very broad.

3. ____ The associations that we might join are simply not very effective.

4. ____ We work with legislators both on our own and through associations. Two voices are simply louder than one.

5. ____ Our interests often conflict with those of similar organizations that might join the most appropriate trade, professional, or civic associations. Indeed, much of our lobbying effort is a form of competition for scarce resources with organizations like our own.

6. ____ We believe it is our civic responsibility to represent our point of view to elected officials.

7. ____ Other (Please Specify) _____

# Notes

## Chapter 1

1. The lesson we wish to draw from this analogy does not include applying this particular solution to the problem of excessive populations of lobbyists or interest organizations.

2. With two exceptions, the data used in this book are available from published sources, as reported throughout the text. The exceptions are the interest organization density and diversity measures, which are reported in chapter 5, and the survey data used in chapter 9, which is archived with the Inter-University Consortium for Political and Social Research.

3. For example, the organizations that reported having PACs were on average somewhat older and smaller than those that did not.

4. Only three lobbyists declined to be interviewed.

5. This sadly illustrates the problem of academic compartmentalization. The first sociologist to apply population ecology models to organizations was Amos Hawley (1950), and a prominent contributor to the contemporary organization ecology research is Howard Aldrich (1979). Currently residing in Chapel Hill, Hawley is retired from the Sociology Department at the University of North Carolina at Chapel Hill, the home department of Aldrich, and Aldrich's office is one floor below that of David Lowery. Yet, we began our analysis with the biological literature, essentially unaware of the work of our intellectual kin.

6. As discussed more fully in chapter 3, organization ecologists rarely study diversity.

## Chapter 2

1. Schlozman and Tierney (1986) have attempted to address this issue, albeit, we will see, in an unsatisfactory manner. As we will see in later chapters, Aldrich and his colleagues (Aldrich and Staber 1988; Aldrich et al. 1990, 1994) have developed much more complete answers, if only for associations.

2. Hansen (1985) restricted his analysis to individual-level contextual issues—the member's assessment of his or her personal situation vis-à-vis the group's goals.

3. Also, their assumptions about the incentive structures of officials do not accord well with the conclusions of others working within the same analytic

tradition. Munger and Denzau (1986), for example, note that politicians' incentives to extract resources from interest organizations in exchange for policy favors is highly constrained by their incentives to seek committee assignments most beneficial to their constituents.

4. The implausibility of such assembly rules forms the core of Elster's criticism (cited in Walker 1991, 46) of Olson's *Logic of Collective Action:* "To assume that there is a collective authority offering incentives often requires another collective action problem to have been solved already."

5. While we follow this tradition, it is worth remembering that this is but one of several different ways in which diversity might be examined.

6. While Walker (1991) resurrected Truman's countermobilization hypothesis in his analysis of membership groups in Washington, he did so to challenge Schattschneider's claim (1960) of a lack of diversity in representation.

7. Schlozman and Tierney (1986) have attempted to test Salisbury's hypothesis. These results are discussed more fully in chapter 6.

8. Even Browne's subthesis on the securing of monopoly status over a narrow set of issues is questionable if Heinz and his colleagues (Heinz et al. 1993, 392–93) are correct that many interest organizations prefer ambiguity in policy outcomes so as to avoid activating quiescent opponents.

9. This outcome parallels Miller and Moe's reconceptualization (1983) of Niskanen's model (1971) as a bilateral monopoly.

10. For more complete reviews of this literature, see Greenwald 1977, Mahood 1990, Petracca 1992b, and Cigler and Loomis 1995.

11. See Schlozman and Tierney 1986, chapter 12, for a recent summary of this literature.

## Chapter 3

1. These theories and methods have been applied to interest organizations only on rare occasions. The most important of these is Schlozman and Tierney 1986 and Walker 1991, on the Washington interest community, and Aldrich and Staber 1988 and Aldrich et al. 1990 and 1994, on national trade associations.

2. The earliest work on organization ecology is somewhat older, reaching back to Hawley 1944 and 1950. But this approach was given new life in Hannan and Freeman 1977.

3. Excellent popular treatments of the traditional literature is provided by Edward O. Wilson in *The Diversity of Life* (1992) and Jonathan Weiner in *The Beak of the Finch* (1994). A sampler of more recent controversies within population biology is provided by Robert E. Ricklefs and Dolph Schluter in *Species Diversity in Ecological Communities: Historical and Geographic Perspectives* (1993).

4. To appreciate the full range of controversies over the definition of species, see E. O. Wilson 1992, 35–50; Stevens 1992; Dupre 1992; Williams 1992; Mayr 1988, 315–58; Mayr 1991, 26–34; and Eldredge and Grene 1992, 25–27.

5. Organization ecologists have tried on occasion to fit organizations within the biological-species concept by analogy. Thus, Hannan and Freeman (1977,

934–35) suggest that the standard operating procedures, governing regulations, and practices of an organization serve many purposes similar to genetics for biological species. The inadequacy of this analogy inheres in its failure to circumvent the differences in the relationship between selection and adaptation between organisms, which recombine genetic information in reproduction, and organizations, which do not.

6. Unlike the biological-species concept, attention to similarity of form renders the definitions of species and populations something less than fully independent; they are defined by reference to each other. But this problem is no less true of E. O. Wilson's general definition of biological species, the same definition used by Darwin.

7. Odum (1969) even advocated extending his biological analysis to consider human interaction with the environment, where the related problem of intentionality is just as prevalent as in ecological studies of organizations. In short, this potential criticism, because it rests on a misunderstanding of population biology models, is not unique to the study of human organizations.

8. Competition, suggests MacIntosh (1992, 64), might take the form of a *scramble*—where there is "competition for a resource in limiting supply, without direct interaction among organisms, in which each secures some portion of the resource"—or a *contest*—"when an organism interacts directly with another and restricts its access to a resource."

9. Indeed, such character displacement has even been used to account for why competition rarely entails overt conflict (Colinvaux 1978, 144).

10. The only change that must be noted here is that because we have defined organizations as species, selection at the level of the individual organization and at the level of the species are collapsed into a single process in the study of human organizations. As a result, our attention to populations is at the guild level rather than the species level.

11. We follow the bulk of organization ecology work by focusing on environmental constraints on the density and diversity of interest organization populations. However, organization ecology research also has given detailed attention to the issue of niche width in response to environmental conditions, or how volatile the environment is over time. For a summary of this research, see Hannan and Freeman 1989, 310–30.

12. However, it is also quite clear that empirical assessment of the competitive exclusion principle has been far less extensive in the study of organizations. As a result, the organization ecology version of the principle must be regarded as an untested hypothesis.

13. We use the qualifier *may* intentionally. In many of the populations of organizations studied by organization ecologists, it is not at all clear how space is conceptualized or if it has a fixed value (see, e.g., Hannan and Carroll 1992, 208–9). Therefore, the focus on simple organization numbers may provide an inadequate conceptualization of the ESA model's space term.

14. In practice, however, organizational ecologists pay far greater attention to space—as measured implicitly by organization number relative to a fixed

boundary—and to legitimacy, and they pay far less attention to energy and stability (Hannan and Freeman 1989; Hannan and Carroll 1992).

## Chapter 4

1. We might initially think that such measures as per capita income tap this concept. But measures of wealth have proven to be weakly related to numbers of lobbyists (Hunter, Wilson, and Brunk 1991). Also, while income may influence decisions of individuals to join groups, it is likely to have little role in the decisions of institutions, associations, or membership groups to engage in lobbying.

2. A possible critique of interest certainty is that while it is expected to influence survival as if it were a resource, it is a joint consumption good and is not, therefore, *expended* like other resources. It might, then, better be viewed as an environmental feature that facilitates usage of the resource of constituent interest. Therefore, including constituent interest and interest certainty in inter-action with each other constitutes a plausible alternative specification.

3. Missing from the model are more general controls, such as population and per capita income, variables that are staples of aggregate analyses of interest organization numbers. Income was discussed in note 1 of this chapter. And while population inevitably will be collinear with some of our measures of latent con-stituency size, the latter are more appropriate theoretically. Manufacturing inter-est organizations represent manufacturing firms, not people. When included in the six interest guild models presented in chapter 7, 1989 per capita income was significant only for agriculture. When 1990 population was added, its estimates in the welfare and construction results were not significant. In the government, environment, agriculture, and manufacturing models, population was highly col-linear with constituent interest. No other coefficients changed markedly.

4. This overstates the case to some degree given comparisons across differ-ent policy domains. Heinz and his colleagues (Heinz et al. 1993) are especially adept at drawing out the implications of such comparisons. Still, they examined only four domains, which provides them with very few degrees of freedom for population-level analysis.

5. For institutions, a similar role is played by sponsors or patrons.

6. It is, of course, possible to provide a more nuanced interpretation, even from a public choice perspective. For example, if interest organizations are substituted for bureaucrats in Niskanen's model (1971) of information mo-nopoly, then such a simple pass-through model would have a firmer theoretical foundation, even if one of doubtful empirical validity.

7. Again, it is possible to construct a better theoretical interpretation of this, even within a public choice framework, by tapping the literature on logrolling and other work. But this was not done in the work of Stigler (1971) and Peltzman (1976), which adopt quite simple models of government (Mitchell and Munger 1991, 520).

8. Lowery and Gray (1993) suggest that it is also possible to reach just the opposite conclusions relying strictly on mobilization theories.

## Chapter 5

1. Hunter, Wilson, and Brunk (1991) employ a related measure—the number of lobbyists registered in each state. Unfortunately, numbers of lobbyists confound the fact of representation of an organization's interest with the intensity of its lobbying effort. Therefore, we focus on organizations registered to lobby rather than on number of lobbyists.

2. Another alternative is numbers of registered organizations in relation to numbers of legislators. But while this measure might be appropriate if we were examining legislator interactions with interest organizations, we are concerned more generally with the interest organization representation *in the governance process as a whole*.

3. In examining the individual state data on interest organizations presented in table 5.1, we find some evidence that might be interpreted as suggesting that the growth observed during the 1980s is somewhat greater among those states with initially greater numbers of interest organizations. For example, the average growth rate in the number of organizations among the five states with the greatest number of organizations in 1980, excluding Florida, was 62.87 percent. In contrast, the average growth rate of the five states with the fewest numbers of organizations in 1980 was only 28.46 percent. This rather sharp difference is complicated somewhat by the fact that Mississippi actually lost lobbying organizations over the ten-year period. When Mississippi is excluded, the growth rate from 1980 to 1990 for the remaining four states with the lowest numbers of organizations in 1980 is a more robust 40.36 percent. Yet the growth rate for both of these sets of states is lower than the 71.46 percent observed earlier for all 50 states. Therefore, the more appropriate conclusion to be drawn is that the increase in the number of organizations is not restricted to only a few states at either end of the continuum running from states having few registered lobbying organizations to those having many. Indeed, this is additional evidence of density dependence, an issue we consider more fully in chapter 7.

4. While conceptually distinct, GSP-BASE is highly correlated with a comparable measure using state population rather than GSP (0.982).

5. The standard deviations for the 44- and 49-state 1990 samples reported in figure 5.2 are 107.73 and 105.30, respectively.

6. This work is reported in Lowery and Gray 1993 and Gray and Lowery 1994b. We no longer view the models presented in these works as capable of "explaining" density for the reasons just noted, although more appropriate ESA model versions of them are evaluated in chapter 7. However, they serve as descriptive snapshots of density relative to economic size, especially for small, dense states.

## Chapter 6

1. Like the work of Schlozman and Tierney (1983, 1986; Schlozman 1984), discussed in this chapter, Walker's study (1991) of interest organizations focuses

exclusively on the Washington population. This means that their population-level inferences are derived from a single case. More troubling, Walker's 1980 and 1985 samples (1991, 5) were drawn from the 1979 and 1984 *Washington Information Directory*'s list of the universe of organizations *that one could join*, a requirement thereby excluding the bulk of the organized interest population—institutions and many associations. Also, counting entries and exits necessarily involves viewing interest organization populations at more than one point in time. While Walker (1991) employed two samples, his analysis is largely restricted to the separate cross sections. A number of state-level studies have been conducted (Thomas and Hrebenar 1992; Hrebenar and Thomas 1992; Hunter, Wilson, and Brunk 1991). However, state populations have been analyzed so far only as annual cross sections, which precludes assessing entry and exit.

2. Because Walker (1991) did not sample institutions or associations, he makes a great leap when he concludes that the "explosion" of membership organizations threatens to outweigh traditional interests. On a related issue, while we cite Schlozman and Tierney (1983) and Walker (1991), our data more directly tap the typology developed by Salisbury (1984). The works are obviously related, however. Institutions and, to a lesser extent, associations tend to represent economic interests, while membership organizations are more likely to be what Walker referred to as citizen organizations (Salisbury 1984, 74).

3. Fully 49.02 percent of all interest organizations in the 50 states in 1990 were institutions, compared to 47.47 percent for our 6-state sample. The corresponding values for associations (22.78 and 22.35 percent) and membership organizations (28.20 and 30.18) were also similar. To generate comparable comparisons for 1980, an estimating routine was employed based on the proportions of 1990 interest organizations by type across economic sectors. When this routine was applied to both our subsample of 6 states and the entire sample of 44 states, similar results were found. Of the organizations in all states in 1980, 38.10 percent were institutions, compared to 37.46 percent for our sample. The corresponding values for associations (31.20 and 30.55 percent) and membership organizations (30.71 and 31.99) were also similar.

4. Given the assumptions underlying our estimates of entry rates, this may slightly overstate the actual influence of entry. Thus, the inferences we draw about the importance of exit, if anything, understate its role. And the regressions we report would remain unchanged since modifying our conservative assumption would have the effect of adding a constant to the dependent variable.

5. We fully appreciate that doing regression with five or six cases is dangerous. However, there is no simpler way to summarize the relationships. For those who remain squeamish, remember that drawing population-level inferences from a single population, which is often done, is equivalent to doing regression with a single case.

6. We have interpreted this finding in terms of Hannan and Carroll's "legitimacy hypothesis" (1992), although we apply it in a highly unusual way. In part, this is a function of our use of cross-sectional data. Within our cross

section, these organizations are not "new" in the sense of being recent innovations.

7. Arkansas, which actually has fewer interest organizations than does South Dakota, is another interesting case because it is one of the few small states that does not have a dense interest organization system given the size of its economy. This fact, in combination with Arkansas's positions in the reported plots, suggests that there may be state, and perhaps regional, differences in numbers of organizations considered natural or taken-for-granted.

8. The same is true for entry or births. Organizations may form as entirely new entities or by splitting from an older organization. In our survey of interest organization leaders discussed in chapter 9, 7.19 percent of association, 13.68 percent of institution, and 10.67 percent of membership group respondents reported that their organizations were born by splitting from another organization.

## Chapter 7

1. Again, because our focus is on organizations, lobbyists registered as individuals were eliminated, as were traditional state agencies (e.g., the office of the governor, etc.).

2. Estimation of the models without the dummy variable still produced generally similar results, although the magnitudes of the coefficients changed markedly.

3. Following Walker (1991, 53, 95), we also tested whether wealthy patrons serve as surrogate constituents for welfare and environmental groups. These analyses also produced supportive results.

4. Again, we might initially think of such measures as per capita income as tapping the concept of energy. But as reported in note 1 of chapter 4, income seems to have little impact at the level of the organization.

5. While this use of a single measure to tap both explanations is appropriate given our specification and use of cross-sectional data, this does not mean the Virginia School explanation could be collapsed into the ESA model. The strictest form of the Virginia School model suggests that politicians generate spending to entice latent interests to organize. In contrast, more traditional interpretations suggest that high levels of spending are a product of lobbying on the part of preexisting interest organizations. Our model agrees with Salisbury's interpretation (1992, 85–86) that interest organizations approach government when their interests are at stake, either when government is doing or may do something that benefits or harms an organization. This does not include global spending, but only very precise interests specific to each guild.

6. We also examined unemployment, thinking that the problems generated by low employment rates might be associated with an array of specific interests and might generate budget crises across state programs and policies as a result of declining revenue. However, when added to the models in table 7.1, the 1975, 1980, and 1990 unemployment coefficients were tiny relative to their standard errors, inconsistent in sign, and changed nothing else in the results.

7. Some might view interest certainty as an element of the stability term of

the ESA model. *Actual* policy change, if it influences interest organization decision making, may constitute a source of instability. However, the *likelihood* of policy change will in most cases be a constant that is quite independent of actual policy change. For example, as policies change in a competitive political system when moving from a GOP to a Democratic and then back to a GOP administration, the probability of policy change could remain constant given that the out party always stands a good chance of winning the next election. This continual uncertainty is a resource for the lobbyist rather than a liability, as would be the case if interest certainty were tapping stability. A more fundamental critique of the interest certainty term is that while it influences survival as if it were a resource, it is a joint consumption good. This is discussed in note 2 of chapter 4.

8. To assess whether the indicator was actually tapping party competition, not patterns of party control, the models were also estimated with the Ranney index unfolded. As expected, the folded index produced stronger results; only two of the unfolded estimates—welfare and environment models—were significant, while all six folded coefficients were.

9. Missing from the models are more general controls, such as population and per capita income. The role of income was considered earlier in note 4 of this chapter. While population inevitably will be collinear with some of our measures of latent constituency size, the latter are more appropriate theoretically. Manufacturing groups represent manufacturing firms, not people. When included, 1989 per capita income was significant only for agriculture. When 1990 population was added, its estimates in the welfare and construction results were not significant. In the government, environment, agriculture, and manufacturing models, population was highly collinear with constituent interest. No other coefficients changed markedly.

10. When the independent variables were regressed on each other, the R-square values were surprisingly modest (below 0.450). However, such tests assess only the *likelihood* of collinearity. The real issue is how much of the variance shared between each independent variable and the dependent variable is shared among the independent variables. Thus, low auxiliary R-squares do not preclude collinearity.

11. While we have no firm answers, it is interesting to speculate about the Olson estimates. They might indicate that, relative to the magnitude of their environmental problems, numbers of environmental interest organizations are depressed in newer, western states because they are more politically conservative. Alternatively, it might reflect a western bias in Sierra Club membership, thereby correcting for this possible source of bias in our constituency size measure.

12. The Olson and Virginia School results are unlikely to be a function of collinearity. When regressed on the other independent variables, neither produced R-square values exceeding 0.62. We also tested models excluding the ESA variables. Two of the Olson and all six of the government size estimates carried the wrong sign. None were significant.

## Chapter 8

1. We do not use the diversity measure focusing on organizational form here, because most discussions of diversity address the representation of varying social and economic interests rather than the organizational basis of lobbying.

2. Collinearity does not account for these results. The R-square values generated by regressing each of the 1990 independent variables on the others were as follows: economic diversity 0.160, economic size 0.091, and economic wealth 0.192.

3. Collinearity was evident among constituent number, its squared value, constituent interest, and interest certainty in the manufacturing model. This necessitated using different specifications for our manufacturing predictions. Thus, the manufacturing estimates change slightly in our baseline scenarios. While the predicted differences are slight, this may make the manufacturing interest organization predictions somewhat more sensitive to our manipulations.

## Chapter 9

1. We use the word *may* deliberately. While most scholars assume that balkanization and bias in representation within domains pose severe difficulties for democratic governance, Salisbury (1992, 98–99) argues that policy outcomes result from more than who shows up in a hearing room to support or oppose pending legislation.

2. As reported in chapter 6, our sample of 6 states mirrors well the distribution of organization types for all 50 states.

3. For example, responses to the four questions used to construct figures 9.1A through 9.1D were combined to form an index of perceptions of balkanization. For all three sets of interest organizations, the index values proved to be quite similar across the six states, and their distribution was not related to the density of their interest organization systems as measured by GSP-BASE.

4. Several respondents called us in puzzlement as to why they were selected, since they did not lobby. Indeed, some said it would be illegal for them to lobby, given their federal tax status. When asked why they had registered, they replied that state law required registration just so they could "hang around the capitol, monitor legislation, talk to legislators, walk the halls," and so on. We indicated that these activities were just what we wanted to study.

5. The percentages reported in the figures are often modestly less than the full set of respondents, due to exclusion of *don't know* and *no response* cases. Including cases with missing data, the surveys generated 99 institution, 142 association, and 156 membership group responses.

6. For a political science example of how this might be done, see Bath's study (1995) of noncompetitive competition among think tanks.

## Chapter 10

1. Rhode Island, unfortunately, did not distinguish between bills and resolutions in its report of legislative actions. To derive a more valid measure of bill activity for Rhode Island, its total number of reported introductions and enactments were discounted for each of the two years by the average of the ratio of resolutions to bills for Connecticut, Massachusetts, and New Hampshire.

2. This coding scheme treats independent governors and legislative chambers with the same number of members from each party the same as if they were controlled by Democrats. A more complex coding scheme might be more precise, but we already have exhausted a rather large proportion of our degrees of freedom.

3. In states with separate adjournment dates for upper and lower chambers, the later date was used. In all cases, this amounted to only a few days' difference.

4. The remaining auxiliary R-square values were as follows: Bowman-Kearney executive centralization 0.421, Bowman-Kearney accountability and management 0.507, opinion liberalism 0.616, legislative days 0.714, party competition 0.533, Herfindahl index of diversity 0.600, percent not-for-profit interests 0.636, Republican governor 0.446, Republican Senate 0.427, Republican House 0.529, split party control 0.521, biennial legislature 0.403, and number of 1991 bill introductions 0.576.

5. We regressed all of the independent variables in the models on the Erikson, Wright, and McIver measure for the 46 states used in our sample, and we used the resulting estimates in an attempt to generate predicted opinion liberalism scores for Alaska, Hawaii, and Nevada. Unfortunately, the prediction equation generated a weak R-square value and the resulting predictions were not especially plausible. Alternatively, we reestimated the model for 49 states while dropping the opinion liberalism variable. The estimates were generally similar to those reported in table 10.2, although modestly weaker. Still, given that opinion liberalism generated significant coefficients in two of our three models, the most prudent course seems to be dropping the three states for which we lack plausible scores on ideology.

6. We checked the plausibility of our claims about the impact of density and diversity by examining the ratio of introductions to enactments of the several pairs of states noted earlier in our assessment of the plausibility of the simulations: Georgia and Virginia, Minnesota and Alabama, Arizona and Colorado, and Tennessee and Wyoming. The differences in the passage ratios between the members of all four pairs match or exceed what we would expect given their numbers of interest organizations or proportions of not-for-profit interests and given the estimates presented in table 10.2.

## Chapter 11

1. The remaining auxiliary R-square values were as follows: Bowman-Kearney executive centralization 0.304, Bowman-Kearney accountability and

management 0.490, Bowman-Kearney representation 0.274, opinion liberalism 0.613, party competition 0.364, Herfindahl index of diversity 0.421, percent not-for-profit interests 0.500, number of interest organizations 0.767, GSP-BASE 0.780, 1982 per capita GSP 0.353, and 1982 state and local share of GSP 0.470.

2. The collinearity diagnostics in the government growth models are the same as those in the economic growth models.

3. Some might wonder whether the same argument about reverse causality applies to the legislative activity models presented in chapter 10. Proposed legislation could be construed as reflecting the constituency interest term of the ESA model. More proposals, then, might be expected to lead to more interests, not the reverse. However, interest organization number was associated with fewer proposals, fewer enactments, and a lower passage rate, not the reverse as implied by this interpretation of causality.

4. The auxiliary R-square values for the variables used in the previous models are of the same general magnitude as those reported in earlier notes. For the variables used uniquely in the four models presented in table 11.3, the auxiliary R-square values were as follows: 1980 number of regulated occupations 0.267, 1979 percent of earmarked taxes 0.195, 1980 AFDC average benefit 0.602, number of welfare interest organizations 0.411, welfare interest GSP-BASE 0.466, 1977 per capita GSP in the welfare model 0.368, 1977 proportion of state and local spending on construction 0.426, 1977 per capita GSP in the construction model 0.293, number of construction interest organizations 0.293, and construction interest GSP-BASE 0.701.

5. Four more cases—New York, Massachusetts, Kentucky, and Wyoming—were lost due to lack of data in the model based on proportion of earmarked taxes. To avoid losing even more cases, the dependent variable measuring change in the proportion of earmarked taxes is measured from 1984 to 1988 for Wisconsin, Oklahoma, and Mississippi.

6. The auxiliary R-square values for the variables used in the previous models are of the same general magnitude as those reported in earlier notes.

## Chapter 12

1. A cautionary note was sounded, however, in our most developed lobbying community—Michigan—where the big lobbying firms are becoming something of a "third force" in state politics. One Michigan lobbyist (phone interview, 29 April 1994) reported that multiclient firms "are now major political players, determining who is running for office, who gets the nomination, how much money they get, etc. To the candidate, the multiclient firm serves the function of the political party in the past. But these firms are enhancing themselves, more than enhancing their clients. They are not really representing an interest or a group; they are representing themselves. As firms, we have an institutional goal to be a political player; we are acting in our self-interest. . . . The multiclient firms are more of an independent force; they are a power unto themselves." Future studies should pay more attention to the large lobbying firms, which are

becoming vertically integrated, controlling campaign finance and electoral strategy as well as engaging in traditional lobbying. Indeed, contract lobbying firms may be a distinct category of interest organization that should be added to our enumeration of membership groups, associations, and institutions.

## Appendix 1

1. Inclusion of the restrictiveness measures in the more complex models presented in chapter 7 produce results similar to those presented here.

2. The inclusion of Florida changes none of the reported slope coefficients or their $t$-values to a great degree, but it is an extreme case that somewhat reduces R-square values (to approximately 0.50).

# References

Abrams, Peter. 1992. Resource. In *Keywords in Evolutionary Biology,* ed. Evelyn Fox Keller and Elisabeth A. Lloyd, 282–85. Cambridge, MA: Harvard University Press.

Aldrich, Howard E. 1979. *Organizations and Environments.* Englewood Cliffs, NJ: Prentice Hall.

Aldrich, Howard E., and Jeffrey Pfeffer. 1976. Environments of Organizations. *Annual Review of Sociology* 2:79–105.

Aldrich, Howard E., and Udo Staber. 1988. Organizing Business Interests: Patterns of Trade Association Foundings, Transformations, and Deaths. In *Ecological Models of Organizations,* ed. Glenn R. Carroll, 111–26. Cambridge, MA: Ballinger.

Aldrich, Howard E., Udo Staber, Catherine Zimmer, and John J. Beggs. 1990. Minimalism and Organizational Mortality: Patterns of Disbanding Among U.S. Trade Associations, 1900–1983. In *Organizational Evolution: New Directions,* ed. Jitendra V. Singh, 21–52. Newbury Park, CA: Sage.

Aldrich, Howard E., Catherine R. Zimmer, Udo H. Staber, and John J. Beggs. 1994. Minimalism, Mutualism, and Maturity: The Evolution of the American Trade Association Population in the Twentieth Century. In *Evolutionary Dynamics of Organizations,* ed. Joel A. C. Baum and Jitendra V. Singh, 223–38. New York: Oxford University Press.

Alvarez, Walter. 1992. Interview. *Dinosaurs!* Public Broadcasting System.

Austen–Smith, David. 1987. Interest Groups, Campaign Contributions, and Probabilistic Voting. *Public Choice* 54:123–40.

Bath, Michael G. 1995. Think Tanks, Patrons, and Funding Niches: *Non*competitive Methods of Competition. Paper presented at the annual meeting of the Midwest Political Science Association, Chicago, Illinois, April.

Bauer, Raymond A., Ithiel de Sola Pool, and Lewis Anthony Dexter. 1963. *American Business and Public Policy.* New York: Atherton.

Baumgartner, Frank R., and Bryan D. Jones. 1993. *Agendas and Instability in American Politics.* Chicago: University of Chicago Press.

Beatty, John. 1992. Fitness: Theoretical Contexts. In *Keywords in Evolutionary Biology,* ed. Evelyn Fox Keller and Elisabeth A. Lloyd, 115–19. Cambridge, MA: Harvard University Press.

Becker, Gary S. 1983. A Theory of Competition among Pressure Groups for Political Influence. *Quarterly Journal of Economics* 98:371–400.

279

Becker, Gary S. 1985. Public Policies, Pressure Groups, and Dead Weight Costs. *Journal of Public Economics* 28:329–47.

Begon, Michael, John L. Harper, and Colin R. Townsend. 1990. *Ecology: Individuals, Populations, and Communities.* Boston: Blackwell.

Benkman, Craig W. 1992. A Crossbill's Twist of Fate. *Natural History* 101 (12): 38–45.

Bentley, Arthur. 1908. *The Process of Government.* Chicago: University of Chicago Press.

Berry, Jeffrey. 1977. *Lobbying for the People: The Political Behavior of Public Interest Groups.* Princeton, NJ: Princeton University Press.

Berry, Jeffrey. 1994. An Agenda for Research in Interest Groups. In *Representing Interests and Interest Group Representation,* ed. William J. Crotty, Mildred A. Schwartz, and John C. Green, 21–28. Lanham, MD: University Press of America.

Berry, William D., and David Lowery. 1987. *Understanding U.S. Government Growth: An Empirical Analysis of the Post–War Era.* New York: Praeger.

Birnbaum, Jeffrey H., and Alan S. Murray. 1988. *Showdown at Gucci Gulch.* New York: Vintage Books.

Boucher, Douglas H. 1992. Mutualism and Cooperation. In *Keywords in Evolutionary Biology,* ed. Evelyn Fox Keller and Elisabeth A. Lloyd, 208–11. Cambridge, MA: Harvard University Press.

Bowman, Ann O., and Richard C. Kearney. 1988. Dimensions of State Government Capability. *Western Political Quarterly* 41:341–62.

Brace, Paul. 1993. *State Government and Economic Performance.* Baltimore, MD: Johns Hopkins University Press.

Brandon, Robert N. 1992. Environment. In *Keywords in Evolutionary Biology,* ed. Evelyn Fox Keller and Elisabeth A. Lloyd, 81–86. Cambridge, MA: Harvard University Press.

Brinig, Margaret F., Randall G. Holcombe, and Linda Schwartzstein. 1993. The Regulation of Lobbyists. *Public Choice* 77:377–84.

Brittain, Jack W., and Douglas R. Wholey. 1988. Competition and Coexistence in Organizational Communities: Population Dynamics in Electronic Components of Manufacturing. In *Ecological Models of Organizations,* ed. Glenn R. Carroll, 195–222. Cambridge, MA: Ballinger.

Brooks, John Langdon, and Stanley I. Dodson. 1965. Predation, Body Size, and Composition of Plankton. *Science* 150:28–35.

Browne, William P. 1988. *Private Interests, Public Policy, and American Agriculture.* Lawrence: University Press of Kansas.

Browne, William P. 1990. Organized Interests and Their Issue Niches: A Search for Pluralism in a Policy Domain. *Journal of Politics* 52 (2): 477–509.

Browne, William P. 1995. *Cultivating Congress: Constituents, Issues, and Interests in Agricultural Policymaking.* Lawrence: University Press of Kansas.

Browne, William P., and Delbert J. Ringquist. 1993. Michigan: Diversity and Professionalism in a Partisan Environment. In *Interest Group Politics in the*

*Midwestern States,* ed. Ronald J. Hrebenar and Clive S. Thomas, 117–44. Ames: Iowa State University Press.

Burian, Richard M. 1992. Adaptation: Historical Perspectives. In *Keywords in Evolutionary Biology,* ed. Evelyn Fox Keller and Elisabeth A. Lloyd, 7–12. Cambridge, MA: Harvard University Press.

Burns, Robert E., and Herbert E. Cheever, Jr. 1993. South Dakota: Conflict and Cooperation Among Conservatives. In *Interest Group Politics in the Midwestern States,* ed. Ronald J. Hrebenar and Clive S. Thomas, 285–304. Ames: Iowa State University Press.

Bush, Winston C., and Arthur T. Denzau. 1977. The Voting Behavior of Bureaucrats and Public Sector Growth. In *Budgets and Bureaucrats: The Sources of Government Growth,* ed. Thomas E. Borcherding, 90–99. Durham, NC: Duke University Press.

Carroll, Glenn R. 1984. Organizational Ecology. *Annual Review of Sociology* 10:71–93.

Carroll, Glenn R. 1988a. *Ecological Models of Organizations.* Cambridge, MA: Ballinger.

Carroll, Glenn R. 1988b. Organizational Ecology in Theoretical Perspective. In *Ecological Models of Organizations,* ed. Glenn R. Carroll, 1–6. Cambridge, MA: Ballinger.

Carroll, Glenn R., and Michael T. Hannan. 1989. Density Dependence in the Evolution of Populations of Newspaper Organizations. *American Sociological Review* 54 (August): 524–41.

Cater, Douglas. 1964. *Power in Washington.* New York: Random House.

Cigler, Allan J. 1991. Interest Groups: A Subfield in Search of an Identity. In *Political Science: Looking to the Future,* ed. William Crotty, 4:99–135. Evanston, IL: Northwestern University Press.

Cigler, Allan J. 1994. Research Gaps in the Study of Interest Representation. In *Representing Interests and Interest Group Representation,* ed. William J. Crotty, Mildred A. Schwartz, and John C. Green, 29–36. Lanham, MD: University Press of America.

Cigler, Allan J., and Burdett A. Loomis. 1995. *Interest Group Politics.* 4th edition. Washington, D.C.: CQ Press.

Clements, Frederic E. 1936. Nature and Structure of the Climax. *Journal of Ecology* 24:252–84.

Coase, Ronald H. 1960. The Problem of Social Cost. *Journal of Law and Economics* 3:1–44.

Colinvaux, Paul. 1978. *Why Big Fierce Animals are Rare: An Ecologist's Perspective.* Princeton, NJ: Princeton University Press.

Colwell, Robert K. 1992. Niche: A Bifurcation in the Conceptual Lineage of the Term. In *Keywords in Evolutionary Biology,* ed. Evelyn Fox Keller and Elisabeth A. Lloyd, 241–48. Cambridge, MA: Harvard University Press.

Connell, Joseph H. 1961. The Influence of Interspecific Competition and Other Factors on the Distribution of the Barnacle *Chthamalus Stellatus. Ecology* 42:710–23.

Conover, Pamela, and Virginia Gray. 1983. *Feminism and the New Right.* New York: Praeger.

Conybeare, John A. C., and Peverill Squire. 1994. Political Action Committees and the Tragedy of the Commons. *American Politics Quarterly* 22:154–74.

Cook, Constance Ewing. 1984. Participation in Public Interest Groups: Membership Motivations. *American Politics Quarterly* 12 (4): 409–30.

Cooper, W. S. 1984. Expected Time to Extinction and the Concept of Fundamental Fitness. *Journal of Theoretical Biology* 107:603–29.

Copeland, Gary W., and Kenneth J. Meier. 1984. Pass the Biscuits, Pappy: Congressional Decision-Making and Federal Grants. *American Politics Quarterly* 12 (1): 2–22.

Coughlin, Peter J., Dennis C. Mueller, and Peter Murrell. 1990. Electoral Politics, Interest Groups, and the Size of Government. *Economic Inquiry* 28 (October): 682–705.

Crotty, Patricia McGee. 1993. Pennsylvania: Individualism Writ Large. In *Interest Group Politics in the Northeastern States,* ed. Ronald J. Hrebenar and Clive S. Thomas, 279–300, University Park: Pennsylvania State University Press.

Crotty, Patricia McGee. 1994. Personal correspondence with Virginia Gray, November.

Crotty, William. 1994. Interest Representation and Interest Groups: Promise and Potentialities. In *Representing Interests and Interest Group Representation,* ed. William J. Crotty, Mildred A. Schwartz, and John C. Green, 1–11. Lanham, MD: University Press of America.

Dahl, Robert A. 1961. *Who Governs?* New Haven, CT: Yale University Press.

Dahl, Robert A. 1982. *Dilemmas of Pluralist Democracy: Autonomy vs. Control.* New Haven, CT: Yale University Press.

Darden, Lindley. 1992. Character. In *Keywords in Evolutionary Biology,* ed. Evelyn Fox Keller and Elizabeth A. Lloyd, 41–44. Cambridge, MA: Harvard University Press.

Davidson, J., and H. G. Andrewartha. 1948. The Influence of Rainfall, Evaporation, and Atmospheric Temperature on Fluctuations in the Size of a Natural Population of *Thrips Imaginis* (Thysanoptera). *Journal of Animal Ecology* 17:200–222.

Dupre, John. 1992. Species: Theoretical Contexts. In *Keywords in Evolutionary Biology,* ed. Evelyn Fox Keller and Elisabeth A. Lloyd, 312–17. Cambridge, MA: Harvard University Press.

Ehrlich, Paul R., and Jonathan Roughgarden. 1987. *The Science of Ecology.* New York: MacMillan.

Eldredge, Niles. 1991. *The Miner's Canary: Unravelling the Mysteries of Extinction.* New York: Prentice-Hall.

Eldredge, Niles, and Marjorie Grene. 1992. *Interactions: The Biological Context of Social Systems.* New York: Columbia University Press.

Elton, C. 1958. *The Ecology of Invasions by Animals and Plants.* London: Methuen.

Endler, John A. 1992. Natural Selection: Current Usage. In *Keywords in Evolu-*

*tionary Biology,* ed. Evelyn Fox Keller and Elisabeth A. Lloyd, 220–24. Cambridge, MA: Harvard University Press.

English, Arthur, and John J. Carroll. 1992. Arkansas: The Politics of Inequality. In *Interest Group Politics in the Southern States,* ed. Ronald J. Hrebenar and Clive S. Thomas, 181–208, 368–71. Tuscaloosa: University of Alabama Press.

Erikson, Robert S., Gerald C. Wright, and John P. McIver. 1993. *Statehouse Democracy: Public Opinion and Policy in the American States.* Cambridge: Cambridge University Press.

Fiorina, Morris. 1992. *Divided Government.* New York: MacMillan.

Fisher, Ronald C. 1987. *State and Local Public Finance.* Glenview, IL: Scott, Foresman, and Company.

Fistrup, Kurt. 1992. Character. In *Keywords in Evolutionary Biology,* ed. Evelyn Fox Keller and Elizabeth A. Lloyd, 45–51. Cambridge, MA: Harvard University Press.

Fleer, Jack D. 1992. North Carolina: Interest Groups in a State in Transition. In *Interest Group Politics in the Southern States,* ed. Ronald J. Hrebenar and Clive S. Thomas, 102–24, 360–63. Tuscaloosa: University of Alabama Press.

Fombrun, Charles J. 1988. Crafting an Institutionally Informed Ecology of Organizations. In *Ecological Models of Organizations,* ed. Glenn R. Carroll, 223–40. Cambridge, MA: Ballinger.

Friedman, Milton. 1962. *Capitalism and Freedom.* Chicago: University of Chicago Press.

Gause, G. F. 1934. *The Struggle for Existence.* New York: Hafner.

Gleason, H. A. 1926. The Individualistic Concept of the Plant Association. *Bulletin of the Torrey Botanical Club* 53:7–26.

Gordon, Deborah M. 1992. Phenotypic Plasticity. In *Keywords in Evolutionary Biology,* ed. Evelyn Fox Keller and Elisabeth A. Lloyd, 255–62. Cambridge, MA: Harvard University Press.

Grau, Craig H. 1993. Minnesota: Labor and Business in an Issue-Oriented State. In *Interest Group Politics in the Midwestern States,* ed. Ronald J. Hrebenar and Clive S. Thomas, 145–64. Ames: Iowa State University Press.

Gray, Virginia, and David Lowery. 1988. Interest Group Politics and Economic Growth in the U.S. States. *American Political Science Review* 82 (March): 109–31.

Gray, Virginia, and David Lowery. 1990. The Corporatist Foundation of State Industrial Policy. *Social Science Quarterly* 71 (March): 3–24.

Gray, Virginia, and David Lowery. 1994a. Reflections on the Study of Interest Groups in the States. In *Representing Interests and Interest Group Representation,* ed. William J. Crotty, Mildred A. Schwartz, and John C. Green, 58–67. Lanham, MD: University Press of America.

Gray, Virginia, and David Lowery. 1994b. State Interest Group System Density and Diversity: A Research Update. *International Political Science Review* 15 (1): 5–14.

Greenwald, Carol S. 1977. *Group Power: Lobbying and Public Policy.* New York: Praeger.

Greisemer, James R. 1992. Niche: Historical Perspectives. In *Keywords in Evolutionary Biology,* ed. Evelyn Fox Keller and Elisabeth A. Lloyd, 231–40. Cambridge, MA: Harvard University Press.

Grier, Kevin B., and Michael C. Munger. 1991. Committee Assignments, Constituent Preferences, and Campaign Contributions. *Economic Inquiry* 29 (January): 24–43.

Grier, Kevin B., Michael C. Munger, and Brian E. Roberts. 1994. The Determinants of Industry Political Activity, 1978–1986. *American Political Science Review* 88 (4): 911–32.

Grinnell, Joseph. 1917. The Niche–Relationship of the California Thrasher. *Auk* 34:427–33.

Haider, Donald H. 1974. *When Governments Come to Washington.* New York: Free.

Hairston, Nelson G., Frederick E. Smith, and Lawrence Slobodkin. 1960. Community Structure, Population Control, and Competition. *American Naturalist* 94:421–25.

Hall, Richard D., and Frank W. Wayman. 1990. Buying Time: Moneyed Interests and the Mobilization of Bias in Congressional Committees. *American Political Science Review* 84:797–820.

Hamm, Keith E., Andrew R. Weber, and R. Bruce Anderson. 1994. The Impact of Lobbying Laws and Their Enforcement: A Contrasting View. *Social Science Quarterly* 75:378–81.

Hannan, Michael T., and Glenn R. Carroll. 1992. *Dynamics of Organizational Populations.* New York: Oxford University Press.

Hannan, Michael T., and John Freeman. 1977. The Population Ecology of Organizations. *American Journal of Sociology* 82 (5): 929–64.

Hannan, Michael T., and John Freeman. 1988. The Ecology of Organizational Mortality: American Labor Unions, 1836–1985. *American Journal of Sociology* 94 (1): 25–52.

Hannan, Michael T., and John Freeman. 1989. *Organizational Ecology.* Cambridge, MA: Harvard University Press.

Hansen, John Mark. 1985. The Political Economy of Group Membership. *American Political Science Review* 79 (1): 79–96.

Hansen, John Mark. 1991. *Gaining Access: Congress and the Farm Lobby, 1919–1981.* Chicago: University of Chicago Press.

Hansen, Susan B. 1983. *The Politics of Taxation.* New York: Praeger.

Hawley, Amos. 1944. Ecology and Human Ecology. *Social Forces* 22 (May): 398–405.

Hawley, Amos. 1950. *Human Ecology: A Theory of Community Structure.* New York: Ronald.

Hayes, Michael T. 1981. *Lobbyists and Legislators.* New Brunswick, NJ: Rutgers University Press.

Heclo, Hugh. 1978. Issue Networks and the Executive Establishment. In *The*

*New American Political System,* 1st edition, ed. Anthony King, 87–124. Washington, D.C.: American Enterprise Institute.

Heinz, John P., Edward O. Laumann, Robert L. Nelson, and Robert Salisbury. 1993. *The Hollow Core.* Cambridge, MA: Harvard University Press.

Heinz, John P., Edward O. Laumann, Robert H. Salisbury, and Robert L. Nelson. 1990. Inner Circles or Hollow Cores? Elite Networks in National Policy Systems. *Journal of Politics* 52 (2): 356–90.

Hrebenar, Ronald J., and Clive S. Thomas. 1992. *Interest Group Politics in the Southern States.* Tuscaloosa: University of Alabama Press.

Hrebenar, Ronald J., and Clive S. Thomas. 1993a. *Interest Group Politics in the Midwest States.* Ames: Iowa State University Press.

Hrebenar, Ronald J., and Clive S. Thomas. 1993b. *Interest Group Politics in the Northeastern States.* University Park: Pennsylvania State University Press.

Hull, David. 1976. Are Species Really Individuals? *Systematic Zoology* 25: 174–91.

Hull, David. 1978. A Matter of Individuality. *Philosophy of Science* 44:335–60.

Hull, David. 1980. Individuality and Selection. *Annual Review of Ecology and Systematics* 11:311–32.

Hull, David. 1988. *Science as a Process: An Evolutionary Account of the Social and Conceptual Development of Science.* Chicago: University of Chicago Press.

Hull, David. 1992. Individual. In *Keywords in Evolutionary Biology,* ed. Evelyn Fox Keller and Elisabeth A. Lloyd, 180–87. Cambridge, MA: Harvard University Press.

Hunter, Kennith G., Laura Ann Wilson, and Gregory G. Brunk. 1991. Social Complexity and Interest-Group Lobbying in the American States. *Journal of Politics* 53 (2): 488–503.

Hutchinson, G. Evelyn. 1957. Concluding Remarks. In *Population Studies: Animal Ecology and Demography,* 415–27. Cold Springs Harbor Symposia on Quantitative Biology 22.

Hutchinson, G. Evelyn. 1959. Homage to Santa Rosalia; or, Why Are There So Many Kinds of Animals? *American Naturalist* 93:145–59.

Kaufman, Herbert. 1985. *Time, Chance, and Organizations.* Chatham, NJ: Chatham House.

Keller, Evelyn Fox. 1992a. Competition: Current Usages. In *Keywords in Evolutionary Biology,* ed. Evelyn Fox Keller and Elisabeth A. Lloyd, 68–73. Cambridge, MA: Harvard University Press.

Keller, Evelyn Fox. 1992b. Fitness: Reproductive Ambiguities. In *Keywords in Evolutionary Biology,* ed. Evelyn Fox Keller and Elisabeth A. Lloyd, 120–21. Cambridge, MA: Harvard University Press.

Keller, Evelyn Fox, and Elisabeth A. Lloyd. 1992. *Keywords in Evolutionary Biology.* Cambridge, MA: Harvard University Press.

Kemp, Kathleen. 1981. Symbolic and Strict Regulation in the American States. *Social Science Quarterly* 62 (3): 516–26.

Key, V. O. 1949. *Southern Politics in State and Nation.* New York: Alfred A. Knopf.

King, David C., and Jack L. Walker. 1992. The Provision of Benefits by Interest Groups in the United States. *Journal of Politics* 54 (2): 394–426.

Kingsland, Sharon E. 1991. Foundational Papers: Defining Ecology as a Science. In *Foundations of Ecology: Classic Papers with Commentary,* ed. Leslie A. Real and James H. Brown, 1–12. Chicago: University of Chicago Press.

Kingsolver, Joel G., and Robert T. Paine. 1991. Theses, Anitheses, and Syntheses: Conversational Biology and Ecological Debate. In *Foundations of Ecology: Classic Papers with Commentary,* ed. Leslie A. Real and James H. Brown, 309–17. Chicago: University of Chicago Press.

Lack, David. 1947. *Darwin's Finches.* Cambridge: Cambridge University Press.

Lack, David. 1954. *The Natural Regulation of Animal Numbers.* Oxford: Oxford University Press.

Latham, Earl. 1952. *The Group Basis of Politics: A Study of Basing-Point Legislation.* Ithaca, NY: Cornell University Press.

Laumann, Edward O. and David Knoke. 1987. *The Organizational State: Social Choice in National Policy Domains.* Madison: University of Wisconsin Press.

Lindeman, Raymond L. 1942. The Trophic-Dynamic Aspect of Ecology. *Ecology* 23:399–418.

Lloyd, Elisabeth A. 1992. Unit of Selection. In *Keywords in Evolutionary Biology,* ed. Evelyn Fox Keller and Elisabeth A. Lloyd, 334–40. Cambridge, MA: Harvard University Press.

Lowery, David. 1987. The Distribution of Tax Burdens in the American States. *Western Political Quarterly* 40 (1): 137–58.

Lowery, David, and Virginia Gray. 1992. Holding Back the Tide of Bad Economic Times: The Compensatory Impact of State Industrial Policy. *Social Science Quarterly* 73 (3): 483–95.

Lowery, David, and Virginia Gray. 1993. The Density of State Interest Group Systems. *Journal of Politics* 55 (1): 191–206.

Lowery, David, and Virginia Gray. 1994a. Do Lobbying Regulations Influence Lobbying Registrations? *Social Science Quarterly* 75 (2): 382–84.

Lowery, David, and Virginia Gray. 1994b. The Nationalization of State Interest Group System Density and Diversity. *Social Science Quarterly* 75 (2): 368–77.

Lowery, David, and Virginia Gray. In press. How Some Rules Just Don't Matter: The Regulation of Lobbyists. *Public Choice.*

Lowi, Theodore J. 1969. *The End of Liberalism.* New York: W. W. Norton.

Lubchenco, Jane, and Leslie A Real. 1991. Experimental Manipulations in Lab and Field Systems: Manipulative Experiments as Tests of Ecological Theory. In *Foundations of Ecology: Classic Papers with Commentary,* ed. Leslie A. Real and James H. Brown, 715–33. Chicago: University of Chicago Press.

MacArthur, Robert H. 1958. Population Ecology of Some Warblers of Northeastern Coniferous Forests. *Ecology* 39:599–619.

MacArthur, Robert H., and Eric R. Pianka. 1966. On Optimal Use of a Patchy Environment. *American Naturalist* 100:603–9.

MacArthur, Robert H., and Edward O. Wilson. 1963. An Equilibrium Theory of Insular Zoogeography. *Evolution* 17 (4): 373–87.

MacIntosh, Robert. 1992. Competition: Historical Perspectives. In *Keywords in Evolutionary Biology,* ed. Evelyn Fox Keller and Elisabeth A. Lloyd, 61–67. Cambridge, MA: Harvard University Press.

Mahood, H. R. 1990. *Interest Group Politics in America: A New Intensity.* Englewood Cliffs, NJ: Prentice Hall.

Malbin, Michael J. 1984. *Money and Politics in the United States.* Chatham, NJ: Chatham House.

Marquis Academic Media. 1978. *Directory of Registered Lobbyists and Information.* 2d edition. Chicago: Marquis Who's Who.

May, Robert M. 1974. Biological Populations with Non-Overlapping Generations: Stable Points, Stable Cycles, and Chaos. *Science* 186:645–47.

Mayhew, David R. 1991. *Divided We Govern.* New Haven, CT: Yale University Press.

Mayr, Ernst. 1988. *Towards a New Philosophy of Biology: Observations of an Evolutionist.* Cambridge, MA: Harvard University Press.

Mayr, Ernst. 1991. *One Long Argument: Charles Darwin and the Genesis of Modern Evolutionary Thought.* Cambridge, MA: Harvard University Press.

McConnell, Grant. 1966. *Private Power and American Democracy.* New York: Alfred A. Knopf.

McFarland, Andrew S. 1984. *Common Cause: Lobbying in the Public Interest.* Chatham, NJ: Chatham House.

McFarland, Andrew S. 1992. Interest Groups and the Policymaking Process: Sources of Countervailing Power in America. In *The Politics of Interests,* ed. Mark P. Petracca, 58–79. Boulder, CO: Westview.

McKeown, Timothy J. 1994. The Epidemiology of Corporate PAC Formation, 1975–84. *Journal of Economic Behavior and Organization* 24: 153–68.

Meier, Kenneth J., and E. Thomas Garman. 1995. *Regulation and Consumer Protection.* Houston, TX: Dame Publications.

Meyer, John W., and Brian Rowen. 1983. Institutional Organizations: Formal Structure as Myth and Ceremony. In *Organizational Environments,* ed. John W. Meyer and W. Richard Scott, 21–44. Beverly Hills, CA: Sage.

Meyer, John W., and W. Richard Scott. 1983. *Organizational Environments.* Beverly Hills, CA: Sage.

Milbrath, Lester. 1963. *The Washington Lobbyists.* Chicago: Rand McNally.

Miller, Gary J., and Terry M. Moe. 1983. Bureaucrats, Legislators, and the Size of Government. *American Political Science Review* 77:297–322.

Mitchell, William C., and Michael C. Munger. 1991. Economic Models of Interest Groups. *American Journal of Political Science* 35 (2): 512–46.

Moe, Terry M. 1980. *The Organization of Interests.* Chicago: University of Chicago Press.

Moe, Terry M. 1984. The New Economics of Organization. *American Journal of Political Science* 28:739–77.

Moe, Terry M. 1987. An Assessment of the Positive Theory of Congressional Dominance. *Legislative Studies Quarterly* 12 (4): 475–520.

Morehouse, Sarah McCally. 1981. *State Politics, Parties, and Policy.* New York: Holt, Rinehart, and Winston.

Mucciaroni, Gary. 1995. *Reversals of Fortune: Public Policy and Private Interests.* Washington, D.C.: Brookings Institution.

Mueller, Dennis G. 1983. *The Political Economy of Growth.* New Haven, CT: Yale University Press.

Mueller, Dennis G., and Peter Murrell. 1986. Interest Groups and the Size of Government. *Public Choice* 48 (1): 125–45.

Munger, Michael, and Arthur Denzau. 1986. Legislators and Interest Groups: How Unorganized Interests Get Represented. *American Political Science Review* 80:89–106.

Niskanen, William. 1971. *Bureaucracy and Representative Government.* Chicago: Aldine.

Odum, Eugene P. 1969. The Strategy of Ecosystem Development. *Science* 164:262–70.

Olson, Mancur, Jr. 1965. *The Logic of Collective Action.* Cambridge, MA: Harvard University Press.

Olson, Mancur, Jr. 1982. *The Rise and Decline of Nations.* New Haven, CT: Yale University Press.

Opheim, Cynthia. 1991. Explaining the Differences in State Lobbying Regulation. *Western Political Quarterly* 44:405–21.

Paine, Robert T. 1966. Food Web Complexity and Species Diversity. *American Naturalist* 100:65–75.

Paolino, Robert. 1991. A Comparative Analysis of State Interest Group Systems. Minneapolis: University of Minnesota. Mimeograph.

Park, Thomas. 1948. Experimental Studies of Interspecies Competition I: Competition between Populations of the Flour Beetle, *Tribolium confusum* Duvall and *Tribolium castaneum* Herbst. *Ecological Monographs* 18:267–307.

Paul, Diane. 1992. Fitness: Historical Perspectives. In *Keywords in Evolutionary Biology,* ed. Evelyn Fox Keller and Elisabeth A. Lloyd, 112–14. Cambridge, MA: Harvard University Press.

Peltzman, Sam. 1976. Towards a More General Theory of Regulation. *Journal of Law and Economics* 19:211–40.

Peterson, Paul E. 1990–91, The Rise and Fall of Special Interest Politics. *Political Science Quarterly* 105 (4): 539–56.

Petracca, Mark P. 1992a. *The Politics of Interests.* Boulder, CO: Westview.

Petracca, Mark P. 1992b. The Rediscovery of Interest Group Politics. In *The Politics of Interests,* ed. Mark P. Petracca, 3–31. Boulder, CO: Westview.

Pimm, Stuart L., H. Lee Jones, and Jared Diamond. 1988. On the Risk of Extinction. *American Naturalist* 132 (6): 757–85.

Preston, Frank W. 1962. The Canonical Distribution of Commonness and Rarity, Part I. *Ecology* 43:185–215, 431–32.

Raup, David M. 1991. *Extinction: Bad Luck or Bad Genes?* New York: W. W. Norton.

Real, Leslie A., and Simon A. Levin. 1991. Theoretical Advances: The Role of Theory in the Rise of Modern Ecology. In *Foundations of Ecology: Classic Papers with Commentary,* ed. Leslie A. Real and James H. Brown, 177–91. Chicago: University of Chicago Press.

Renshaw, Vernon, Edward A. Trott, Jr., and Howard L. Friedenberg. 1988. Gross State Product by Industry, 1963–86. *Survey of Current Business* 68 (May): 30–45.

Richards, Robert J. 1992. Evolution. In *Keywords in Evolutionary Biology,* ed. Evelyn Fox Keller and Elisabeth A. Lloyd, 95–105. Cambridge, MA: Harvard University Press.

Ricklefs, Robert E., and Dolph Schluter. 1993. *Species Diversity in Ecological Communities: Historical and Geographic Perspectives.* Chicago: University of Chicago Press.

Roeder, Phillip W. 1994. *Public Opinion and Policy Leadership in the American States.* Tuscaloosa: University of Alabama Press.

Rose, Arnold M. 1967. *The Power Structure: Political Process in American Society.* London: Oxford University Press.

Rosenthal, Alan, and Rod Forth. 1978a. The Assembly Line: Law Production in the American States. *Legislative Studies Quarterly* 3:265–91.

Rosenthal, Alan, and Rod Forth. 1978b. There Ought to be a Law! *State Government* 51:81–87.

Rothenberg, Lawrence. 1992. *Linking Citizens to Government: Interest Group Politics at Common Cause.* Cambridge: Cambridge University Press.

Rottenberg, Simon. 1980. *Occupational Licensing and Regulation.* Washington, D.C.: American Enterprise Institute.

Sabatier, Paul A. 1992. Interest Group Membership and Organization. In *The Politics of Interests,* ed. Mark P. Petracca, 99–129. Boulder, CO: Westview.

Salisbury, Robert. 1969. An Exchange Theory of Interest Groups. *Midwest Journal of Political Science* 13 (1): 1–32.

Salisbury, Robert. 1984. Interest Representation: The Dominance of Institutions. *American Political Science Review* 81 (1): 64–76.

Salisbury, Robert. 1990. The Paradox of Interest Groups in Washington: More Groups, Less Clout. In *The New American Political System,* 2d edition, ed. Anthony King, 203–30. Washington, D.C.: American Enterprise Institute.

Salisbury, Robert. 1992. *Interests and Institutions: Substance and Structure in American Politics.* Pittsburgh: University of Pittsburgh Press.

Salisbury, Robert. 1994. Interest Structures and Policy Domains: A Focus on Research. In *Representing Interests and Interest Group Representation,* ed. William J. Crotty, Mildred A. Schwartz, and John C. Green, 12–20. Lanham, MD: University Press of America.

Salisbury, Robert, John P. Heinz, Edward O. Laumann, and Robert L. Nelson. 1987. Who Works with Whom? Interest Group Alliances and Opposition. *American Political Science Review* 81 (4): 1217–35.

Schattschneider, E. E. 1960. *The Semisovereign People.* New York: Holt, Rinehart, and Winston.

Schlozman, Kay Lehman. 1984. What Accent the Heavenly Chorus? Political Equality and the American Pressure System. *Journal of Politics* 46 (4): 1006–32.

Schlozman, Kay Lehman, and John T. Tierney. 1983. More of the Same: Washington Pressure Group Activity in a Decade of Change. *Journal of Politics* 45 (2): 351–73.

Schlozman, Kay Lehman, and John T. Tierney. 1986. *Organized Interests and American Democracy.* New York: Harper and Row.

Shugart, William F., and Robert D. Tollison. 1986. On the Growth of Government and the Political Economy of Legislation. *Research in Law and Economics* 9:111–27.

Signor, Philip W. 1990. The Geologic History of Diversity. *Annual Review of Ecology and Systematics* 21:509–39.

Simberloff, Daniel S., and Edward O. Wilson. 1969. Experimental Zoogeography of Islands: The Colonization of Empty Islands. *Ecology* 50:278–96.

Singh, Jitendra V., and Charles J. Lumsden. 1990. Theory and Research in Organizational Ecology. *Annual Review of Sociology* 16:161–95.

Stevens, George C. 1989. The Latitudinal Gradient in Geographical Range: How So Many Species Coexist in the Tropics. *American Naturalist* 133 (2): 240–56.

Stevens, Peter F. 1992. Species: Historical Perspective. In *Keywords in Evolutionary Biology,* ed. Evelyn Fox Keller and Elisabeth A. Lloyd, 302–11. Cambridge, MA: Harvard University Press.

Stigler, George. 1971. The Theory of Economic Regulation. *Bell Journal of Economics and Management Science* 2:3–21.

Tansley, A. G. 1935. The Use and Abuse of Vegetational Concepts and Terms. *Ecology* 16:284–307.

Taylor, Peter. 1992. Community. In *Keywords in Evolutionary Biology,* ed. Evelyn Fox Keller and Elisabeth A. Lloyd, 52–60. Cambridge, MA: Harvard University Press.

Thomas, Clive S., and Ronald J. Hrebenar. 1990. Interest Groups in the States. In *Politics in the American States,* ed. Virginia Gray, Herbert Jacob, and Robert B. Albritton, 123–58. Glenview, IL: Scott, Foresman, and Company; Boston: Little, Brown, and Company.

Thomas, Clive S., and Ronald J. Hrebenar. 1991. The Regulation of Interest Groups and Lobbying in the Fifty States: Some Preliminary Findings. Paper presented at the annual meeting of the Midwest Political Science Association, Chicago, Illinois, April.

Thomas, Clive S., and Ronald J. Hrebenar. 1992. Changing Patterns of Interest Group Activity: A Regional Perspective. In *The Politics of Interests,* ed. Mark P. Petracca, 150–74. Boulder, CO: Westview.

Thomas, Clive S., and Ronald J. Hrebenar. 1994. Interest Group Power and Impact: Exploring the Issues and the Variables. Paper presented at the annual meeting of the American Political Science Association, New York, New York, September.

Thomas, Clive S., and Ronald J. Hrebenar. 1995. Understanding Interest Group

Power: Lessons from Developments in the American States since the Mid–1980s. Paper presented at the annual meeting of the Midwest Political Science Association, Chicago, Illinois, April.

Tierney, John. 1994. Research on Interest Representation: Questions and Approaches. In *Representing Interests and Interest Group Representation,* ed. William J. Crotty, Mildred A. Schwartz, and John C. Green, 37–45. Lanham, MD: University Press of America.

Trott, Edward A., Jr., Ann E. Dunbar, and Howard Freidenberg. 1991. Gross State Product by Industry, 1977–89. *Survey of Current Business* 71 (December): 43–59.

Truman, David. 1951. *The Governmental Process.* New York: Alfred A. Knopf.

Volterra, Vito. 1926. Fluctuations in the Abundance of a Species Considered Mathematically. *Nature* 118:558–60.

Walker, Jack L., Jr. 1983. The Origins and Maintenance of Interest Groups in America. *American Political Science Review* 77:390–406.

Walker, Jack L., Jr. 1991. *Mobilizing Interest Groups in America: Patrons, Professionals, and Social Movements.* Ann Arbor: University of Michigan Press.

Watt, Alex S. 1947. Pattern and Process in the Plant Community. *Journal of Ecology* 35:1–22.

Weiner, Jonathan. 1994. *The Beak of the Finch.* New York: Alfred A. Knopf.

Weingast, Barry R., and Mark J. Moran. 1982. The Myth of Runaway Bureaucracy. *Regulation* 6:33–38.

West-Eberhard, Mary Jane. 1992. Adaptation: Current Uses. In *Keywords in Evolutionary Biology,* ed. Evelyn Fox Keller and Elisabeth A. Lloyd, 13–18. Cambridge, MA: Harvard University Press.

Wiggins, Charles W., Keith E. Hamm, and Charles G. Bell. 1992. Interest-Group and Party Influence Agents in the Legislative Process: A Comparative State Analysis. *Journal of Politics* 54 (1): 82–100.

Williams, Bruce A., and Albert R. Matheny. 1984. Testing Theories of Social Regulation: Hazardous Waste Regulation in the American States. *Journal of Politics* 46:428–58.

Williams, Mary B. 1992. Species: Current Usages. In *Keywords in Evolutionary Biology,* ed. Evelyn Fox Keller and Elisabeth A. Lloyd, 318–23. Cambridge, MA: Harvard University Press.

Wilson, David Sloan. 1992. Group Selection. In *Keywords in Evolutionary Biology,* ed. Evelyn Fox Keller and Elisabeth A. Lloyd, 145–48. Cambridge, MA: Harvard University Press.

Wilson, Edward O. 1992. *The Diversity of Life.* Cambridge, MA: Harvard University Press.

Wilson, James Q. 1973. *Political Organizations.* New York: Basic Books.

Wilson-Gentry, Laura A., Gregory G. Brunk, and Kennith G. Hunter. 1991. Institutional and Environmental Influences on the Form of Interest Group Activity. Paper presented at the annual meeting of the American Political Science Association, Chicago, Illinois, April.

Wright, John R. 1985. PACs, Contributions, and Roll Calls: An Organizational Perspective. *American Political Science Review* 79 (2): 400–414.

Wright, John R. 1990. Contributions, Lobbying, and Committee Voting in the U.S. House of Representatives. *American Political Science Review* 84:417–38.

Young, Ruth C. 1988. Is Population Ecology a Useful Paradigm for the Study of Organizations? *American Journal of Sociology* 94 (1): 1–24.

Zeigler, L. Harmon. 1983. Interest Groups in the States. In *Politics in the American States,* 4th edition, ed. Virginia Gray, Herbert Jacob, and Kenneth Vines, 97–132. Boston: Little, Brown, and Company.

Zeigler, L. Harmon, and Hendrik van Dalen. 1976. Interest Groups in State Politics. In *Politics in the American States,* 3d edition, ed. Herbert Jacob and Kenneth Vines, 93–136. Boston: Little, Brown, and Company.

Zeller, Belle. 1954. *American State Legislatures.* 2d edition. New York: Thomas Y. Crowell.

Zucker, Lynne, G. 1989. Combining Institutional Theory and Population Ecology: No Legitimacy, No History. *American Sociological Review* 54 (August): 542–45.

# Subject Index

Adaptation
  in evolutionary biology, 45, 49
  in organization ecology, 49
    competition, 51
Area (space)
  concept in ESA theory, 52–54, 69–71, 139
  curvilinear size-competition relationship, 70
Area-species curve, 53

Balkanization of interests
  economic explanation of, 30–31
  political science explanations of, 25–30
  support in aggregates of interest organization survey, 181–85
  sustained conditions for, 177
Biological-species concept, 37–38
*Book of the States, The,* 202, 232
Bowman-Kearney factor analysis, 204–5, 221
Bush/Denzau hypothesis, 219

Capacities
  state-level institutional variables, 204–5
  at state level to process bills, 203
Certainty
  in energy component of ESA model, 72
  interest, 148–49
Character displacement, 51
Coalition building, 200
Collective action, 112–13

Communities
  ecological, 38–39
  interest organization
    assembly rules, 19
    density in, 54, 88–89
    diversity of, 48–49, 254
    diversity using ESA model of, 56
    impact of, 239–41
    population ecology in study of structure of, 75–77
    structure of, 25
  plant, 48
Competition
  conditions for increased, 70
  density dependence with, 179
  distribution of aggregate survey responses of, 189–94
  driven by resource scarcity, 179
  in ecosystems, 42
  expressed through niche partitioning, 47–48, 78–79
  interest organization survey responses of, 184–89
  in organization ecology, 50–51
  for organization survival, 65
  political party, 204
  in population ecology, 42
  within species, 54
  *See also* Density dependence; Niche partitioning
Competitive exclusion principle
  applications in organization populatin ecology, 51
  in biology, 46–47
  in interest organization analysis, 64–65, 196–97

293

# Author Index